THE
QUALITY SCHOOL

Other books by William Glasser

Control Theory in the Classroom
Control Theory
Schools Without Failure
Reality Therapy
Positive Addiction
The Identity Society
Mental Health or Mental Illness?
Stations of the Mind

THE
QUALITY SCHOOL

Managing Students Without Coercion

Second, Expanded Edition

William Glasser, M.D.

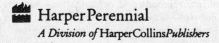

HarperPerennial
A Division of HarperCollins*Publishers*

HarperCollins books may be purchased for educational, business, or sales promotional use. For information please write: Special Markets Department, HarperCollins Publishers, Inc., 10 East 53rd Street, New York, NY 10022.

FIRST EDITION

Designed by Rhea Braunstein

Library of Congress Cataloging-in-Publication Data
Glasser, William, 1925–
    The quality school / William Glasser.—2nd, expanded ed.
      p. cm.
    Includes bibliographical references
    ISBN 0-06-096955-5
    1. School management and organization—United States.
2. Quality control—United States.   3. Motivation in education.
4. School improvement programs—United States.   I. Title.
LB2805.G534 1992   92-52634
371.2'00973—dc20

97 98 RRD - H 20 19 18 17 16

The population of Apollo consists of students who refused to fit into the structure of the regular high schools in Simi and had stopped trying to learn in these schools. Before coming to Apollo, they had also been so rebellious that they were no longer welcome where they were.

They are not rebellious at Apollo. Eighteen years of hard work by Brad and the staff has resulted in a totally noncoercive atmosphere. When I came to Apollo as a consultant four years ago, they had succeeded in eliminating almost all discipline problems. What has yet to be accomplished is to get the students as involved in quality education as they are in following the school rules.

During the time I have been at the school, I have talked extensively to the students both in and out of class and have met with the staff individually and in groups. All that I have learned from them confirms what I say in this book. For example, most of the students had been diagnosed when they were young as having a variety of learning disabilities. Yet in the noncoercive, need-satisfying atmosphere of Apollo, they all seem able to read and write well enough so that if they worked harder they could do quality work. Here and there we even see bits and pieces of the superb work that they are able to do when they see quality in what they are assigned—but we have yet to persuade most of them to do this with any consistency.

I cannot predict that, starting as far behind as we do at Apollo, we will ever have a quality school such as I describe at the end of this book. On the other hand, we have yet to try to implement many of the ideas in this book, especially the idea of student self-evaluation, and it is possible that we will go much further in the direction of quality than now seems possible. I appreciate the opportunity to work and continue to learn at Apollo and will make every effort to improve what has started so well.

Contents

Acknowledgments

I cannot begin to acknowledge all the teachers and administrators who help me as I struggle to bring the ideas of control theory and reality therapy to the schools. If I attempted to name names, I would surely leave out many and inadvertently hurt people who have helped as much as those named. Still, there is one person, Jim Griner, principal of the Brimfield Elementary School, Brimfield, Illinois, a man I hardly know, who helped much more than he probably realizes.

In response to a booklet outlining these ideas that I published three years ago, Jim sat down and wrote a rigorous, sixteen-page critique. He was highly supportive and, at the same time, extremely skeptical. He suggested flatly that, in the early form in which he read them, many of the ideas just would not work. But the tenor of his input was "Right on! Please show us how to make them work."

Based on this particularly thoughtful response, as well as on the input of many others, I have struggled to refine the ideas presented here so that they may be more workable than they were in their initial form. I have read and reread Deming, and I continue to believe that quality is the answer to many societal problems and that quality schools are possible. Thanks, Jim, and thanks to all of you who have done so much to help.

Although I acknowledge the Johnson City, New York, schools in the text, I also wish to acknowledge the work of others like William Spady and John Champlin who are deeply involved in Outcome

Based Education (OBE), a successful model which many ideas in this book support.

Finally, I want to thank my wife, Naomi, for her continuing encouragement and her "quality" editing of still another manuscript. Marriage is full of pleasant surprises. I had no more idea that she had these skills when we married than she did that I would write books.

Preface

Shayle Uroff,[1] who helps Brad Greene to describe work being done at the Apollo School, gave me the following:

A boss drives. A leader leads.
A boss relies on authority. A leader relies on cooperation.
A boss says "I." A leader says "We."
A boss creates fear. A leader creates confidence.
A boss knows how. A leader shows how.
A boss creates resentment. A leader breeds enthusiasm.
A boss fixes blame. A leader fixes mistakes.
A boss makes work drudgery. A leader makes work interesting.

As you read this book, return to this page periodically and reread these statements. They will help keep you on track.

Author's Note

Many educators who have read the first edition of this book have contacted me to find out how to begin the process of moving their school to a Quality School. To assist them, I have worked out a process called: The Quality School Training Program. This program is described in the last chapter of this book. For any further information please contact:

The Institute for Reality Therapy
7301 Medical Center Drive
Suite 104
Canoga Park, CA 91307
(818) 888-0688; Fax: (818) 888-3023

PART ONE

CHAPTER ONE

Quality Education Is the Only Answer to Our School Problems

Picture the students in a required academic class at a randomly selected secondary school as a gang of street repair workers. If they were working as hard as the students do in class, half or more would be leaning on their shovels, smoking and socializing, perfectly content to let the others do the work. Of those who were working, few would be working hard, and it is likely that none would be doing high-quality work.

It is apparent, however, that students have thought about quality and have a good idea of what, in their school, is considered quality. I have talked at length to groups of high school students about this subject, and most of them see quality in athletics, music, and drama, a few see it in advanced placement academics or shop classes, but almost none see it in regular classes. While they believe they are capable of doing quality work in class, all but a very few admit that they have never done it and have no plans to do it in the future. The purpose of this book is to explain how to manage students so that a substantial majority do high-quality schoolwork: Nothing less will solve the problems of our schools.

If we accept that the purpose of any organization, public or private, is to build a quality product or perform a quality service, then we must also accept that the workers in the organization must do quality work and that the job of the manager is to see that this occurs. In school, the students are the workers, and right now almost none are doing quality work in class. Those who manage in the schools—teachers who manage students directly and administrators who manage teachers and some students—are in most instances highly dedicated, humane people who have tried very hard but have yet to figure out how to manage so that students do significant amounts of quality work.

Is this problem unsolvable? Should we, as we seem to be doing, give up on the idea of many students doing quality work and instead increase the amount of low-quality work— as we do when we settle for trying to reduce the number of dropouts? But if quality education is what we need, does it make that much difference whether a student stays in school and "leans on his shovel" or drops out and "leans on his shovel"?

Or should we look for organizations in which almost all the workers are working hard and doing a quality job and try to apply to the schools what the managers in these places are doing? Although not widely known or applied in this country, there are far better management practices than most school managers know about. This book describes these highly successful practices and explains how school managers can learn to use them. What is significant about these practices is that they are specifically aimed at persuading workers to do quality work. In today's competitive world, only organizations whose products and services are high quality thrive, and our schools are far from thriving.

Among those who have taught managers to manage so that almost all workers do high-quality work, one name stands out. To quote from Dr. Myron Tribus, one of his disciples:

> The man who taught the Japanese to achieve high quality at low cost (after World War II) is an American, Dr. W. Edwards Deming. . . . The Japanese faced an "export or

die" situation. They had a reputation for shoddy products. . . . With the aid of the MacArthur government, they located Dr. Deming, and he proceeded to teach them the methods rejected by our managers. The rest is history.[1]

What this history tells us is that the Japanese workers, led by managers trained by Dr. Deming, for the first time in modern history made very high-quality products, especially automobiles and electronics, available at a price the average person could afford. Given the opportunity to get high quality for the same price as low quality, consumers are stampeding toward "made in Japan," and the result is that Japan is now the world's richest country.

I must mention that today, many years after Dr. Deming introduced his ideas so successfully in Japan, some people have become critical of both how the Japanese now manage and of American managers who claim to be using the same ideas.[2] When this criticism is examined, however, it becomes clear that what is being criticized is not what Dr. Deming teaches but rather the distortion of his noncoercive ideas by managers who are only paying lip service to Deming as they return to the traditional, coercive management practices that have been associated with the problems Deming has shown how to solve.

This book will explain how Dr. Deming's ideas can be brought undistorted into our schools so that the present elitist system, in which just a few students are involved in high-quality work, will be replaced by a system in which almost all students have this experience. Once they do have this experience, which for almost all of them would be a totally new one, students will find it highly satisfying. They will no more turn down the chance to continue doing this kind of work than does the well-managed factory worker. But further, as I will soon explain, students are not only the workers in the school, they are also the products. Once they see that they themselves are gaining in quality, they will make an effort to continue this option, just as we continue to buy the quality products of Japan.

Deming, now ninety-one years of age, labored for thirty years in Japan before more than a few American industrialists paid attention to him. More are now listening because they have become aware that paying attention to what he has to say may mean their very survival, but teachers and administrators have no such incentive. They have every reason to believe that they will survive whether or not they change what they have done for so long. So as much as Deming's ideas are likely to increase the quality of our education, moving "managing for quality" into practice in our schools will not be easy.

To help administrators and teachers to accept these new management ideas, I will explain the principles of control theory, with which I have been identified for the past ten years. Control theory reveals, far better than any existing theory, both why and how all of us behave. It explains both why Deming's ideas, when they are used correctly, work so well and how these ideas can be brought into schools. I do not believe those who manage students will make any major changes in what they do if they do not clearly understand the reasons for these changes. Therefore, control theory, as it relates to managing for quality, will be explained in detail beginning in Chapter Four.

To me there is a remarkable parallel between the American manufacturers who ignored Deming's suggestion that they make quality their number-one priority after World War II and our seeming lack of concern today that only a few students in any secondary school do what we, or even they, would call high-quality schoolwork. Like the automakers in the seventies who concentrated on building low-quality, high-profit cars and might have gone bankrupt had competition been unrestricted, our schools have focused on trying to get more students to do enough work, even though that work is almost never high quality, to reach the low-quality standard required for graduation. But, for reasons I will explain in this book, as long as our goal is to "get more of them to do enough to get through," we will only fall further behind.

This claim is confirmed by the disturbing reports printed almost daily in our newspapers that show American college students to be in the minority among graduate students in math and science in our own country; foreign students predominate. And as flawed as any machine-scored tests may be, the latest studies show that American thirteen-year-olds, whose scores on achievement tests have been dropping steadily, now rank below almost all their counterparts in the rest of the world in math and science.[3]

As difficult as this is for most teachers to believe, I contend that this continuing drop is caused by the fact that our traditional system of managing students sends a clear message to almost all students that low-quality work is acceptable. Probably fewer than 15 percent of those who attend do quality academic work in school, and even many of these do far less than they are capable of doing. We fail to realize that the way we manage ignores the fact that very few people—and students are no exception—will expend the effort needed to do high-quality work unless they believe that there is quality in what they are asked to do.

While the manager cannot make people do quality work—control theory contends that no one can make anyone do anything—it is the job of the manager to manage so that the workers or the students can easily see a strong connection between what they are asked to do and what they believe is quality. And as long as we continue to embrace expediency ("get them through") as an excuse to compromise on quality, our schools, already behind, will continue to slip.

That we are not doing this is supported by the fact that many public school teachers, desperate for better education for their own children, are strapping themselves financially to send their children to private schools, which they believe are doing a better job of quality education than the public schools. This is not to say that private schools are actually better than public schools, but only that they are perceived to be so by many people, including many teachers.

It would be extremely difficult to come up with an exact definition of quality education that would apply to all situations. Even without being able to define it, however, we can almost always recognize quality when we see it. Ask any school administrator to take you through the school and show you some high-quality work in any subject area, and I am certain that you will agree that what you are shown is quality. What is similar about all this work is that none of it could be graded or evaluated by machines—quality never can. Further, as I will explain later when I discuss control theory, it is almost impossible for us to do or see anything without making a fairly accurate appraisal of the quality of what we see or do.

Throughout the rest of this book, I will continue to use the industrial analogy of workers and managers because I think it is both accurate and appropriate. The students are the workers of the school, and high-quality work, whether it is waiting on tables or academics, is the difference between the success or failure of the organization. The teachers are the first-level managers, and the administrators are middle- and upper-level managers. As in industry, the productivity of any school depends mostly on the skill of those who directly manage the workers—the teachers. But according to Deming, their success depends almost completely on how well they, in turn, are managed by the administrators above them.

In his 1982 book, addressed to industry but whose message applies even more urgently to the schools, Deming says, "This book teaches the transformation that is required for survival, a transformation that can only be accomplished by man. A company cannot buy its way into quality—it must be led into quality by top management. A theory of management now exists. Never again may anyone say that there is nothing new in management to teach."[4]

Most of those concerned with the problems of our schools have not focused as specifically on how students are managed as I will in this book. When pressed for a solution, both professionals and nonprofessionals say better teaching is the answer, without realizing that much of what they consider better teaching is really better managing. They call for better teaching because we all remember, regardless of the course, working harder and learning more from some teachers than from others. We also remember thinking how good it would have been to have had more teachers like those.

Our main complaint as students (and this has not changed) was not that the work was too hard, but that it was boring, and this complaint was and still is valid. "Boring" usually meant that we could not relate what we were asked to do with how we might use it in our lives. For example, it is deadly boring to memorize facts that neither we, nor anyone we know, will ever use except for a test in school. The most obvious measure of the effective teachers we remember is that they were not boring; somehow or other what they asked us to do was satisfying to us.

Here perhaps is a major difference between a teacher who understands his or her role as a manager and one who does not; the manager is willing to expend effort to assign work that is not boring because he or she knows that it is almost impossible for bored workers to do high-quality work. As I will explain in Chapter Four when I introduce you to control theory, the teacher who is a good manager is not boring because he or she has figured out how to teach in a way that makes it easy for students to satisfy their basic needs when they do the work. If teachers do not teach in need-satisfying ways, then they almost all resort to coercion to try to make students learn.

As this book will attempt to explain, effective teachers manage students without coercion. While less effective teachers may be just as concerned about students personally, when they teach they slip into the coercive practices that destroy their effectiveness. Coercive teachers are the rule, not the exception, in our schools. But, if increasing the number of teachers who manage students without coercion, like the good teachers we remember, is the solution to this pressing problem, no one in power seems to want to address this issue.

For example, none of the recommendations in *A Nation at Risk* focused on how teachers managed students. That report claimed that what we needed was a longer school day and year, stiffer graduation requirements, and more homework, all coercive practices.[5] Since it failed to address the fact that longer hours and harder courses with the same teachers for whom students were not now doing quality work would change nothing, it is hardly surprising that this report has not led to any significant improvement in the schools.

What has surfaced that seems effective is a new focus on changing the school structure, and the most popular new configuration is the magnet school. Here, both teachers and students have more choice: Teachers can teach more of what they enjoy, and students can learn more of what interests them. When this occurs, there is no need for coercion. There is already clear evidence that both students and teachers work harder and do more quality work in magnet schools than they do in the less flexible, more coercive neighborhood schools in most school systems.

But, published research documents that magnet schools and other structurally innovative schools can also fail if traditional coercive management prevails. For this reason, many of these schools are now doing much less than they are capable of doing. This is not because their structure is faulty but because, after a good start, many teachers who made a successful effort to improve the way they managed students are being hampered by administrators who tell them that the quality work both they and their students are doing is not acceptable.

And it is not acceptable to administrators, according to the research of Linda McNeil, Professor of Education at Rice University, because it does not include enough of the low-quality schoolwork that state-mandated achievement tests measure.[6] Nothing of high quality, including schoolwork, can be measured by such standard, machine-scored tests. If we were interested in measuring what these successful, magnet school teachers are doing, this could easily be done through in-depth interviews, observation of a statistically significant sample by qualified observers, and follow-up studies to see if future academic performance was enhanced by this good work. It is symptomatic of our present self-destructive system that students are made aware in a wide variety of coercive ways that low-quality work that can be measured by machines is the top administrative priority of almost all school systems.

This is beautifully illustrated by the following academic equivalent of the Boston Tea Party:

A group of seniors at Torrance's academically rigorous West High School intentionally flunked the latest California Assessment Program test in an attempt to send a message to administrators who they believe place too much emphasis on the exam. . . . At the school Wednesday, student body President Kelle Price, who said that she did not intentionally fail the test, said some seniors became disgruntled when some teachers interrupted classes to prepare them for the [state] tests. She said students also believed that administrators—who visited classes to stress the importance of doing well—were too concerned with maintaining the school's image. . . . At West High, there was much debate Wednesday about who—if anyone—places too much emphasis on the tests. Bawden [the principal] blamed the state Department of Education and the press which does not publish other indicators of a school's performance. . . . Bill Franchini, who heads the Torrance Teachers Association, . . . blamed it on a trickle-down effect, saying the pressure starts with the state department . . . and works its way down through the local school districts, principals, teachers and eventually students. "I think they [students] are feeling like pawns in a game that is much bigger than they are," he said.[7]

These assessments are all correct. Intelligent students who want high-quality education are rebelling against the coercion from the top down to do well on low-quality tests. Coercion begets coercion. Anyone who knows history knows this is true.

It is important to be aware that one of the reasons for the success of magnet schools is that there are not too many of them. If there were an attempt to increase their numbers without increasing the number of teachers drawn to them by the opportunity to be free and innovative, there might not be enough teachers to supply many more of these magnet schools. We should keep in mind that the power of innovation is not that it increases the number of effective people, but that it gives the effective people we have a better chance to demonstrate their effectiveness. What magnet schools do that works is far more than structural. When they work, it is because they are also better managed. When they fail, it is usually because they are managed in the traditional coercive way that has produced the low-quality work that predominates now.

Therefore, the shortage of effective teachers is not a problem that can be solved by a new structure. It is caused by how we train and manage teachers and can only be solved by improving the way we do this, no matter what the structure of the school. Teachers who are effective managers will be effective in any school setting, but they will be less effective if they are managed differently from the way they manage students. The good teachers we remember should be especially revered because in most cases they had the strength to manage students far better than they themselves were managed.

If through better administration we can increase the number of effective teachers, we will soon see a wide variety of structural improvements in many schools, improvements made possible and brought about by the increased numbers of more confident, more professional teachers and, because of them, more hard-working students doing quality work. Creating large number of magnet schools before improving school management to the point where many more students are involved in quality work is putting the cart before the horse.

This book is about managing schools for quality and, in doing so, moving any school toward being what I will call a quality school. I will focus on how teachers can manage students more effectively and on how administrators can use the same methods to manage teachers. The management method I will suggest is very different from the school management now in place in most schools. As I have already begun to explain, it is based on control theory and utilizes the proven quality methods of W. Edwards Deming. It is almost unused in schools, although it is being used with great success in a few corporations. The Ford Motor Company may be a particularly apt example.

However, I doubt if the corporations who have improved their management and who are now struggling to maintain what they have accomplished have any idea that what they are doing is explained by a coherent, easily understood theory. As good as Deming's ideas are, it is my belief that they will not spread as widely as needed, or even continue to be used as much as they are, unless many more managers, especially those who manage our schools, realize that they are based on an understandable and usable new theory that is far different from the one most managers use now.

Although there may be the beginnings of a management revolution in a few major industries, these changes are far from widespread, and almost none have reached the schools. Here, as in most industries, teachers and students are being managed in the same way they always have been, the same way that people have been managed for centuries, by a method based on an ancient, "common-sense" theory of how we function, which is best called stimulus-response.

But, as I will show when I begin to explain control theory in Chapter Four, stimulus-response theory is wrong. When it is used to manage people, it leads to a traditional management method that I will call boss-management. Boss-management is ineffective because it relies on coercion and always results in the workers and the managers becoming adversaries. Bossing rarely leads to consistent hard work and almost never to quality work, and nowhere is this more obvious than in the schools. Managing for quality demands a new noncoercive method of management that I call lead-management. I will begin to explain this method in detail in Chapter Three.

As many of you know, this is not the first time I have written about the use of control theory in the schools. *Control Theory in the Classroom* focused on how the knowledge of this new theory can persuade teachers to use cooperative learning to replace lecturing and individual desk work.[8] But while the feedback on this important change has been very positive, progress has been slow. And it is now apparent to me that progress will continue to be slow until we are able to change from boss-management to lead-management.

Cooperative learning works well because through it students gain power. Lead-managers support this approach because they have discovered that the more they are able to empower workers, the harder they work. In contrast, bosses want to be in charge. They are not comfortable giving workers as much power as cooperative learning requires.

Moving to lead-management, however, means breaking with tradition, and this is always hard to do. In the schools it will be especially hard, even harder than in industry. As Chapter Two explains, this is because embedded in education is a major obstacle not found in most places where people work.

CHAPTER TWO

Effective Teaching May Be the Hardest Job There Is

It is unlikely that we will ever move from boss-management to lead-management unless we overcome the obstacle that stands in the way of making this necessary change. This is our failure to understand how difficult it is to teach effectively. We continue to think that if we just buckled down and really tried, we could easily boss our teachers into doing better. Nothing could be further from the truth. What makes this obstacle so difficult to overcome is that most people, educators included, do not see it as an obstacle. Unless it is clearly seen for what it is, there is little chance that we will overcome it and it will continue to block what we must do, which is to change the way we manage both students and teachers.

Almost everyone in our society shares a huge misconception about teaching. By "everyone" I mean not only the general public, but also teachers as well as parents, administrators, school board members, politicians, educational news reporters, and even the college professors who run teacher-preparation programs. What almost all fail to understand is that being an effective teacher may be the most difficult job of all in our society.

Before I explain why this is so, let me define what I believe effective teaching is. An effective teacher is one who is able to convince not half or three quarters but essentially all of his or her students to do quality work in school. This means to work up to their capacity, not to "lean on their shovels" as so many are doing now. All the measures of school failure that are widely reported—for example, dropout rates, low test scores, and the refusal to take hard subjects like math and science—are the result of students failing to expend the effort to do quality work. The few teachers who can consistently persuade almost all their students to do quality work are, without doubt, succeeding at the hardest job there is.

In order to explain why effective teaching is such a hard job, first I must briefly discuss work in general. I think it is safe to say that almost all work falls into one of two major categories: managing things or managing people.

When we manage things, the essence of the job is to perform an operation on a thing or even on a person (who may be acting as passively as a thing) that improves its value. What is characteristic of a thing (or a person behaving like a thing) is that, hard as the operation may be, the thing never actively resists the person managing it. Diamond cutting, for example, requires great skill but the diamond never resists the cutter. It is passive, having no agenda of its own. A medical patient and a person sitting in a hairdresser's chair are by choice more like things than people in that they resist neither the doctor nor the hairdresser. In fact, they usually try to help the person working on them to do whatever he or she is trying to do.

Jobs in which things are managed—such as carpenter, postal worker, computer programmer, musician, truck driver, architect, and even surgeon—are in some sense much easier than jobs managing people. It is helpful if a musician has a good piano, a programmer a good computer, a truck driver a good truck, an architect good drafting tools, and a surgeon a good patient, but it is not essential. Depending upon their skills and the amount of energy they are willing to expend, they can do their jobs and be judged by others as doing it well even if the things they work on or with are flawed or the people they are trying to improve are less than cooperative. When we manage things, which have no personal agenda, we are much more in control of what we do than when we manage people. It is the well-defined, impersonal, consistent skills of the thing manager that are central to the job. For example, most skillful cabinetmakers work the wood in very much the same way.

This control makes managing things, no matter how much skill or creativity is required, much easier than managing people. Regardless of the skill and creativity of the manager, managing people depends for its ultimate success on the cooperation of the people being managed. The less the people being managed are willing to do as the manager says, the harder the job of managing them is. Teachers are people managers, and most everyone will agree that students as workers seem to be most resistant of all to being managed.

While managing workers or students to increase the quality of their work is less well defined than managing things, there is still great similarity between the skills used by effective managers of both kinds. If teachers become well acquainted with control theory, which explains that all of our behavior is an attempt to satisfy basic needs like love and power, effective management skills will not be hard to learn. For example, while students may appear to be very different from each other, they are all driven by the same needs. The teacher who understands this will focus a great deal of effort on managing in a way that the students can satisfy their needs by doing schoolwork. When they do, and in the process discover that it is in their best interest to do quality work, the teacher's needs are satisfied also.

A graphic example of both the workers and the manager satisfying their needs was seen in a recent America's Cup competition: The crew of the winning boat and the skipper, Dennis Connor, had exactly the same need-satisfying agenda—to win. The crew followed Connor's orders without question from start to finish of each race and were overjoyed when they won. While I am sure there are a few similar examples, blind obedience is by far the exception, not the rule, when it comes to managing the vast majority of workers.

With the exception of teachers, most managers manage workers who, unless they are seriously underpaid, accept that what they are asked to do is reasonably need-satisfying. Unlike students, if they did not want to do what they were told, they would not take the job in the first place or, if they take the job anyway, they will either quit or the manager will fire them. Of course, many dissatisfied students do quit or are thrown out of school, but not before they have attended for a long time, resisting teachers every inch of the way. Other workers who do not like their jobs do not usually last as long.

There are some exceptions to the general rule that most managers deal with workers who are fairly cooperative. For example, a small number of people hold on to jobs they hate and often do poor work because they do not know how to get a better job. This is especially common when their jobs are protected by civil service rules or unions. The major exception to the rule that most workers are fairly cooperative is in the classroom. Here we have teachers and administrators trying to manage huge numbers of students who actively and passively resist what they are asked to do. From the superintendent down, all school managing is difficult, but teaching—the daily face-to-face managing of many resistant students—is not only the hardest job in the school, it is the hardest job there is.

To clarify what I mean, let me compare effective teaching with practicing medicine. Medicine is generally thought to be a very exacting profession and, for that reason, physicians are rigorously and thoroughly trained more so than are teachers. And when physicians work, they are assisted by a variety of highly skilled and often well-paid professionals and technicians. Most physicians work in the finest workplaces that money can buy, are better compensated for what they do than all other professionals, and are treated with respect by all segments of the community. Obviously, physicians labor under far better working conditions than do teachers, and good working conditions, like good training, make any hard job easier.

But what makes medicine so much easier than teaching is more than training, pay, and working conditions. Even if teachers had better working conditions, they would still have to struggle with students who are much more resistant than patients. Patients are usually cooperative because, unlike the way many students view teachers, they almost always see their doctors as need-satisfying people. And if, as rarely happens, patients are not cooperative, few fault the doctor for refusing to treat them. Doctors, therefore, are much more in control of what they are allowed to do than teachers, and the more in control a person is, the easier that person will perceive the job.

Another integral part of what makes a job hard is how much a manager is subject to blame for doing a poor job. Those whose job it is to manage things are usually clearly at fault and quickly blamed when they do a poor job. For example, a truck driver who runs out of gas or a plumber who fails to fix a leak is quickly blamed for this obvious failure.

But it is almost always in the power of such managers to do a good job. Those who manage things, much more than those who manage people, are in control of what they do. This means that although they are clearly subject to blame when they do a poor job, they can almost always avoid blame if they make the effort to do a good job.

On the other hand, those who manage people are less obviously at fault when the people they manage do a poor job. For a long time, the tendency has been to blame the worker more than the manager. A poor student or even several poor students tend to be blamed more than their teachers. But as we are now inundated with students doing badly in school, more and more teachers, who do not believe they are at fault, are being blamed for what they do not know how to correct or being blamed for what they cannot correct because they themselves are managed badly by administrators above them. Being blamed for what you cannot correct or do not believe you can correct is extremely frustrating.

This does not mean that people managers, even administrators and some teachers, should not be held responsible when those they manage do not perform. The thrust of this book is that through better management and the move to quality education, it is possible to teach much more effectively than many teachers do now. However, the point I am trying to make here is that when a teacher is blamed for what he or she believes is almost impossible to do—for example, teach the academically unmotivated student—the teacher perceives this blame as unfair, and this makes the job especially hard.

Another factor that makes teaching such a hard job is the lack of adequate pay for such hard work. If we accept the fact that we need many more effective teachers, we also have to face the fact that a large part of what makes a job easy or hard is the pay. Digging ditches at twenty-five dollars an hour isn't easy, but it's a lot easier than it would be at five dollars an hour. Teaching will never be a high-paying job, but low pay makes it much harder than it needs to be.

Teaching also is hard because there is no relationship between how effectively a teacher teaches and the pay he or she receives for doing it. There is, therefore, no direct financial incentive for expending the time and energy needed to do this hard job better. A good argument against giving teachers a financial incentive for performance is that there is no way yet to measure performance that teachers themselves will agree is fair. For example, a teacher may do a good job all year and sell her class on the value of quality work, but the payoff of her hard work may not be obvious until the following year, when her former students buckle down.

Any system of rewards that is perceived by the workers as unfair will create bitterness and resentment. This is already a problem with merit pay and in the mentor-teacher system, and the more pay is based on arbitrary criteria, the more this problem will grow. It is not an insoluble problem, however. At the end of this book, I offer a solution for increased pay for increased performance that I believe most teachers will consider fair.

Another factor that makes effective public school teaching in this country much harder, as compared to other countries, is that we do not have the strong cultural support of education that is taken for granted in countries like Korea, Japan, France, and Germany. We have a wide variety of subcultures, many of which do not value the education offered in our schools. If they do value it, they do not value the way it is offered. While it may be overstating the case to say that some of our subcultures are anti-intellectual, we certainly have many families in which what is commonly referred to as "book learning" is not highly prized.

Even our colleges are publicized more for athletics than for academics. We take pride in the fact that someone who did not do well in school or who had little schooling—the so-called self-made man or woman—can go far in our society. A person running for high office with a Ph.D. might find it to be as great a handicap as a moral indiscretion. This ethos may be democratic and less elitist than foreign cultures, but it does not help our teachers. They have a much harder job than teachers in some foreign countries because foreign students are much more likely to be persuaded by their families to work hard in school and to do as the teacher says.

Obviously, the less resistant the students, the easier the teacher's job. It would seem, therefore, that those in the state departments of education, who are at the top of the school management hierarchy, would do all they could do to create curricula that students would not resist. But as Professor Linda McNeil points out, (and supported by the rebellious West High Students described in Chapter One) this is hardly the case.[1]

Instead, as students' "achievement" is more and more being called into question by the public and has become a political issue, state after state is "measuring" achievement on the basis of "objective" tests and finding the scores too low. Driven by the fear that they will be blamed for these low scores and their power will thereby be threatened, most state departments are desperately introducing teaching "reforms" that are directly (and, I believe, blindly) aimed at raising test scores.

As Professor McNeil's research clearly shows, teachers are being asked more and more to objectify and standardize their teaching. As they do, education is being fragmented and mystified, and large areas that might in any way be controversial, and therefore interesting, such as the Vietnam War, are being omitted. As this happens, the result from the teachers' point of view is that they are more and more being treated as nonintellectual "things" and less and less as capable professionals. McNeil writes:

> Such reforms render teaching and the curriculum inauthentic. If we are to engage students in learning, we must reverse this process. When school knowledge is not credible to students, they opt out and decide to wait until "later" to learn "what you really need to know." Mechanical teaching processes knowledge in a way that guarantees it will be something other than credible. Centralized curriculum, centralized tests of outcomes, and

standardized teacher behaviors can only frustrate those
teachers whose passion for teaching has shown students
(and the rest of us) what education should be about.[2]

To conform to this new and widespread concern that all
that is taught be measured, teachers, as the managers of students, are required to turn their backs on a basic control
theory axiom: For workers, including students, to do quality
work, they must be managed in a way that convinces them
that the work they are asked to do satisfies their needs. The
more it does, the harder they will work.

Instead, teachers are required to stuff students with fragments of measurable knowledge as if the students had no
needs—almost as if they were things. Education is defined as
how many fragments of information these "student-things"
can retain long enough to be measured on standardized
achievement tests. Most competent teachers recognize, however, that this approach has little or nothing to do with what
they consider quality education, but their input is either ignored or depreciated by the politically motivated standardiz-
ers and fragment measurers who are now in charge.

Because this low-quality, standardized, fragmented approach is so unsatisfying to students (and teachers), more and
more students are actively resisting and this resistance is seen
as a discipline problem. School administrators then fall into
the trap of thinking that discipline problems, not unsatisfying
education, are the cause of low levels of achievement. This
explains the increased emphasis on strict rules of deportment
(more coercion), which further define a good student as a
passive thing rather than an involved, questioning, even at
times dissenting learner.

When this happens, as Professor McNeil found at a school
she studied,

Any deviations from administrative directives for maintaining order were dealt with by school discipline policies that frequently did not punish offenders directly but punished all students together. Both teachers and students felt herded. Many attempts to control behavior were so disproportionate to the offense that they seemed to be acts of desperation and, in turn, made students rebel in such petty ways as littering in the halls and cafeteria.[3]

Teaching is difficult under the best educational conditions, and this failure to take into account the needs of students or teachers makes what is already a hard job almost impossible. Any method of teaching that ignores the needs of teachers or students is bound to fail. Most of us are now well aware that we are increasingly paying the price for that failure in the increased use of drugs, more delinquency, and greater numbers of teenage pregnancies—to cite some of the more obvious problems.

Teachers, who must manage better than all other managers if they are to succeed at all, are being asked to accept educational working conditions that almost ensure that they will fail to persuade at least half, and usually more, of their students to do even low-quality work. For the competent teacher, it has become a miserable Catch-22: If I teach conceptually and challenge them to think and defend their ideas, which is the way I know is right, my students have a chance to succeed in learning something worthwhile, but they may not do well on the tests that measure fragments and I will be labeled a troublemaker and a failure. On the other hand, if I teach the way I am told, my students will fail to learn anything that I, and most of them, believe is worthwhile, but I will be praised as a successful team player and they will be blamed as incompetent.

Caught in this trap, many teachers are giving up on what

they believe and accepting the political view that students should be treated as things and stuffed with fragments of knowledge. To teach this way, they emphasize facts and "right" answers, avoid controversy and discussion, give a great deal of homework, test frequently, and tailor what they teach to state testing programs. In doing so, they become much more impersonal than they would like and teach less of what their students want to learn than they feel is right. Nothing makes a job harder than feeling that you have to give up on what you believe.

There are probably other obstacles to overcome if we are to make the switch from boss- to lead-managing. But if we can overcome this one, we have a good chance of overcoming others. If we continue to take the skill and art of teaching lightly, believing that almost anyone can do it, and end most formal training when teachers start to teach, we will not make progress. Teaching is a very hard job that needs ample compensation and considerable on-the-job training for the lifetime of the teacher. Less than this will not suffice.

CHAPTER THREE

We Need Noncoercive Lead-Management from the State Superintendent to the Teacher

Having seen that teaching is perhaps the most difficult of all management jobs, we are now ready to take a detailed look at the crucial factor in educational reform: replacing boss-management with lead-management so that we can begin the move to quality. Boss-management is wrong because it limits both the quality of the work and the productivity of the worker. And further, as I will explain shortly, its use actually produces most of the discipline problems we are trying to prevent.

In education, where it is used almost exclusively, boss-management has effectively limited the number of students who do acceptable work (many less do quality work) to about 50 percent in the best neighborhoods and up to 90 percent in schools where there is little support for learning in students' homes. Therefore, given the hardest of management jobs, teachers as well as administrators are burdened with a method of management that limits their ability to succeed no matter how competent they are in other respects.

Boss-management is not complicated. Reduced to its essentials, it contains four basic elements:

1. The boss sets the task and the standards for what the workers (students) are to do, usually without consulting the workers. Bosses do not compromise; the worker has to adjust to the job as the boss defines it.

2. The boss usually tells, rather than shows, the workers how the work is to be done and rarely asks for their input as to how it might possibly be done better.
3. The boss, or someone the boss designates, inspects (or grades) the work. Because the boss does not involve the workers in this evaluation, they tend to settle for just enough quality to get by.
4. When workers resist, the boss uses coercion (usually punishment) almost exclusively to try to make them do as they are told and, in so doing, creates a workplace in which the workers and manager are adversaries.

Viewed as a whole, it is obvious that boss-management is much more concerned with the needs of the boss than of the workers. Because this is so obvious, many bosses have been able to see that boss-management is counter productive. There is now some softening of this hard line, mostly in high-tech and service industries where the educational and persuasive skills of the worker are paramount to the success of the company. Schools, however, are one of the few "industries" in which boss-management is used pretty much as outlined above.

The most obvious reason for the overwhelming preponderance of boss-managers is tradition. It is "natural" for the strong to try to dominate the weak, and students are always younger and less knowledgeable (therefore weaker) than the teacher. Administrators, especially, tend to see students as subordinates, a situation tailor-made for the boss-management approach. And since schools have always been boss-managed, most teachers and administrators do not question what they do and are not even aware that a better, noncoercive method of management exists.

In industry, we now have extensive research to prove that boss-management is much less effective than lead-management,[1] but this research has had little effect on much of industry and almost no effect on the schools. I believe there are two reasons for this, both of which I address in this book:

1. Managers do not know control theory and do not know why lead-management works. They therefore tend to distrust it even when they see it working.
2. Managers do not realize that what Deming has taught and demonstrated is that quality is the key to increased productivity.

There is always the fear, especially in education among the measurers and fragmenters who prevail at the top, that if we are too concerned with quality, students will cover less ground. Deming has shown that the opposite occurs: Quality always leads to increased productivity. Many people do not believe this because what Deming has accomplished is so contrary to "common sense."

Boss-management is also difficult to challenge because in most schools there are enough students willing to work that any teacher can say, "Look at all the students who are doing well because they are doing what they are told." But the success of these students is not due to the way they are managed: It is because of the homes they come from. It occurs despite how they are managed: If boss-management were effective, many more students would be successful.

The get-tough, coercive boss approach is the main way in which schools deal with problem students. The persuasive, lead-management approach is not known well enough even to be considered. But even if teachers were aware of this approach, they would be leery of it because they fear it lacks control. Boss-managers are not comfortable with the idea of giving up the control they believe is inherent in their traditional boss approach.

But as much as boss-management promises control, in schools it totally fails to deliver on this promise. There is no shortage of students in most schools who neither work nor follow rules. Teachers who become frustrated by these resistant students tend to request sanctions like detention, suspension, and corporal punishment, but as they use these, they become more boss-like and less effective. They fail to recognize that many students have become hardened to these limited sanctions and have no fear of them. From the students' standpoint, the need-frustrating pain of memorizing low-quality fragments is as great or greater than the pain of whatever sanction they might suffer at the hands of the teacher.

What teachers also fail to see is that these very sanctions stand in the way of achieving the quality that is essential to a highly productive workplace. This is because as soon as a boss uses coercion, especially punishment, the boss and the worker become adversaries. There is no way to avoid this happening. And while people will work for an adversary (huge numbers do and some even work hard), they do so because of their own needs. The boss is ignored, avoided, disliked, or ridiculed and is seen as either unnecessary or as an obstacle to getting the job done.

In such an atmosphere, which prevails in many work situations (schools have no monopoly here), workers will work, but very few will consistently do the high-quality work of which they are capable. Too often, work becomes a wasteful contest. The boss tries to get as much from the workers as possible while giving as little as possible, and the workers give as little as possible and still try to get what they want. This contest uses up a great deal of energy that could be better channeled into productivity and quality.

In school, the adversarial teacher-student relationship that is destructive to quality starts quickly. As early as first grade, any child who does not do as the teacher says is almost always boss-managed, and the coercion starts. It does not make much difference whether it is done subtly or overtly: The child knows when he or she is being coerced. As soon as this occurs, the child's main agenda becomes resistance, the personal power struggle between teacher and pupil begins, and education is left behind. It becomes a vicious cycle: The child learns less and resists more; the teacher coerces more and teaches less. For many children this adversarial relationship is in place by elementary school, and their formal education becomes secondary to a never-ending power struggle in which all involved are losers.

Teachers in elementary schools, however, are much less likely to use boss-management destructively than in the secondary school. The "keep-quiet-and-do-what-you-are-told" boss approach flowers in the higher grades, where teachers are pressured to "produce" and where, with well over a hundred students each day, they have little opportunity to get to know their students personally. By the end of the seventh grade, more than half the students believe that teachers and principals are their adversaries. Quality education thus becomes unavailable except to the dwindling minority who are willing to fit into the boss-defined system. Believing, correctly in most cases, that the system will never adjust to what they want or even try to find out what that is, many students drop out altogether, many more than are reported because our present statistics do not include substantial numbers of middle school dropouts.[2]

Boss-management works better if the boss uses rewards instead of punishment. Even though control remains in the hands of the boss, this tends to reduce the adversarial atmosphere that is the hallmark of boss-management. Schools, however, are largely unable to reward students, so that the best part of boss-management is mostly unavailable to students. There are, for example, no immediate rewards comparable to those in industry, such as pay increases, help from subordinates, promotions, better offices, good parking, and time off.

Even good grades, essentially the only tangible school reward, are far from immediate. Most schools depend on hazy, long-term rewards, such as the promise that students will get into a good college and get a good job if they work hard and get good grades. This is probably true, but these goals are so far in the future that fewer than half of the capable students are willing to work hard now to achieve them. Young people, especially, will not work hard for distant rewards. If they are to put out a lot of effort, they want an immediate payoff.

Therefore, it is almost impossible to coerce students to work hard enough to do quality work when they see school as nonsatisfying. What is needed instead of coercion is a great deal of creativity and patience, both of which tend to be in short supply. This does not mean that all boss-management is ineffective, but it is least effective where workers do not see the job as satisfying. It is most effective where workers and the boss have the same agendas and where the boss uses rewards more than punishment, a situation more prevalent in elementary school than in secondary school.

While boss-management is ineffective at all levels, the higher the level at which it is employed, the more damage it does to the quality of the work and the productivity of the worker. For example, teachers who use boss-management exclusively will limit the learning in their classes. A principal who is a dedicated boss-manager will make it so hard for teachers to use lead-management that the whole school will be negatively affected. A superintendent following this philosophy will cast a shadow on the whole district, and when boss-management is the philosophy in the state office, as it is in the many states that are now demanding that standardized fragments of learning be measured, the whole state will suffer.

As Deming says, "The goal is clear. The productivity of our systems must be increased. The key to change is the under-standing of our managers, and the people to whom they re-port, about what it means to be a good manager."

Lead-Management Is the Basic Reform We Need

In contrast to the coercive core of boss-management, per-suasion and problem solving are central to the philosophy of lead-management. The lead-manager spends all his time and energy figuring out how to run the system so that workers will see that it is to their benefit to do quality work. In Deming's words:

1. A manager is responsible for consistency of purpose and continuity to the organization. The manager is solely responsible to see that there is a future for the workers. [It is our responsibility as a society to manage our schools so that almost all students get a high-quality education.]
2. The workers work in a system. The manager should work on the system to see that it produces the highest quality product at the lowest possible cost. The distinction is crucial. They work *in* the system; the manager works *on* the system. No one else is responsible for the system as a whole and improving it.[3] [This means that the adminis-trators, much more than the teachers, are responsible for improving the system.]

Keeping these points in mind, following are the four essen-tial elements of lead-managing:

1. The leader engages the workers in a discussion of the quality of the work to be done and the time needed to do it so that they have a chance to add their input. The

leader makes a constant effort to fit the job to the skills and the needs of the workers.

2. The leader (or a worker designated by the leader) shows or models the job so that the worker who is to perform the job can see exactly what the manager expects. At the same time, the workers are continually asked for their input as to what they believe may be a better way.

3. The leader asks the workers to inspect or evaluate their own work for quality, with the understanding that the leader accepts that they know a great deal about how to produce high-quality work and will therefore listen to what they say.

4. The leader is a facilitator in that he shows the workers that he has done everything possible to provide them with the best tools and workplace as well as a noncoercive, nonadversarial atmosphere in which to do the job.

To demonstrate how these elements would work in practice, let me apply them to the teaching of algebra, a subject that many students are having difficulty learning in our predominantly boss-managed math classes. In these classes a boss-teacher sets the agenda, and the students have no say in this process. The students pass the course if the first time they take the test they are able to achieve a minimum score; even low-quality D work is passing. Large numbers of students are failing, however, because they do not do even this much or cannot do it on the only test given.

In contrast, a lead-teacher would start by discussing algebra, defining it, and explaining why it is taught and how the students could use it in their lives. If available, a videotape would be shown in which successful people from various cultural backgrounds explain how they use algebra in their lives and why it was worthwhile for them to learn it. The lead-teacher would tell the class that any student who makes an effort can learn algebra well.

After answering students' immediate questions, the teacher would then explain that much of the work would be done in small cooperative groups (a very need-satisfying way to teach) in which students would help each other. The teacher would try to assign at least one capable student to each cooperative group and would teach these student leaders how to model the problem-solving techniques for the rest of the group. The teacher would emphasize that the purpose of the groups is to help them all to understand algebra, not just to get the problems done. Schools would make an effort to train all the teachers who use cooperative learning to use it well.

The teacher would ask for students' input as to when they are ready to take the tests, based on their results on practice tests that would always precede the real exams. Students who did well on the tests would go on; students who did not do well would then have the chance to continue working on the tested material until they mastered it. Competency and quality would be the rule: Time would never be a factor. The ideal of a quality school would be that no student willing to do the work would need to be concerned about running out of the time needed to learn. This would mean that no one would be asked to go on to new material until he or she had demonstrated a good understanding of what had been covered so far.

In practice, this approach would present difficulties. How would a teacher handle faster and slower students in the same classroom? What we do now is to let the slower students struggle. They either fail or end up doing work of very low quality, hardly a sensible solution to this problem. Or they drop algebra, enroll in general math, and never learn higher mathematics. My solution is to find out early who is not able to keep up in the standard one-year course and offer a two-year course concurrently into which these slower students could transfer. While some of the one-year students might do higher-quality work than the two-year students, quality would also be maintained in the slower course. The difference would be less in the quality of the work than in the time to do it.

In the two-year course, all students who worked would be given sufficient time to complete each unit of the course with competence. As they did, they would gain confidence and begin to work a little faster, and many would go on to higher math. (At present, students who fall behind lose confidence and simply give up.) Students from the one-year course could transfer into the two-year course at specified intervals during the year, knowing that the same quality standards would apply. This might mean that the faster students would have a chance for an additional elective, or they could be enlisted to help tutor the slower students both in and out of class. Given a chance to teach, they would improve their already high-quality skills. An added incentive to do this would be the chance to earn the A+ grade that I will explain in Chapter Eight. In this way, almost all who are willing to try would eventually learn to do quality algebra. And using the approach described here, many more than now would be willing to try.

From the beginning, all students, both as individuals and as a group, would be asked to evaluate the quality of their class-work, homework, and tests and to put this evaluation at the top of all they do. How they would do this would be discussed and agreed on as part of the continual give-and-take that would take place in a lead-managed class. Following Deming, the emphasis would be on involving the students in the evalua-tion of their own work for quality, and they would be encour-aged to keep their own quality record so that they would always know exactly where they were.

The lead-teacher's job would be to facilitate continually, which would mean talking to students and listening to their input on how to keep the classroom a good place to learn and how to make improvements. Once the students discovered that they could actually do quality work in algebra, they would find a satisfaction with math that almost no students get now in their boss-managed classes. It is only the discovery that "I can do quality work" that leads to motivation, a subject I will discuss in detail in the next chapter. There would be no coercion and, therefore, no discipline problems, as they do not occur in a noncoercive atmosphere.

When the above principles are put into practice in school or elsewhere, the worker cannot help but see that the manager is as concerned with the workers' needs as with his or her own. And when the workers are students, they realize that the person they are working for is a teacher, not a boss. This is why lead-managing is so applicable to education: The very definition of good teaching is embodied in the four elements of lead-management.

While in theory the basic tactics of the two types of managers differ markedly, in practice boss-managers are rarely all boss. Few boss-managers approach their job with the coercive zeal of a marine drill sergeant, and even a drill sergeant will at times use some persuasion. On the other hand, lead-managers may be tempted to blend a little coercion into their basic lead approach, but, if they do, they risk losing their effectiveness. For this reason, the best lead-managers make a constant effort never to coerce. Even a little coercion will taint the lead atmosphere and render it adversarial because the manager will be seen as a phony. It takes a long time to persuade workers who have been boss-managed to accept that they can work in a problem-solving, give-and-take atmosphere free of coercion. If there is any coercion at all, this acceptance time is greatly extended.

This does not mean, however, that the lead-manager does nothing if a worker fails to put forth effort or breaks the rules of the workplace. There is much the lead-manager can and should do: His skill is doing it without coercion. How a teacher or administrator can accomplish this will be explained in detail in the final chapters of this book, but basically, when there is a dispute between the leader and the worker, the leader makes it clear to the worker that this is a problem they can solve together. The leader emphasizes that problems are never solved by coercion: They are solved by all parties to the problem figuring out a better way that is acceptable to all. If the first solution does not work, the problem is addressed again. Coercion is never an option, so it is almost impossible for the leader and the workers to become adversaries.

While being an effective leader may initially take more time and effort than bossing, in the end it takes much less time and effort because workers find that when they are managed by a leader, quality work is very satisfying. It is certainly possible to learn how to be an effective lead-teacher, but few teachers will make the effort to do so unless they themselves experience the benefit of this approach. This means that lead-management and the concepts of quality will not flourish in our classrooms unless they are implemented at the level of the school principal. He or she is the crucial element in educational reform.

The principal who wants to be a successful lead-manager must learn the social and administrative skills needed to be a buffer between the bosses above and the teachers he or she lead-manages. It would be good if these ideas were accepted at levels above the principal, and I am sure that this will be the case at times. But once we leave the school, the central office power struggles of educational politics almost always intrude. Bossing and kowtowing are so deeply ingrained at the top of the system that my hope for educational reform is to find enough principals willing to give up bossing and start leading.

Boss-management has failed and will continue to fail because it is not based on how we function. The following chapters present a control theory explanation of how we function that shows clearly why lead-management and the quality ideas of W. Edwards Deming work. If this explanation makes sense to you, then maybe together we can begin to make the changes that are needed.

An Important Word About Style

I have stated that lead-managers are not coercive, but most of us remember great teachers whose style seemed to go against this tenet. Jaime Escalante, the calculus teacher in the movie *Stand and Deliver,* seemed the antithesis of the lead-teacher: he threatened, cajoled, cursed, ridiculed, graded almost capriciously, threw students out of class, put down their interest in other activities such as playing in the band, gave huge amounts of homework, and worked students to the point of exhaustion. A few rebelled, but most revered him and accepted that what he did was for their own good.

What we must realize is that there is a very fine distinction between coercion, which is never caring, and a coercive style of teaching that is, at its core, very caring. If the workers see the manager as caring, then they can accept whatever he does, no matter how coercive it may seem on the surface. To workers, caring means that they believe their welfare is more important to the manager than either his welfare or the welfare of those above him in the organization. Further, they see the manager as desperate, not vindictive. They know that they are not used to doing quality work and that he is only attempting to get them to work harder than most have ever worked before. But they will not see this if they do not also see that the manager himself is working harder than they are used to seeing managers work. The message must come across loud and clear from the manager: No matter how hard I ask you to work, I work as hard or harder.

Therefore, the essence of good managing is caring and hard work. Acting, posturing, dramatizing, shouting, gesturing, and criticizing are styles a manager may choose as he or she attempts to add drama and excitement to what can easily become a boring process. As long as the essence is preserved, any style is within the confines of lead-management. Great leaders all have a style that works for them, and I doubt that it can (or should) be taught or even successfully imitated. It is their unique, creative approach to the difficult problem of persuading people to do what they are reluctant to do.

I believe, however, that the majority of great teachers do not use the coercive style that Escalante used so successfully. When you study great teachers, as I hope you will have a chance to do, you will learn much more from their caring and hard work than from their style. To be a successful lead-manager, you will have to develop your own style; it is the only style that will work for you.

CHAPTER FOUR

Control Theory and Motivation

In school, boss-management is a major reason why so few students are involved in high-quality honors or advanced-placement classes. And as long as boss-managers prevail, there is little chance we will ever be able to increase this small number because boss-managers totally misunderstand what has become one of the most common management buzzwords: motivation. Boss-managers firmly believe that people can be motivated from the outside: They fail to understand that all of our motivation comes from within ourselves.

Boss-teachers and administrators constantly lament that students are not motivated, but what they are actually saying is that they do not know how to persuade students to work. And as long as they continue to believe in coercion, they never will. When it comes to understanding motivation, boss-managers are looking for something that does not exist. But they keep looking because they, like almost everyone else, accept the stimulus-response theory. According to this theory, our behavior is almost always motivated by a stimulus that exists outside of ourselves. For example, most people believe that students stop talking because the teacher asks for silence or that jail sentences deter crime. But control theory points out that this is not the case. Students keep quiet only when they believe it is to their benefit to do as the teacher asks; otherwise they keep talking. And our jails are filled with lawbreakers who have been there before and have not been deterred by that experience.

It is always what we want at the time that causes our behavior. The outside event (stimulus) may seem to be the cause, but it never is. Some students do not stop talking when the teacher asks; short of applying force (gagging them or dragging them from class), there is nothing any teacher can do to make them. Boss-teachers tell students every day to work hard; even though they are punished, many students still do not work hard. In fact, many do even less after they are punished. This fact does not faze boss-teachers; they continue to believe they can make students do what they are told, if only they can figure out a firmer way to tell them. One indication of this is that more teachers than the general public, (56 percent compared to 50 percent) believe that they should have the right to spank children.[1]

A friend of mine stopped believing in external motivation when he was held up at gunpoint and found himself refusing to give the gunman his wallet because he did not want to lose his driver's license and credit cards. He was amazed that he ignored one of the most powerful stimuli of all, a gun. We can argue that he is lucky to be alive, but the fact is that the gunman, a firm believer in boss-management, did not get the wallet. Even a gun does not always make you boss.

This does not mean that people threatened with a gun do not usually do as they are told: Most of the time they do. But the reason they do is not just because of the threat. It is because they decide that, all things considered, it will be better for them at the time not to resist. But they resent being threatened and will do only the bare minimum of what is asked. Managers can count on coercion to achieve only the simplest tasks: Resentful workers will not do anything well that is the least bit complicated.

The same goes for reward: It is not the reward but the

person's evaluation of how much he or she wants the reward that determines behavior. Managers who use rewards achieve more than managers who use punishment because rewards tend to be more need-satisfying, but workers may still resent the manager's power to give or withhold the reward. They may challenge that power by not doing as much as the manager wants, even at the risk of losing the reward altogether.

I am not saying that what happens outside of us means nothing, far from it. What happens outside of us has a lot to do with what we choose to do, but the outside event does not cause our behavior. What we get, and all we ever get, from the outside is information; how we choose to act on this information is up to us. Therefore, the information that the students get from the teacher, which includes how this information is given, is very important. In fact, this whole book is about its importance. But the students are the ones who make the ultimate judgment about how important it is to them. The more important they think it is, the more they will do what they are asked and the better they will do it.

If I point a gun at you and ask for your wallet, that whole sequence for you is information. You will do, and only do, what you think is best. Most of you will give up your wallets because you decide your life is more important than your wallet, but some of you, like my friend, will not. The difference between a lead-manager and a boss-manager is in the information each gives to the worker or student, and this is a huge difference. In practice, it is the main difference between students working or "leaning on their shovels." The message from the boss-manager is always coercive, be it reward or punishment, because the bosses think that this is the best way to "motivate" workers. Bosses like to point guns more than they like to raise salaries and are always looking for bigger guns. Effective lead-managers never use coercive messages but instead try to give the workers the kind of information that will persuade them to do as they are directed because it is as much or more to their benefit as it is to the manager's.

But if they know control theory, lead-managers also know what information that we, as humans, are always looking for. Using this knowledge, an effective lead-manager makes an effort to combine what workers are looking for (actually what all humans are looking for) with what he or she is asking them to do. If the manager succeeds, it is very likely that the workers will decide not only to do the work but to do it well.

When boss-teachers complain that nothing they do seems to motivate students to work hard, what they are really saying is that they have not succeeded in giving these students the right message. Given the usual coercive messages, "unmotivated" students ignore them and choose not to work. But the fact that students choose not to do schoolwork does not mean they lack motivation: No human being is unmotivated. In fact, every living creature is highly motivated all the time. Students are no exception to the control theory axiom that all living creatures are always motivated by the basic needs of their species. But every living creature, including students, is not necessarily motivated to do what you, I, or anyone else thinks they ought to do. There is certainly no basic need to do schoolwork.

If, however, what we are asked to do also satisfies one or more of our basic needs, a great deal of work gets done. If we care for the manager, we may even do what is distasteful to us because pleasing the manager strongly satisfies our basic need for love and friendship. This means that as much as we dislike it, we may learn grammar because we care for the teacher who teaches it. But if we stop caring for this teacher, we may stop learning grammar. Students will do things for a teacher they care for that they would not consider doing for a teacher they did not care for.

But there is a limit to what we will do for someone we care

for if it is distasteful to us. In fact, much misery is caused by our failure to understand that we cannot get other people, even if we love them and they love us, to do what we want them to do if it is extremely unsatisfying to them. Many parents have struggled painfully to try to "make" a child they love change his or her ways because they "know" that what they want the child to do is better for that child than what the child is doing.

Time may even prove the parents right. However, when they are engaged in what is too often a losing battle, for example, when a teenager starts to stay out half the night even on school nights, the parents may worry and suffer beyond belief. But the more the parents act the boss and try to coerce the child into coming home at a reasonable hour, the less control they seem to have and the more miserable they are.

The crucial difference between boss-managers and lead-managers is mainly in how they understand motivation. Bosses refuse to accept that they cannot "motivate" the workers with what they believe will cause the workers pain or give them pleasure, especially when they also believe that what they are asking is good for the workers. Following this belief, bosses constantly look for new sanctions or rewards to "make" the workers work. Leaders, on the other hand, know that they cannot make the workers work hard if the work is seen as unsatisfying or they are seen as unconcerned about the workers' needs.

To understand what motivation actually is, it is necessary first to understand that control theory contends that all human beings are born with five basic needs built into their genetic structure: survival, love, power, fun, and freedom. All of our lives we must attempt to live in a way that will best satisfy one or more of these needs.

Control theory is a descriptive term because we try to control our own behavior so that what we choose to do is the most need-satisfying thing we can do at the time. Although we can control only our own behavior, it is obvious that much of what we choose to do is an attempt to control others. For example, many of us attempt to stop people we love from destroying themselves with addicting drugs. But to do this we can control only what *we* do. Control theory, therefore, is the explanation of this constant attempt to control both ourselves and others, even though in practice we can control only ourselves.

Keep in mind that "control" in this context means to control as in steering a car or following a recipe. It does not mean to dominate by using force or the threat of force, as a police officer does to subdue a criminal. And although we may say, "I forced myself," we do not really use force on ourselves. What we mean is that it was particularly difficult for us to choose to do as we did.

Our genes, which in essence are the biological instructions for what we are to become, not only dictate what our structure is to be (for example, our eye color) but also (and this claim is unique to control theory) how we, as humans, must attempt to live our lives. Just as a northern migrating bird must always attempt to fly south for the winter, we, too, must attempt to live our lives in ways that we believe will best satisfy our needs. If what we are asked to do in school does not satisfy one or more of these needs or we do not care for the teacher who asks us to do it, then we will do it poorly or even not at all.

From birth, our behavior is always our best attempt at the time to do what we believe will best satisfy one or more of our needs. We can no more deny that these needs exist and are constantly on our mind (whether we are aware of it or not), than we can deny the shape of our nose or the color of our eyes. And regardless of our cultural background, we are all members of the same species, and all of us have the same genetic needs. We spend our lives trying to learn how to satisfy these needs, but most of us do not have a clear idea of what they are, especially when we are young. What we always know, however, is how we feel. And what we actually struggle for all of our lives is to feel good. It is from our ability to feel, essentially from our ability to know whether we feel good or bad, that most of us gain some idea of what our needs are.

Because they are well able to tell the difference between pain and pleasure, newborn babies quickly learn to express themselves so that those who take care of them can tell whether they are feeling good or bad. Parents may not know exactly how to help a baby feel better, but they almost always know how the baby feels. Very quickly, babies become better at expressing what is wrong and parents become more adept at guessing what it is.

It does not take long before parents are also able to figure out how to help the baby to feel better, which is the same as saying how to help the baby satisfy his or her needs. Using the information constantly available to them about how they feel, children learn as they grow what feels good and what feels bad. As they do, they learn to satisfy their own needs or to get help from others (like their parents) if they cannot do it for themselves.

Even before starting school, most children are told by their families that school is good for them, and they expect school to feel good. And in the beginning it usually does feel good: For most children, kindergarten is a very need-satisfying experience. As they progress, however, what they do in school does not feel as good as it did in kindergarten. When they question this dropoff, they are told that what they are taught is still good for them because it will help them later. The strong implication is, "Continue working hard, but also be patient because there will be less that feels good immediately and more that will not feel good until later."

The problem is that the genetic needs themselves know nothing about later: They are continually pushing us to do what feels good now. You can tell your stomach that you are not going to feed it because you want to lose weight, but you cannot stop your stomach from telling you that it wants food right now. A measure of our strength, often called strength of character, is how much we can learn to tolerate pain or delay pleasure while doing what is "good" for us in the long run. As stated in the last chapter, if we have a supportive family and can satisfy our needs at home, getting through a frustrating day at school or work is a lot easier.

Even with strong family support, it's hard to get through many bad days. Without this support, it may be impossible. Not enough students have the strength to keep working hard if they encounter day after day of painful frustration, and many subjects, taught now in the fragmented way described in the first chapter, are miserably boring. Since we all want to suffer as little possible, many students who feel bad choose to stop working in school.

A good lead-manager is able to predict how much pain a worker will put up with in the present and still keep working hard for a future payoff. Right now school managers are making this prediction very accurately: Far too many students are refusing to work hard for what seems to be a too-distant payoff. What teachers have no way of knowing is how much family support their students have. Too many teachers mistakenly believe their students have more family support than they actually have.

This is an easy mistake to make because teachers, like all of us, tend to draw on their own experience, and most teachers had more family support when they were young than their students do. You probably did not have much use for higher math when you took it, and you were well aware that there were more enjoyable things to do than study for a math exam. But you studied anyway because you decided, based on information you got from your family, whom you believed, that this effort was necessary if you were to get some power later on. You may not have known about your need for power, but you were aware that your future might depend on doing well in math.

If you had known about your basic needs, you might have been even more willing to work and may have even been willing to work with less family support. Later I will discuss teaching students control theory so that they might use its concepts to make better choices in their lives, especially to work hard in school and to stay away from addicting drugs. It is always helpful to know about our needs, especially our need for power, because we can use this knowledge to help us accept short-term pain when there is a good chance that this sacrifice will lead to power and long-term pleasure later.

For those in the position of managing people, knowledge of needs is more than helpful, it is essential. For example, when I present my ideas to teachers and administrators, I usually interview six junior or senior high school students in front of a large audience. Because for young people the need for power is very difficult to satisfy, I always ask, "Where in school do you feel important?" This question always seems to the students to come from outer space; they look at me as if I had asked something ridiculous. Even for the very good students, who are the group usually selected to be interviewed, feeling important (powerful) in school is an experience that few seem to think relates to them.

However, when I persist, most students tell me that they feel important in their extracurricular activities: Sports, music, and drama are most frequently mentioned. Almost never mentioned are academic classes. When asked why this is so, they say that in the extracurricular situations, where they work together as a group or on a team, they work harder and accomplish more because they help each other and have more fun. They also emphasize that they are both more comfortable and less bored in these situations because it is accepted that they socialize while they work, which is unacceptable in their regular classes. From the standpoint of control theory, these students are saying that it is very hard for them to satisfy their needs in academic classes because most work is done alone and there is little or no class discussion.

To remedy this, I strongly suggested in *Control Theory in the Classroom* that we teach students in cooperative groups in their academic classes. Learning together as a member of a small learning team is much more need-satisfying, especially to the needs for power and belonging, than learning individually. Good lead-managers recognize that when they can promote and support worker cooperation, they have laid the foundation for quality work. Since I have already argued extensively for this approach in my earlier book, it need not be repeated in this one.

If we attempt to manage people without taking their needs into account, we will ask them to do things without considering whether or not those things are need-satisfying either now or later. Lead-managers know that the more immediately need-satisfying the work is, the harder people will work. Of course, everything we ask students to do in school cannot be immediately satisfying. But at the least, it has to lead to later satisfaction, and students need to know when and where this satisfaction will come. Lead-managers make a point to give students this information. To the extent that the work is not satisfying now or later, students will not do it and the manager will fail.

In terms of how they handle the need-satisfaction of those they manage, there is a marked difference between boss-managers and lead-managers. Boss-managers tell people what they should do and often how to do it. They also tell them that it is the best thing for them to do at the time. To the extent that they take the workers' needs into account, boss-managers imply that doing what they are told is the best way for workers to feel good (or to satisfy their needs).

Basically, the boss-teacher is not that concerned with the students' needs. This type of teacher does not work at making friends with students and sees the work as more important than the atmosphere in which it is done. Contrary to what Deming advises, the boss-teacher works on the students, not on the system. In this tense situation, where low grades abound, it is hard for all but a few students to satisfy their needs. Far too many stop trying altogether.

To be fair, boss-teachers are willing to reward workers who work hard and do well, but, as discussed in the previous chapter, except for good grades there are few rewards available that mean much to students. Whatever other rewards they use, the bosses tend to decide on them on their own and rarely try to find out from their students if these rewards are what the students want. The bosses decide what the rewards should be, and often they are not as need-satisfying to the students as the bosses believe. Basically, boss-managers tell the workers that they know what is best for them and that they are willing to use what power they have to coerce the workers to get the work done, regardless of their needs.

While some people may have stronger needs than others, for example, some people seem to want more love or more power than others, in most cases this difference is not significant. Just as most adults are between four and seven feet tall, most of us want similar amounts of love, power, fun, and freedom, and all of us will struggle fairly hard to survive if we are in danger. For all practical purposes, there are few significant differences among us in what we need. Where we differ significantly is in how successful we are in getting it.

I think it is safe to say that some students are lucky enough to be born into homes, usually affluent, where their parents boss them less than most children are bossed. In this less coercive atmosphere, they learn more ways to satisfy their needs than those who are bossed more. Children from affluent homes not only tend to be bossed less but they also get more help from their parents as they learn to satisfy their needs. They also have the opportunity to live in better neighborhoods and to go to "better" schools. In these schools they are also bossed less than students from less affluent homes. They work harder to please their parents because they can count on more love and attention, and they and their teachers have similar academic agendas. Because of all these factors, school is more satisfying for them than it is for less affluent students. Students from affluent homes do most of the quality work that is done in public school.

For the less advantaged, boss-management both at home and in school is a double disaster: First, such students have learned fewer need-satisfying behaviors than children from advantaged homes, and they come to school both less willing and less able to do the work. They are, therefore, more easily frustrated. This means that almost from the start they do not do as well in school, even though they are inherently just as capable as the advantaged students who do better. Second, less advantaged students are bossed more than the lucky students by people who assume that this will "motivate" them to do better. In this oppressive (to them) boss atmosphere, they refuse to work even more; as they continue to be pushed and punished, they learn to hate school. Unfortunately, school for most of them is the only place outside of home where they can learn significant ways to satisfy their needs. In the end they get much less from school than they need, and many become both a burden and a danger to the society in which they live.

By late middle school or early high school, there is a state of almost total antagonism between the teachers and the non-working students, who sometimes number as many as 90 percent of the students in schools in economically deprived neighborhoods. When such high numbers are involved, this angry atmosphere takes too much energy to maintain. Both sides tend to slip into a kind of sullen, apathetic truce: "I won't bother you if you don't bother me." This truce is fragile. When it is broken, which happens frequently when either teachers or students get excessively frustrated, anger explodes from one or both sides.

This is also the sad state of affairs for up to half the students in even our best public secondary schools. The atmosphere may be less explosive, but the sullen antagonism is just as high. And unless we eliminate the boss-management that does not address itself to the needs of students, we will stay right where we are or lose even more ground. We need to accept the fact that, right now, the majority of boss-managed students see little chance to satisfy their needs by working hard in school, and we cannot boss them into doing more.

Many teachers, however, point out that years ago "all" students worked hard because they were punished if they did not. There may be some truth in this, but it is more likely that students who did not work were punished so much that they left school or were thrown out. Because of large early dropout rates, before World War II the upper grades contained a higher percentage of students who wanted to learn than they do now.

Today, as it has become obvious to almost all families and to many students, rich or poor, that having a chance for a good life requires a diploma, more students than ever are staying in school. But staying in a school where they do not believe they can satisfy their needs means that they will not work hard or do quality work. A well-researched article on the "dropout" problem states:

> American Business is spending $30 billion a year training employees in reading and math skills that they should

have received in high school. . . . If the problem of school dropouts and a faltering educational system is not met head on it is not just individuals but the entire nation that is at risk, said David P. Gardner, President of the University of California System and the head of a blue-ribbon panel studying the issue. . . . "The task must be faced and the price must be paid," Gardner said, "We are out of alternatives."[2]

We have to recognize that although we cannot make students work harder, either lead-management in school or family support at home will lead to harder-working students. If both are present, the student is almost certain to do well in school. If neither is present, the student will probably be a nonachiever in school and no amount of coercion will change that. It would, of course, be wonderful if more families were supportive of the value of education. But what schools can and should do is manage students in a way that they can better satisfy their needs by what they do in school.

Like boss-managers, lead-managers have the goal of getting their workers to work hard, but to do this they continually keep the needs of the workers in mind. I illustrated this in Chapter Three with the description of how a hypothetical algebra teacher could persuade many more students to learn the material. I think it would be worthwhile to review that example and show how this approach relates to the basic needs. From the first day, the lead-teacher attempts to create a work situation that is warm and friendly and totally noncoercive. Students quickly realize that this teacher is not their adversary and is not trying to satisfy his or her need for power by bossing them.

As long as they are willing to work hard, the teacher will fight to protect them from others who would boss them. For example, if the students are learning but also noisy, the lead-teacher will protect them from an administrator who thinks that the only good work is quiet work. Classes may be noisy because the lead-teacher teaches in cooperative groups, and research shows that when there is a lot of interaction, often noisy, students learn more. The teacher also encourages students to work together at home as many will not do homework if they have to do it alone. In the classroom, the teacher goes from group to group and gets to know each student in a way that would not be possible simply by lecturing or assigning individual deskwork. While getting to know the students, the teacher is continually looking for a better way to teach and asking for their input on what this way might be.

The lead-teacher emphasizes that while algebra is difficult, it is far from impossible. It requires no special talent, and all who work will be able to learn it well. Both in class and in their homework, the teacher tries hard not to let students settle for anything less than getting their work correct, even if they do only one problem. But even more important than getting the problems right is understanding what they did to get them right. The emphasis is always on knowing how to do the math and where it may be applied in their lives.

The lead-teacher also explains that the only purpose of grades is to show what the students know. (Grades will be discussed extensively in Chapter Eight.) A low grade does not mean failure; it means that the student has not yet learned enough. Until the final grade, all grades are temporary: Any low grade along the way can and should be raised. By demonstrating that they know more than they did, students will get a higher grade to replace a low one. The teacher explains that he or she personally hates low grades and loves to give higher ones: All the students have to do is to be willing to do the work. The teacher thus shows that grades will be used to empower, never as a weapon or as punishment. This is in marked contrast to boss-teaching: Students often feel powerless and frustrated over grades when low grades are used punitively and never raised.

Although the emphasis is on hard work, the class atmosphere is never grim. The mood that the lead-teacher tries to create is one of enjoyment: As long as we have to work, let's have some fun along the way. Lead-managers, however, are much more willing than boss-managers to allow the workers to have a part in determining what is the best way to do the work. To accomplish this, the lead-teacher spends a small part of almost every class asking for students' input on how more can be learned or what can be done to make the class more enjoyable. The teacher does not reject the idea of rewards but believes that the class should set its own rewards if it judges that it is doing good work. Students are encouraged to plan activities both in and out of class as a reward for doing good work, and the teacher attends some of the out-of-class get-togethers as part of the commitment to the whole social process of which he or she is an important part.

The lead-teacher recognizes that the needs most satisfied by this way of teaching are for all of us the hardest to satisfy—power and belonging—and is always trying to help students satisfy these needs as they work. Lead-teachers accept what boss-teachers find hard to accept—the more power the teacher is given, the less he or she should use to boss students. The real power comes from students' perceptions of the teacher as competent to do the job, which is to show and model what is to be done and to create a good environment in which to work. Students appreciate the fact that the lead-teacher never threatens or punishes but says that if there are problems, "We will work them out." The lead-teacher's need for power is satisfied by a job well done, not by having students be subservient.

Assuming that the administrators manage teachers in the same way that I suggest teachers manage students, what has been proposed here may sound marvelous to some teachers.

They may also say that I have described a pipe-dream: "No one would let me teach this way or treat me like this." What they are saying is that this kind of teaching and managing goes against the traditional boss-manager premise that seems to dominate education: Neither students nor teachers can be trusted to do what is best for them; they have to be told what to do and coerced into doing it. Therefore, even when lead-teachers get results, as they consistently will, what they do to get these results might be seen as a threat both to those who boss them and to the boss-teachers who teach alongside them.

Even if her students are working, the lead-teacher may be told that her discipline is lax because there is laughter in her class. If she is creative, as she must be to teach in a need-satisfying way, she will be told that she is deviating from the time-tested (deadly) way to plan her lessons, which is to lecture and give ditto work for students to do by themselves at their desks. One group of high-performing students told me they were being "ditto'd to death" in their high school.

The lead-teacher will also be criticized for caring too much and told that too much personal involvement is unprofessional. She will be admonished to keep the state assessment tests in mind and to fragment the subject so that students will do better on these tests, even though this approach fails to capture the attention of over half the students. She will quickly learn that in schools (as well as in a world) dominated by boss-managers, she will be unpopular for what she believes and especially for what she does. She will see many boss-teachers failing miserably, but still most of those who run the system will continue to support what the boss-teachers do as right and criticize her as wrong.

It is this kind of boss-thinking that leads to the totally destructive premise that school needs to be a struggle between the teachers (bosses) and the students (workers), and if the bosses relax even for a moment the students will destroy the school. But the sad truth is that many of our schools are already very close to being destroyed: Some of our central city schools are no longer even semblances of places of learning. The more we depend on boss-managers to solve the problem, the more we will lose of what little we have.

It is my contention that successful teachers and administrators, whether they are aware of it or not, use control theory, which I will further explain in the two following chapters. But most teachers will not make an effort to learn control theory unless they are firmly and warmly supported by administrators who also have become conversant with it. If teachers' attempts to become lead-managers are only tolerated, boss-management will prevail. Teachers need to be led, which means to be encouraged and praised by administrators who go into their classes and compliment both them and their students for any quality work they do. Lead-managers must actively promote need-satisfaction at all levels of the system; any less will not work.

CHAPTER FIVE

The Quality World

In the last chapter, I explained that we are all motivated by five basic needs that are built into our genetic structure. Our behavior is always our best attempt at the time to satisfy one or more of these needs. It is important to remember that even though our needs are essentially the same, the behavior we choose to satisfy them may be quite different. For example, one student may gain power by excelling in math and another by disrupting his math class. As we have seen, given the way our schools are managed, differences in family support may be the best explanation for why this happens.

While probably accurate, this explanation is of little help to the teacher who is trying to teach a disruptive student. The teacher cannot increase the support of that student's family. But understanding the disruptive student's need for power can certainly help. If the teacher can persuade the disruptive student to work hard enough to get even one good grade, the student may feel so good that he or she stops disrupting and starts to work for more good grades. Or if the teacher decides that the student is lonely and is being disruptive to get attention, the teacher may be able to assign work in a small cooperative group in which the student can get some of the desired attention.

These, however, are big "ifs." In practice, frustrated students are very difficult to manage successfully. This is because, to solve problems, most teachers depend upon coercion. This approach not only fails to work, but almost always makes the problems worse. If we cannot persuade students (without coercion) that it is to their benefit to do quality work in school, we will do nothing to improve the schools. Those who run our schools must realize that most of the problems have been caused by boss-management, and they must begin the process of changing to lead-management. Problems will then be prevented, and only through prevention will we make progress.

Take the example of seat belts: It took a long time before people accepted them as a good idea. And while we should all support medical research into the treatment of trauma, seat belts will prevent problems such as brain damage that medicine may never solve. It may take a long time for lead-management to be accepted. But, having gone as far as we can in trying to improve education through coercion, we should now turn to quality as the best way to prevent problems. To do this, however, we need to understand the control theory concept of the quality world.

While our underlying motivation is always an attempt to satisfy one or more of the five basic needs, few of us are actively aware that these needs exist. When we are lonely and miserable, we do not complain that our need for belonging is unsatisfied: We look for a friend. When we are hungry, we do not complain that we are having difficulty surviving: We look for a meal. We look because we know we will feel good when we find what we are looking for, not because we think we have to satisfy this need or that.

As previously mentioned, what we know at birth and will know all of our lives is how we feel. It may be a while before we are actually aware of the concepts of pain and pleasure, but from the beginning we know the difference between these two basic feelings, and very quickly we learn specifically what feels good and what feels bad. Beginning shortly after birth, we learn to remember all that we do, or all that happens to us, that feels very good. We then collect these very pleasurable memories into what is best called a quality world, and this memory world becomes the most important part of our lives.

For most of us, this world is composed of pictures (or perceptions, to be more exact) and represents what we have best enjoyed in our lives. These pictures become the standards for what we would like to enjoy again and again if we could. If we attempt to manage people without knowing about the part the quality world plays in their lives, we will not be effective.

To clarify this important idea, consider a newborn baby: It will be obvious that the baby is almost helpless and will quickly die if not cared for. The baby has needs but has no idea of what they are or how to satisfy them. But she is already well aware of how she feels, and she has (or soon learns) some very primitive behaviors like screaming or cooing that help those who care for her to guess how she feels.

The baby also has senses. She does not know what they are or even what they sense, but in a minimal way she can see, hear, touch, smell, and taste. And finally, the baby has considerable capacity to learn from her behavior, minimal as this may be, that what she does may change what she senses. For example, very early in life when she feels the pangs of hunger, she learns to scream. Assuming that the baby is cared for by her mother, the mother soon figures out that the baby needs to be fed and feeds her.

As this process occurs repeatedly, the baby begins to learn that there is a relationship between her hunger pangs, her choice to scream, and the pleasure of getting fed. She also begins to sense, and then learn, that "something" out there feeds her. What she also quickly learns is that she can control the "something" out there through her screaming so that the "something" consistently does things that make her feel better.

Eventually the baby learns specifically who is out there, that this person has a name, "Mother," and that Mother helps her whenever she hurts. As this learning process continues, the baby uses all of her senses like a multisensory camera to take a picture of a loving, helping mother and stores this very satisfying picture as one of what will become her special collection of need-satisfying memories—the quality world. In this place in her memory, for the rest of her life, this child will store the most need-satisfying or quality pictures of everything she perceives. Most of us have a picture of our mother in this special world for much, if not all, of our lives.

Unlike the basic needs that are about the same for all of us, the pictures in our special world are very specific and completely individual. No two of us could possibly have the same pictures because no two of us live the same lives. It is called the quality world because it contains our best or highest-quality pictures or perceptions of the people, things, and situations that we have learned feel especially good in the real world. As we live, this special world grows, and eventually we have a collection of wonderfully satisfying pictures or perceptions in our head. If we were able to live in a real world that was exactly like this Shangri-la of our memory, life would be perfect.

Even though it is never more than a small part of our memory, this quality world is the most important part of our lives. What makes it so important is that these are the pictures we make an effort to pursue all of our lives. If something is not pictured in this quality world, we will not expend much effort pursuing it. The reason that many students do not work hard in school is that they do not have a picture of schoolwork in their quality world. Unless we can manage them so that many more are persuaded that schoolwork belongs in this world, we will not solve the problems of our schools.

When we are young, whenever we hurt, most of us will turn to the picture of our mother in our quality worlds. When we do, we immediately look for her in the real world to help us get rid of the pain. Because mother is for almost all children, and many adults, a very need-satisfying picture, we will listen carefully to what she says. In the same way, we will listen to all the other people we picture in this world. If a person is not pictured in our quality world, however, we will rarely do anything difficult that he or she may ask us to do.

Most small children come to school ready to work because people they love have told them to obey their teacher. In the beginning, the teacher may not be in the children's quality world. If what she asks them to do is not satisfying or she uses a great deal of coercion, they may never admit her. And they will pay less and less attention to what she asks them to do. Mother may get the process started, but the teacher has to get into the child's quality world to keep it going. As far as the direction of our lives is concerned, the most important pictures in our quality world are pictures of people. We will listen to and trust these quality people because we have learned that they are very much a part of why we feel good.

While we can live for years without learning exactly what our basic needs are, by age two or three we begin to suspect that there are some general conditions like love and survival that are strongly related to how we feel. When we engage in loving behaviors with people like our parents, we feel good, and when we are hungry and eat good food, we also feel good. From this it is easy to relate our parents to love and food to survival. Soon we begin to understand how important freedom is, and through laughter we quickly learn about fun even though few of us realize it is a basic need. And when people listen to us or pay attention to what we do, we feel good and begin to get the idea that we have a little power. We soon discover, however, that power is not easy to acquire. More people would rather that we listen to them than pay much attention to us. It is so hard to find power that many of us have difficulty accepting it as a need. Once we become aware of a need, we place it as a general picture in our quality world and attach it to the specific quality pictures that are very important to all of us.

It is easy to see that a need-satisfying picture may relate to all of the basic needs. From a caring, responsible mother, for example, we are better able to survive, gain love, feel powerful through her support, have fun as we laugh with her and find the joys of freedom as she encourages us to strike out on our own. It is similar for a caring teacher or manager. A good lead-teacher may become a strong picture in our quality world because he or she teaches survival skills, becomes a good friend, shares a few laughs, and gives us freedom to learn as we see best. Where a teacher may have more difficulty than our mother is in helping us to satisfy our need for power because the teacher does not have as much time as our mother to listen to us. This means that a teacher or manager who wants to get into our quality world must continually encourage the students or the workers to express themselves and then to listen carefully to what they have to say.

It is in this area, listening, that lead-managers differ greatly from boss-managers. Lead-managers try constantly to empower the workers by listening to what they have to say. Boss-managers are less secure. They fear that if they listen too much to the workers, they will lose some of their power. By remaining aloof, they try to make sure that the workers do not lose sight of the fact that they are in charge. It is not that lead-managers are not ultimately in charge, but that they avoid making their power an issue as they manage. They try to get the workers to understand that although they are in charge of the workplace as a whole, their job is not so much to boss as it is to help the workers overcome any obstacles that may stand in the way of doing quality work. Lead-managers also make it clear to the workers that the reason they want quality work is to make sure that everyone has a secure, well-paid job. The foundation of successful managing is conveying the message to the workers that the higher the quality of their work, the more they will be in charge of their work. And because high-quality work (and certainly this includes schoolwork) leads to economic security, they are more in charge of their lives.

Workers do not usually want to run the company, but, driven by their needs for power and freedom, they want some say as to how they do their work. If they do not have any control over what they are asked to do, they feel powerless: They will not put a picture of the job or the manager into their quality world, and they will not do quality work. Because most students are boss-managed and do not believe that they are important or are in charge of what they are asked to do, they will not put either the teacher or what is taught into their quality world.

Persuading students to do quality work is even more difficult than persuading workers to do the same. Partly this is because workers are paid, but mostly it is because many more workers than students are able to see the quality in the work they are asked to do. For example, a cleaning person can more easily see the quality in a job as menial as mopping a floor until it is spotless than a student can see the quality of learning history or English. Although industrial managers have the job of persuading workers to expend the effort to do quality work, they rarely have to explain what quality is. The workers can usually recognize quality when they see it. With schoolwork, however, this does not happen as often. The quality of academic work like history, English, and math is not apparent to most students until they begin to do it. This was well brought out in *Stand and Deliver,* a movie that illustrates many of the points I am trying to make in this book.

We are usually able to recognize quality work because we have some standard quality words—for example, neat, clean, prompt, durable, shiny, functional, smooth, attractive, valuable, tasteful, competitive, polite, sensitive, thoughtful, and accurate—in our quality world. When we use any of these words to describe a job or a product, it is likely that we will see that job or product as quality. Most of these same words also describe quality schoolwork, but the connection is not nearly as clear. To help students recognize the quality of what they do, good teachers spend time and effort teaching the relationship between these standard words and the quality of the work they assign.

Lead-teachers explain what they mean by quality schoolwork and post quality papers for students to inspect. Further, to convince students that what they do has quality, a part of all assignments, both individual and group, is for the students to assess the quality of what they do. As long as the students are cautioned to avoid harsh criticism, which is almost always destructive, they might also be asked to assess the quality of the work that others do and to discuss how they came to their conclusions. It is from these discussions that students get a tangible idea of what quality is and what has to be done to achieve it.

For example, in English, a lead-teacher might first assign an essay to a student and then ask the student to assess the quality of the completed essay. The student might rate it as high quality because it is neat, no words are misspelled, and the grammar is correct. But the teacher may give the essay a lower rating because it is not written in an interesting way. Or a history student may rate a completed assignment as high quality because the dates and places are all correct, even though the student does not understand the historical reason for what happened.

The reverse may also happen. The student may hand in an essay with poor grammar and spelling, even sloppy erasures and crossouts, and give the work a high rating because the ideas are expressed creatively and with emotional impact. The teacher may downgrade the essay because of the obvious technical errors. Or a history student may know the historical significance of events but be downgraded by the teacher for not knowing the exact dates or places. Obviously, quality in schoolwork is not nearly as clear-cut as it may be on a student's after-school job.

When there is a difference between the student's and the teacher's assessment of the quality of an assignment or test, the teacher should discuss this difference with the student. From these discussions students learn to judge what determines quality work. It is also very important that students be given a chance to improve their work: If we are not going to try to improve what we do, there is little sense in assessing it. Even if the teacher and student have the same assessment, it is still worth discussing because there could be different reasons for the same assessment. Good managers do their best to teach what quality is, especially in situations where it is not obvious and schoolwork is frequently one of those situations.

In many of the schools in which I have worked, both teachers and students take for granted that most of the work will not be high quality. And as long as we do not make an effort to teach students what quality work is, this will continue. Lead-managers do not accept that students cannot do quality work, but they are aware that many students do not know what it is and have almost never done it. They know that until a student or a worker becomes aware of what quality is and has experienced enough to find it need-satisfying, there is little chance it will be pursued with determination.

Another aspect of lead-teaching that differs from lead-managing in industry is that the teacher needs to make more of an effort than the industrial manager to get into the workers' quality world. Industrial workers are more likely than students to do quality work because they are more concerned with survival, and they are also much less dependent on the manager than students are on the teacher. For example, once most workers learn what to do, they are perfectly capable of continuing to do it well if they wish; as long as they do the job well, the manager may pay little attention except, if the manager is wise, to give an occasional compliment. On the other hand, as soon as students do something well, they go on to something new and are closely involved with the teacher in the whole process. Schoolwork changes frequently, and the quality of the teacher is as important as the quality of the work. Students will not work hard for a teacher who is not firmly embedded in their quality worlds. A teacher must expend more time and effort trying to satisfy a student than an industrial manager needs to do for a worker.

Students tell me that a good teacher is deeply interested in the students and in the material being taught. They also say that such a teacher frequently conducts class discussions and does not lecture very much. Almost all of them say that a good teacher relates to them on their level; the teacher does not place herself above them, and they are comfortable talking with her. They also tell me that a good teacher does not threaten or punish and that they have little respect for teachers who do. What they are actually saying is that these are their criteria for admitting a teacher into their quality worlds.

Students also tell me that they appreciate teachers who make an effort to be entertaining. To maintain student interest month after month in potentially boring courses, good lead-teachers try to inject humor, variety, and drama into the lessons. How to be entertaining cannot be taught: Each teacher must work it out in his or her own way, but it is another way to gain admission into students' quality worlds. While this was not mentioned in Chapter Two, the desirability that a teacher be entertaining is a further indication of how difficult it is to be an effective teacher.

Even if a teacher is willing to make the effort to be entertaining, boss-administrators tend to frown on these teachers and on their efforts. Bosses who thrive on coercion believe in the virtue of "no pain, no gain," and they do not fret if a boring teacher uses threats to keep students in line. They do not realize that boredom is the enemy of quality and that part of their jobs is to do more than encourage: It is to nurture teachers as they struggle to put fun and interest into their work. Good administrators will use humor as they deal with students and, through this model, encourage teachers to do the same.

In a good marriage, both husband and wife have satisfying pictures of each other and of their marriage in their quality worlds. Because of these pictures, they work hard to solve any problems that arise. If, however, the problems become overwhelming and the partners cannot find satisfaction in the marriage, one or both will take the picture of the other out of their quality worlds. When this happens, they divorce. They may not go through the legal process and may even continue to live together for religious, family, or economic reasons, but one or both may be miserable, and the marriage as a satisfying relationship is over.

The same thing can happen in school. Once a student takes the picture of school out of his or her quality world, the student becomes "divorced" from school. For a variety of reasons, the student may not actually leave school, but he or she will not work to get even a minimal education. Just as judges many years ago could legally force married people to stay together except when there was adultery, we can force students to stay in school. We can even try to force them to do schoolwork, but we will almost never succeed. We cannot force people to put pictures in or take pictures out of their quality worlds.

While it is possible that husbands and wives who have removed each other's pictures from their quality worlds will get back together, it rarely happens. It is also possible to persuade an alienated student to start working in school again, but this, too, rarely happens. If a "divorced" student is to get started again in school, it usually has to be in a new school, just as remarriage is usually with a new partner. Continuation schools are havens for "divorced" students. When these schools succeed, they are lead-managed. It is in these schools that we find most of the lead-management that exists in education. Boss-management has, in fact, led to the need for these alternatives.

One example of a lead-managed continuation school is the Apollo School, where I am presently a consultant.[1] This continuation high school is in the quality worlds of most of its students because we manage without any attempt at coercion. Because students see their school as need-satisfying, there are almost no discipline problems. Even though they are doing more work and better work than they have done for years, many students do not have a strong picture of schoolwork in their quality worlds. They do very little of what either we or they would call quality work and do not even attend as much as we would like. Nevertheless, as long as they keep school in their quality worlds, we believe that we can persuade them to do more. Our long-term goal is for Apollo to become a quality school.

Continuation schools like Apollo are expensive. In business, research shows that it takes five times as much money to find a new customer than to keep a current one satisfied. In school, we start with almost all satisfied customers but spend much less time and effort keeping them satisfied than we do trying to get them back when we have almost lost them. Most students start school with a picture of schoolwork in their quality worlds, and our main effort should be to keep it there. When we do this, we will eliminate the need for expensive alternatives.

School problems do not start immediately. Unless they are so unfortunate as to get a coercive boss-teacher in the first year of school, beginning students are generally eager to do what the teacher asks them to do. They come to school with pictures of school, teachers, and schoolwork, like reading and arithmetic, in their quality worlds because their mothers and others they love have told them that school is good for them and that they will like it. Most kindergarteners and first graders discover that what they have been told is true, and they work hard. Head Start programs have been successful because they increase the strength of the school pictures in many children's quality worlds.

Finding school enjoyable and also wanting to please their parents, young students put the pictures of their caring need-satisfying teachers firmly into their quality worlds. As I have said, the people pictures are most important here. But after the early grades, the number of children who find school satisfying starts to drop significantly. This is because the coercion gets stronger, and students do not feel nearly as good as they did in the lower grades.

For most children, this process accelerates and reaches a peak in the seventh, eighth, or ninth grade, when many students choose to begin removing teachers, schoolwork, and finally school from their quality worlds. Taking this last picture out is not easy, and even those who drop out are rarely willing to remove it completely. Although the picture of school gets very small, most students keep some vestige of it in their quality worlds. They may not like schoolwork or teachers, but they still retain the idea that school itself has value and that they need it.

When asked what is good about school, students all over the country tell me that, good or bad, it is where their friends are. In saying this, they are also telling me that, if the teachers were friendly, few of them would leave school. But when their teachers are coercive where schoolwork is concerned, as has been the experience of most of those who have taken the picture of schoolwork out of their quality worlds, students say that teachers do not care. The students then stop working or leave school altogether. Unless we can get rid of coercion, we will not make even a dent in the problems of education. Anything that smacks of coercion will not be admitted to anyone's quality world.

Many teachers get involved in the same process. Will Rogers is famous for saying, "I never met a man I didn't like," but most teachers have met plenty of students that they don't like. Just as students take teachers out of their quality worlds, teachers take nonworking students out of theirs. As, increasingly, neither sees the other as need-satisfying, the vicious cycle that we see in almost all of our schools begins. This cycle of increasing dislike, distrust, and hostility leads to the adversarial relationship between students and teachers that is so destructive to the purpose of school.

Teaching is a very hard job even when many students are trying, but getting "divorced" students to start working again—a difficult task that many secondary teachers face in almost all their classes—is what makes teaching the hardest of all jobs. We need to learn to become noncoercive lead-managers so that students will find school satisfying enough to keep a picture of it in their quality worlds. The focus must be on prevention. No matter how hard we try to "remotivate" nonworking students who have removed the school picture, I do not think we will ever have much success.

CHAPTER SIX

How We Behave: Quality Work Feels Good

Most successful managers have the luxury of discharging non-productive workers and looking for better replacements. School managers do not have this option. Poor students cannot be discharged or replaced; large numbers of these students, who produce almost nothing of value, remain in school. To be successful, a school manager has to manage so that almost all the students behave in a way that produces quality work through graduation. To reach this goal, teachers and administrators must learn much more than most of them do now about how we actually behave.

My explanation of control theory has so far covered why we behave, our needs, and the pictures in our quality worlds. In this chapter I will explain how we behave, a subject much more complicated than most of us realize. First, it is important to accept that all we do from birth to death is behave and that, for all practical purposes, all of our behavior is chosen. We choose to do what we believe will best control the world around us so that it becomes closer to one or more of the pictures we select from our quality world. Our biggest problems arise when we try to control other people. In that sense, we are all trying to be managers, and when we fail it is usually because we depend too much upon the coercive methods of the boss-manager.

Most of us do not realize that no matter how much coercion

we use, we cannot consistently control other people: In fact, it is an axiom of control theory that the only person any of us can consistently control is ourselves. When others do as we ask, it is because they find it more satisfying than anything else they can do at the time. Even when we threaten them, we cannot be sure they will obey, as the holdup example in Chapter Four illustrated. Instead of accepting this axiom and concentrating on managing so that workers can satisfy their needs while doing what we ask, we try again and again to make others do as we want, regardless of how satisfying it may or may not be for them.

For example, if my need for power is satisfied by my son's doing well in school, I may continually badger him to do his homework. But if he refuses, there is nothing I can do to make him do it: All I can actually control is the way I choose to ask him. I can threaten, bribe, sweet-talk, punish, reward, promise the moon, all in the hope that one of these will be persuasive, but I can never be sure that any of these will be. If my son does his homework, it will be because he decided that this was the most satisfying thing that he could do at the time.

Among the most destructive of all our coercive practices is our overuse of personal criticism. We spend too much time telling people we manage that what they are doing is wrong, that they should have done something else in the past instead of what they did, and that their plans for the future are faulty. When we criticize, we often have the advantage of second-guessing, which makes our position safe but increases the anger of those criticized.

More than anything else, if we are to manage successfully, we must do all we can to get in and stay in the quality world of those we manage. The problem with criticism is that it persuades the people we criticize to take us out of their quality world. They see our criticism, constructive as we may think it is, as an attack. It is not constructive to them.

As stated, we cannot consistently control other people; we can control only ourselves. Therefore, the basis of effective lead-managing is to deal with others knowing that you cannot control them, that all you can do is to give them the kind of information that has a good chance of persuading them that the work you ask them to do will feel good as they do it. In practice, workers do not work to satisfy their needs; most do not even know what their needs are. What they want is what we all want—to feel good. If we can help them to feel good, they will listen very carefully to what we ask them to do and, most of the time, will do it.

As we manage workers, especially students, we need to be aware that there are two important aspects of feeling good: immediate and delayed. We all like to feel good all the time, but, as we grow, most of us learn the lesson of the little red hen. We find out that it often pays to endure some immediate short-term pain in order to have a good chance for some later long-term pleasure. Keeping this in mind, what actually leads a worker or a student or anyone to initiate a new behavior is:

1. The behavior the student or worker is presently choosing does not feel very good.
2. The student or worker believes there is something different to do that, sooner or later, will feel better than what he or she is doing now.

The key here is the phrase "sooner or later." Students almost always know what will feel better immediately. If they are bored, they know it will feel good in the short run just to get up and walk out of class. But an effective manager will persuade them that, although an effective behavioral change may not feel good in the short run, there is a very good chance it will feel good in the long run. The little red hen did not enjoy much of the work involved in getting the bread into the oven but she had her eye on the future and it paid off for her.

Whether what the student does feels good immediately or later, what actually initiates all behavioral change is the pain associated with the difference between what the student wants from his or her quality world and what is going on in the real world. The greater or more sudden this difference, the more urgent and energetic the change in behavior will be. A student who is bored may accept the boredom because he or she does not see anything else to do that would be that much better. But a student who is put down by a teacher or a classmate may explode with anger.

In the process of living, most of us have to learn over and over that what feels good in the short run may soon dissipate, that an effective life depends much more on what feels good in the long run than in the short run. In school, much of what students are asked to do does not feel good right away. Because of this, a lead-teacher always tries to manage in a way that the students put the teacher into their quality worlds as a need-satisfying picture. To get into the students' quality worlds, the teacher must have a track record of asking the students to do what feels good in the long run and of asking them to do it in a way that feels good right away. This means that lead-teachers add kindness, courtesy, and humor to whatever they ask students to do.

But besides the immediate caring that gets the job started, the lead-manager will not be effective by only promising long-term satisfaction. Slowly and carefully the manager must help the worker, at the beginning of the job, to gain at least a little short-term satisfaction by providing what the worker appraises is a good place to work. From this, and from caring, the lead-manager can eventually build up to the point that the worker is willing to wait for the long-term satisfaction involved in doing a quality job. Once the workers gain the confidence in the manager's ability to provide the leadership necessary for their long-term satisfaction, they become more and more willing to put up with short-term pain and frustration. It is from this confidence that students become willing to accept the delay in satisfaction that is so much a part of education.

For example, suppose the manager says politely, "I would appreciate it very much if you would sweep the floor, and I have this new electric broom on trial loan. Tell me if it's worth buying." In this way, the manager acknowledges that sweeping is not the best job while involving the worker in the decision to make it better. Few workers would refuse to sweep under these conditions. I am exaggerating to make the point that by consulting the workers, good managers constantly keep the workers' need for power in mind.

Control theory explains another aspect of our behavior that is critical for managers to understand. As stated earlier, it is important to accept that we choose all of our conscious behavior. If a student does not work in school, that student is choosing not to work. When a teacher attempts to deal with that student, the teacher is also choosing what he or she does.

For example, when students disrupt and refuse to quiet down, many teachers get very upset. But without understanding the control theory explanation of behavior, an upset teacher will not realize that the upset is how he or she is choosing to deal with frustration. By recognizing that it is a choice, the teacher will learn to choose far better behaviors than to upset. This aspect of control theory is difficult to understand because when we are upset, we do not feel that we are choosing our misery. Although few people have heard about this concept, it could be very valuable because the idea of making a better choice, instead of continuing to suffer, quickly becomes a very attractive idea to most people.

To clarify why most of us choose so much upset, control

theory explains that behavior is far more than a simple action or activity like moving our legs and arms when we drive a car. It is actually a combination of four separate behavioral components: actions, thoughts, feelings, and physiology. When we look at what we are doing, it is often difficult to appreciate not only that our feelings and physiology are always a part of every behavior, but also that these components are always linked with our actions and thoughts into a whole, or what is best called a total, behavior.

Without control theory, we tend to look at behavior as made up of a single component—action—or two components—action and thinking. But behavior is never limited to these two components. Can you conceive of a time when you were just thinking and engaging in no action or having no accompanying feelings or being totally devoid of physiology? Except in a deep coma, can your body function without concurrent thoughts? Even when you are asleep, don't you dream as well as move and feel?

Therefore, by saying that we choose all of our behavior, I mean that all behavior is always some blend of acting, thinking, feeling, and physiology. Although we can actually choose two of the four parts of any total behavior, we cannot keep these parts (acting and thinking) separate from the total. Total is total. No matter which part or parts I choose, the other parts are always present.

For example, I can choose to take a walk and also choose, in the beginning, to try to think of nothing but the exercise I will get as I walk. I focus consciously on the action component while I am walking, and I tend not to think much about the other three components: thinking, feeling, and physiology. But I cannot walk unless I initially choose to think, "Start walking," and continue to think, "Keep on walking." After a while, I usually choose other thoughts, and if I get very relaxed, thoughts may intrude from unconscious sources that

I do not choose. In almost all cases, I can choose to ignore these extraneous thoughts or certainly choose not to act on them, but I cannot walk (or do anything else) without thinking.

Can I also choose to feel good when I walk? The best I can do when I start out is to think, "I hope I feel good while I walk." But I cannot choose to feel good in the same direct way that I can choose the activity of walking and also choose most of the thoughts that go through my mind as I walk. If I want to feel good while I walk, I must choose to walk at a time and a place, and perhaps with a person, that I know from experience are need-satisfying. If I force myself to get out of a warm bed on a cold, rainy morning, it is very unlikely that I will enjoy the walk.

I cannot choose an action such a taking a walk and feel good if it does not satisfy a need. This is impossible. Both our feelings and physiology work automatically and are proportional to how much or little the thoughts and actions we choose are need-satisfying. For all practical purposes, we cannot feel good or be healthy if we are not mostly choosing thoughts and actions that lead to need-satisfying total behaviors.

For example, suppose someone asks how you are feeling as you are walking. You say, "I feel fine." Then the person asks, "Are you choosing to feel fine?" Here, if you are honest, you might reply, "No, I'm choosing to walk. But since I almost always feel good when I walk, I guess the best I can say is that I'm choosing to do something that usually feels good, and it feels good today."

Suppose the questioner persists by asking, "Suppose you stopped walking right now, could you still feel good?" You would have to say, "I don't know. It all depends on what I'd be doing instead." What you are saying is that you cannot separate what you are doing (actions and thoughts) from your feelings or your physiology. You try to do things that feel good and are healthy, but you do not have nearly as much direct control of how you feel or of your physiology as you do of your actions and thoughts. Sometimes, for reasons you cannot control—like getting bitten by a dog as you walk—the walk turns out miserable.

When students do not work, most teachers are frustrated because they have a picture in their quality worlds of students working hard. Because they are frustrated, they try to choose a managerial behavior that will persuade the students to start working hard. But in this situation, most teachers do not know what to do. Many of them choose to threaten, a coercive choice that often increases the problem and their frustration. But if this is a choice, they also have a choice to ask themselves, "What might be the best way to solve this problem without coercion?" As soon as they think this, they open their minds to better ways to solve the problem because we have almost complete control over our thinking.

Suppose a teacher tells the class that she is disappointed that so few of them are working and that she would like to hear suggestions from them during a class discussion about what could be done to persuade more of them to work. She might say to them, "I am tired of yelling at you. Help me to solve this problem." Suppose the class is doing spelling, and students suggest that the teacher divide the class into four teams and hold a contest to see which team can spell the most words. The idea works, and the students begin to work hard.

How will the teacher feel? How will the class feel? Is the total behavior of discussing a problem better than yelling? Again the answers are obvious. We frequently choose behaviors like yelling and threatening, which do not work and which necessarily feel miserable, but we do not have to choose these behaviors. Once we catch on to the concept of total behavior and understand we always have direct control over our actions and thoughts, we tend to choose actions and thoughts that lead to new and more effective total behaviors that will always have as their feeling components good feelings. But to get these good feelings, we have to choose to act and think in more need-satisfying ways than those that did not get us what we want.

It is interesting that while almost none of us has been able to learn how to choose to feel good directly, almost all of us can make a direct choice to feel bad, to suffer misery, pain, and even sickness. We seem to be able to do this to some extent almost from birth, and we learn a wide variety of additional ways to do this all of our lives. When we are severely frustrated, choosing misery is a very common way of trying to relieve the frustration.

At birth and throughout our lives, we can deal with frustration by choosing anger. We are actually born with the capacity to choose anger; even a very little baby can express a great deal of anger. But anger is only the feeling part of an almost infinite variety of total behaviors of which anger, or angry feelings, may be the most recognizable behavioral component.

From now on, I will call this total behavior *angering* because it makes sense to me to use a verb, not an adjective, to describe behavior. For example, a person may be old or tall, both adjectives, neither of which has anything to do with his or her behavior. But if the person is angry, this is the feeling part of the total behavior he or she is choosing. As it is also a total behavior, I use the verb forms *angering* or choosing *to anger* because the feeling is the most obvious or recognizable part of this total behavior.

For the most part, the choice to anger is not an effective way to persuade others to give us what we want. It works well when we are very small: An angering baby can usually succeed in getting his parents to jump around as they try to relieve his frustration. But as we grow older, parents and others are less and less intimidated by the information that we are angering. This would usually include coercive actions and thoughts like yelling and threatening and a pounding heart, dry mouth, dilated eyes, and tense muscles, which are the physiology of angering.

We begin to learn early to substitute a wide variety of misery and sickness for the angering because we have found that the people we need are better controlled through their "compassioning" when we give them the information that we are "miserabling" (to keep it all in verb form). Parents, for example, are much more effectively controlled by a child who chooses to depress or to sick than by a child who tantrums. The choice to sick or to miserable can be learned: There are plenty of role models around. But the child may also figure this out independently, as we are capable of figuring out new behaviors, even miserable ones, when we are frustrated.

In industry and school, managers sometimes have to deal with people who anger, but more often they have to deal with people who are depressing, hurting, or sicking as their way of handling frustration on or off the job. By realizing that this is a choice, the manager is much better able to deal with these puzzling behaviors successfully. For example, teachers are aware that young girls of elementary school age often complain of a stomachache before an important test. In control theory terms, what they are doing is stomachaching. They create the upset stomach to avoid taking the test because they see themselves as good students and fear a low grade on the test. Stomachaching is their way of getting out of the test.

Teachers who understand control theory would be able to deal with this effectively. They would know that stomachaching was a choice, and they would concentrate on helping the young students to make better choices. Simply telling them that no single grade is that important and that they will have another chance if they do not do well will usually "cure" the stomachaching. And, of course, if the students do not do well, they must be given the second chance. A lead-manager is never deceptive.

Again, the choice to sick or to hurt is the students' way of dealing with the threat of failure, which is the coercive core of boss-teaching. It is the students' attempt to defend themselves against a need-frustrating coercive system. If it works, as it often does, students learn a self-destructive way to deal with frustration that may last all their lives.

There are certain total behaviors, like drinking, that people choose frequently because they can count on feeling very good when they choose them. What we commonly call vices— drugs, some sexual activity, gambling, overeating—are all total behaviors that people choose when they want to make sure they feel good at least for the short term. But again, the good feeling is not achieved directly: It is still the result of an action that is chosen. And it is not a sure thing. I can eat and/or drink too much and get sick, I can be refused sexually, and I can lose steadily at gambling and not enjoy it at all.

When we have few long-term satisfactions, we are especially attracted to actions that feel good for a while and over which we have a great deal of personal control. This is why there are so many alcohol and drug abusers: Getting high is something we can do easily and immediately all by ourselves. That we are in total control and do not need anyone else is the cornerstone of addiction.

To understand why self-destructive total behaviors like addictions feel good, we must understand that there is a normal physiology of good feelings that is part of every need-satisfying total behavior. Suppose you buy a lottery ticket and then win a big prize. The moment you hear that you have won, you feel ecstatic. Any quick and massively need-satisfying behavior like winning a lottery feels very good because natural pleasure chemicals like endorphins are poured into their brain receptors as the normal physiologic component of this behavior.

What addicting drugs do is to mimic these same chemicals and fill the same receptors in the brain. As they do, they give you the feeling that you have suddenly and massively satisfied your needs. Once you experience this easy, chemically induced pleasure, it becomes hard to forget. The desire to experience it again and again is what leads so many people to pursue an addiction.

One of the most difficult of all management problems is the use of addicting drugs in the workplace by both workers and managers. There are obviously no easy solutions to this problem but the answer lies in increasing the lead-manager approach to managing at all levels. The more work is managed in a way that the workers can obtain long-term satisfaction of their needs through doing quality work, the less they will be attracted to drugs. The more students feel both bored and bossed in school, the more they will be attracted to the easy, immediate pleasure of drugs.

The most sensible school approach to preventing drug abuse is prevention through need-satisfying instruction when the student is young and has not tried drugs. Once dissatisfied students experience the easily attainable good feelings associated with drugs, the less they will be willing to do the work that is necessary for the long-term satisfaction of their needs in school. Students are well aware of the dangers of drugs, but they may ignore them if they are unable to feel good through success in school.

Lead-teachers do not coerce: They talk to their students and work out ways to solve problems. Their students have no need to choose self-destructive total behaviors like acting out, depressing, and drug use. All of these are students' weapons in the adversarial struggle that is characteristic of a boss-managed school. Unlike boss-teachers, lead-teachers do not get angry when they are frustrated because they do not attempt to coerce students into doing what they do not want to do.

Boss-teachers and administrators who grow frustrated and find that angering does not "motivate" many students also choose to suffer a lot. Depressing, headaching, backaching, stomachaching, sicking, and drinking are commonly chosen by frustrated managers, including educators. In many cases, if they did not choose to suffer, they would be too angry to do their job. In some cases, their suffering controls some students, but students are usually the last group to feel compassion for the pain of a frustrated teacher.

What we learn at an early age and never forget is that people who care for us personally or legally can be controlled by our paining or sicking. We also learn that we can control ourselves through choosing paining or sicking. We learn for example, to substitute depressing for angering because it is a much safer thing to do. If we anger, we may do something destructive like hurt someone and even spend time in jail. When we choose to depress, we do not usually have the energy to destroy anything or hurt anyone so that depressing is one of the safest ways to deal with a frustration we cannot seem to solve. Most of us learn to depress early in life, and later we learn similar miserable behaviors like headaching and worrying, which serve the same purpose for many of us. Exactly how we do this is too complicated to explain in this book, but that we do it in many cases is obvious.[1]

Caring for employees who pain and sick is now a very large part of the modern workplace. The newspapers carry many ads soliciting people to make a claim against an employer for "causing stress" on the job. It may be that some employers treat workers so badly that they have no other choice but to choose to suffer, but this is rare. More likely, workers do not like the job because they see themselves as insignificant or powerless at work, a situation in which many boss-teachers, who teach in difficult schools, find themselves. Then they learn to choose a total behavior that includes suffering or sicking so that they can receive compensation from a "compassionate" workers' compensation system.

After they have been compensated, usually not adequately in their opinion, they usually make some sort of a recovery, but not always. Sometimes, through the suffering, they get what they consider to be enough control over their lives so that they never choose to recover. The unfortunate result of this growing failure to deal more effectively with paining or sicking is that huge sums of money are paid to doctors, lawyers, and others who make a living helping these people. All of this huge expense and waste of talent is created by a boss-managed system that is coercive and frustrating. What we need is more lead-management so that this money could be paid to employees for quality work instead of draining most of it away from the workers as we do now. Unfortunately, suffering or disability, for those who choose it, has a huge payoff; its only serious flaw is that it is miserably uncomfortable. This is the price, however, that millions of people, old and young, are willing to pay.

Suffering teachers, also, are hardly the best people to handle frustrated students. And as long as students are frustrated, teachers will be frustrated too. There is no way a manager can be happy if the workers do not produce. Teachers need to learn that only by choosing to teach in a need-satisfying way can they satisfy both their own needs and the needs of their students.

Managers, including teachers, who want to be successful have to learn to counsel workers who choose angering, depressing, or some other miserabling that seems to be getting in the way of their doing quality work. Counseling is talking to workers or students with the purpose of helping them to choose more need-satisfying total behaviors as they work.

For example, a teacher may find it almost impossible to teach grammar to an angry, often truant student who tells the teacher that she hates school and does not want to be in the teacher's class. Is there any doubt that the student is choosing not to try to learn? While she may not be aware of the fact that she is also choosing her anger, from her standpoint, as long as the teacher pressures her to learn what she does not want to learn, has she any other choice but to mobilize the angering that she frequently chooses when she is frustrated? If she does not show her anger, wouldn't she be acting and still be angry underneath? Can she stop her heart from pounding or her hands from sweating if she is confronted with her flaws? No. These are the natural emotions and physiology that go along with the rebellious actions and thoughts that led to the confrontation.

But, as I will explain in greater detail in a later chapter when I discuss counseling nonproductive students, it does no good for the manager to focus on the students' feelings or physiology. This is because we cannot directly change either of these components. The manager needs to be sensitive and compassionate to the students' upsets, yet focus as much as possible on the behavioral components the students can change—their actions and thoughts. Unless the student previously mentioned changes her actions and thoughts so that she does better in her English class, there is little likelihood that she will stop feeling angry or upset in that class.

Counseling an upset worker whose work is not satisfactory becomes one of the tests of managing that lead-managers have a good chance to pass and boss-managers almost always fail. This is why many managers, especially teachers, are so puzzled. They see themselves as noncoercive human beings who are caring and sensitive, and they make an effort to talk to their students or workers warmly and noncoercively where work is not directly concerned. But when they go back to managing "in order to get the work done," they become coercive and send a mixed message to the workers. The coercive side of this mixed message almost always erases the counseling side. The workers, sensing the coercion much more than the noncoercion, do not buckle down and do the quality work, which is the only way to solve the problem.

Therefore, as important as it is to be compassionate to the workers' feelings and health, if the manager does not focus on helping the workers without coercion to act and think more effectively on the job, the manager will not be successful. I will explain in detail how to do this in Chapters Nine and Ten, when I discuss how to handle students who do not follow the rules.

Although our modern, media-dominated society sends the message that we should all be happy all the time, there is nothing wrong with being frustrated. No one can live in Shangri-la. When we are frustrated, we must try to act and think more effectively, and in so doing find a total behavior that will reduce or end the frustration. What we can do, and only we can do it (a machine cannot), is create a new behavior. Everything that exists in the world that is the result of human effort was created by someone who was frustrated with the status quo. Even the expressions on our faces or the timbre of our voices is constantly being created as we to try to communicate what we want to express in the best possible way.

If we were more aware of this process and more open to the creative ideas that are continually bubbling up inside us, we would be better able to deal with frustration. A manager who encourages the expression of creativity in workers will find that this unique ability can solve many problems that are resistant to the prosaic solution of just working harder.

When we put all this information together—the needs, the pictures in our quality world, our total behavior, and our ability to create completely new behaviors—we have the basics of control theory. As we have seen, it is called control theory because it states that we are always trying to control our behavior in a way that best satisfies our needs. And as we do, we must realize that we should not waste time and effort trying to control other people. It is not until we become knowledgeable and accepting of control theory that we finally realize that all we can control is our own behavior: We cannot directly control anyone else.

The more a manager focuses on the needs that are hardest to satisfy—belonging and power—and figures out how to manage in such a way that these needs are satisfied, the more successful he or she will be. Managers who manage in a way that empowers workers are by far the most successful because it is harder for most of us to satisfy our need for power than any of our other needs. This is especially true in school: Students who feel powerless make up the vast majority of those who do not work in school.

Control theory is not abstract. It is usable everyday in our lives and is especially useful for managers. Although teaching effectively is the hardest of all managerial jobs, it can be made easier if teachers are willing to try to incorporate control theory into the way they approach the job.

CHAPTER SEVEN

Quality Schoolwork

Anyone who understands control theory would predict what Deming has found to be true: Workers will not work hard unless they believe there is quality in what they are asked to do. Working hard will not satisfy our need for power when we are engaged in doing what we believe is a low-quality task: Busy work, for example, is the epitome of low-quality schoolwork. Although quality may be a hard concept to define, most of us recognize it when we see it, and most students do not see it in the work they are asked to do in their academic classes. On the other hand, they easily see the quality inherent in most of their extracurricular activities. They recognize quality music and drama, and they know a good football team when they see one.

When they volunteer for extracurricular activities, students work hard because they want the fun, freedom, power, and sociability that are associated with these activities and that are actually what gives them quality. In fact, because these activities are voluntary, they become more attractive; freedom of choice adds quality to what we choose. If all students were expected to play football, there would obviously be much less quality to this activity. But whether our activities are voluntary or not, when we fail to recognize that there is quality in what we do, we will not work hard to do it.

For example, on any given day in an average nonvoluntary

academic class like tenth-grade English, fewer than ten students will be working hard. The rest will be doing little more than sitting there.[1] If you ask the nonworking students why they are not working, they will that say the class is boring, that they don't need it, or that no one cares what they think. While the work may have value to the teacher, the students do not see much value in what they are being asked to do.

If you ask the slackers why the few students who are working are making the effort, they will make a few disparaging remarks about the type of students who work (*nerds* is the current word), but it will be apparent that they really don't know the answer. Then ask those who are working why they are doing so. They will say that they need a good grade or that they don't want to disappoint their parents much more often than they will say that the work has value or quality. More than almost any workplace, school, with its many compulsory academic subjects, suffers from its inability to project an image of quality to the work the workers are asked to do.

When students say that they hate school, much of what they are saying is they hate being asked to work hard at something that does not fulfill their needs. Many of these same students will say that what they want is to get out of school and go to work. Right now there are unskilled and semiskilled part-time jobs available, and many young people are working much harder at after-school jobs at fast-food restaurants than they do in school. This is because most of them see what they are asked to do at work, menial as it is, as more need-satisfying than schoolwork. While the money is satisfying, there is another factor operating that is more subtle. For most of them, it is easier to see the quality in what they are asked to do at work—for example, be clean, courteous, and quick—than to see the quality of the reading and calculating they do at school. I don't believe this would continue if these students felt that they had to work the rest of their lives at a fast-food restaurant, but in the short run what is high quality at McDonald's is more obvious to them than what is high quality in English or math.

On the other hand, and this may seem contradictory, if you ask students working at McDonald's if they want a good education, the answer will be Yes. They have a vague picture in their quality worlds of what they conceive to be a good education, but I believe few of them have any idea of what it actually is. It is easier for them to see quality on the job than at school. To find out why requires a few more questions.

If you ask if it takes hard work to get a good education, students will again answer Yes. They are still not clear about what a good education is, but whatever it may be, they think it takes hard work to get it. Further, if you ask them if they are smart enough to get a good education, almost all will answer Yes, even if they do not know exactly what it is they have to be smart enough to do.

But if you then ask them if they are working hard in school, most will answer No. What they are saying is that, as much as they want the vague something that to them is a good education and know it takes hard work to get it, they do not have any clear idea of how schoolwork, as they now know it, relates to what they want. Until they have a much clearer idea about what a quality education is and how it can be attained from what they are asked to do, students will not work hard in school.

This is hardly a problem exclusive to schools. It is a problem inherent in any work situation where there is little emphasis on achieving quality. For example, the American auto industry produced low-quality cars for years and years, and no one seemed to care. In the same vague sense that students want a "good" education, both the auto workers and those who managed them wanted to build a "quality" car. Unfortunately, however, they did not know what a good car was anymore than most students have a clear, tangible idea of what a good education is. But once cars made in Japan, Germany, and Sweden began to come into this country, it became obvious what a quality car was.

As soon as customers woke up to the fact that there was a car with more quality than they had thought possible, many of them stopped buying American cars even when the imports became more expensive. Even many American auto workers started buying foreign-built cars. Suddenly people knew what a good car was, and they wanted one.

Now American automakers have finally become aware that to survive they must build a better car, and Deming has been helping them. To do it, however, they have had to change to the beginnings of lead-management; the traditional boss-managers could not coerce the the workers into making the effort to build a better car in quantity. Many American cars are much better because of this management change. The workers now recognize that there is more satisfaction and more job security in building a better product, and they seem to be willing to work harder and more carefully than they did before. Unfortunately, it will not be as easy to find a recognizable quality education model as it was to find a high-quality car, but once quality is recognized as the answer to the problems, we will at least begin to look for these models—an important first step.

The Johnson City Schools (Al Mamary, Superintendent) in Johnson City, New York, are probably the best model in the United States of what could be called quality schools. Even in Johnson City, however, the staff would be the first to admit that there is still work to be done before all the students put schoolwork into their quality worlds. But we need more than a few models like Johnson City: No one paid attention to the quality foreign cars until they arrived in quantity. Even the schools that border on Johnson City have paid little attention to the good work going on next door to them.

As mentioned in earlier chapters (and documented by Linda McNeil), the problem is that even the possibility of finding quality in education has been made much more difficult by the increasing boss insistence that all academic subjects be fragmented into small "objective" bits to be measured on achievement tests. Some students work hard to master this low-quality material because they see it as necessary for college, which is very much a picture in their quality worlds. Most, however, see no quality in the type of study needed to do well on these tests, and students who do not have a firm picture of college in their quality worlds will not study very hard for them. This is a major reason why scores are slipping: Fewer and fewer students are willing to do this much work when there is nothing in the work itself that has much value to them.

As Linda McNeil pointed out, we are making the serious mistake of assuming that a high-quality school is one where students are orderly and get low-quality "passing" scores on non-quality achievement tests. Led (really misled) by state departments of education, we are striving to do in our schools what, had it continued, would have destroyed the auto industry. Ill-designed, poorly-built cars were able to pass minimal inspection standards; not knowing better or having no better ones available, people bought them. People are still supporting our schools, but their discontent is increasing. If better models were more widely available and publicized, as Johnson City should be, people would demand the same from their school systems.

Until the foreign imports started to penetrate the market,

the American auto industry failed to recognize that the domestic cars were low in quality. In the same way, our boss-dominated educational establishment fails to recognize that quiet, conforming students who pass achievement tests that measure minimal knowledge and low-quality skills are not doing the high-quality schoolwork we need. Few of us may be able quickly or easily to define quality education, but most of us recognize that it is not what is measured by machine-scored achievement tests.

When I talk to students, as I do frequently, I have begun to ask them questions about quality. There is no doubt that they know both what quality is and that to achieve it takes a great deal of hard work. When I ask them whether they have done much quality work in school, at first many say that they have. But when I ask them how many times they have actually worked hard enough to do the best work they possibly could, almost none, including the very good students, say that they have ever done as much as they are capable of doing. I think it is safe to say that very few students expend the effort to do quality work in school.

But I think it is also safe to say that those who manage our schools do not manage for quality and that most teachers do not even think of quality when they address the students in their classes. On their minds are the goals of those who manage at the top of the system: raising the test scores; getting more students through; keeping discipline problems low. There is no way that anyone will ever confuse these minimal goals with quality. The result is that less than 15 percent of all students do quality work. When quality suddenly appears in classes where it had never been before, as in the movie *Stand and Deliver,* it is so unusual that it borders on the unbelievable and becomes the stuff of real-life drama.

When we do quality work, we carefully evaluate what we

are doing and come to the conclusion that it is worth working hard to continue to do it because it feels good. What few managers realize is that the coercion boss-managers use prevents this necessary self-evaluation because the workers or students spend most of their time and effort evaluating the boss instead of evaluating their own work.

For an illustration of this point, consider the example in Chapter One of the students at West High in Torrance who purposely failed the state assessment tests because they resented the amount of time that preparation for these low-quality tests took from the high-quality work that they felt they should be doing. The students focused their resentment on the boss-administrators they saw as pushing this meaningless assessment program. They then did what we all tend to do when we are being coerced: wasted time and effort evaluating the coercers and trying to outwit them. If they had not been coerced, these students would have ignored the tests and spent this same time and effort furthering their education by evaluating their own work and raising its quality. And they still would have done reasonably well on the tests they made so much effort to mess up. When effort is diverted from the task to be done, as happens in every coercive situation, quality must suffer.

Let me give another example to illustrate this difficult point. Suppose you are involved in a minor car accident and you recognize that it was partly your fault. But the other driver comes on very strong and blames you for the whole thing. Immediately you forget about the part that was your fault and defend yourself by trying to place all the blame on the other driver. The same thing happens in school. Even though most of what students are asked to do in school has the potential for quality, students so resent being coerced that they spend their time hating school instead of evaluating their work and trying to improve it.

When we are coerced, we usually refuse to take ownership of the work we are asked to do. But for students to do quality work, it is crucial that they see that it is for their benefit, not the benefit of their teachers, school system, or parents. Think of the times in your life when you did high-quality work. Didn't you do it because you were supported and encouraged enough so that you were willing to evaluate what you were doing and work to get better and better? As you improved, didn't the work itself became more and more important to you? Or did you do it because you were badgered and wanted to get rid of the pressure from the manager or teacher?

In education more than industry, it is the rare student who can recognize quality when he or she starts a new subject. In the movie *Stand and Deliver,* the true story of a group of Hispanic-American high school students who successfully learned calculus, it is clear that the students did not have any idea that there was quality to calculus when they started. What they recognized quickly, however, was that their teacher, Jaime Escalante, was a high-quality teacher, and they began to accept that if he taught calculus, it, too, must have quality.

These students first put Escalante's picture into their quality worlds, and when they began to succeed at learning this difficult subject—a feat few had ever dreamed they could do— they added calculus to this same world. Finding this effort need-satisfying, they began to work harder than they had ever worked in school. I am sure many teachers have had a similar experience: First they were accepted as quality instructors; then their students got successfully involved in what was taught and began to experience the pleasure of achieving quality. It was this pleasure that led students to continue to do the hard work that led them to the top rung of scholastic success.

As stated earlier, to be accepted into students' quality worlds the teacher has to become a lead-manager: Those you manage must sense your concern that the work you ask them to do be done in a way that satisfies their needs, especially their need for power. Even if, in the beginning, there is not much need satisfaction possible in the work you ask them to do, your concern that there be some need satisfaction helps persuade students to see you as a quality teacher. In a quality school system, you will also be seen as part of a whole system that is concerned that all students get involved in quality education.

Quality is not the image that most school systems project because they make the serious mistake of accepting what is obviously low-quality schoolwork starting in the very early grades. A student in any grade from first to twelfth may turn in what is to him, and to anyone else, a minimal assignment or test and hope that this is the end of that task. Most of the time this is the case: We accept what the student turns in, whether or not we believe that he could do better. We deal with the low quality by giving the student a low grade. This is the end of both his and our work on that paper or test.

A quality school would not accept low-quality work from any student. (Refer to the description in Chapters Three and Four of how a lead-teacher would teach algebra.) Beginning in the first grade and continuing through school, the subject of quality and how it relates to school work would be discussed with students so that they have a clear idea that quality work, at least as the teachers and administrators see it, is the goal of the school. Examples of quality work would be posted, and students would be encouraged to judge what they do for quality.

As stated in the first chapter, this is not hard to do. Most students and teachers would agree that the work exhibited in their school is high quality. In actuality, the problem is to judge what quality is not as much as what it is. This process should begin the day school starts and continue to the end of the year.

Once students have an awareness of quality and are told that quality work is the goal of the school, they should be asked if they would accept this goal. They would immediately ask if hard work was involved, and they should be told that it is: There is no way to achieve quality without hard work. In *Stand and Deliver,* Escalante made no secret of the amount of work that would be involved, but since the work began to be need-satisfying, most students were willing to do it. Students should also be told that they, as much as their teachers, will be the judge of the quality of what they do. Then it should be explained both to them and to their parents why raising the state test scores a point or two or reducing the dropout rate a few percentage points are no longer the goals of this school: The new goal is quality in all that takes place in school.

While the teacher must be the final judge of the quality of the work students do, I suggest that, starting in the first grade, students be asked to evaluate all their work in writing and sign it before turning it in. I have talked to high school students about quality work, and most of them would be willing to do this ongoing evaluation. If it were started early in a lead-managed elementary school, I think almost all students would accept this procedure. Some high school students, however, many of whom admitted that they had never done any quality schoolwork, said that they would not do this evaluation of their work. When I asked them why, they told me that this was not their job, it was the teacher's, another example of boss-managed students focusing on the teacher instead of on the material to be learned. When pushed as to why it was not their job to evaluate their own work, they told me that if they began to assess their work honestly, they would have to work much harder.

Control theory explains that what these students were really saying was that if they willingly took a good look at what they usually do in school, their need for power would make it very hard for them to write "low quality" on an assignment and sign it. As long as they do not do this, it is easy to blame the teacher, especially if the teacher is coercive, for boring assignments or low grades and to avoid taking responsibility for the low-quality work they do. What I think some of the students were also saying was that they do not want to take responsibility for assessing assignments that they do not think have the potential for much quality. Busy work will have to be eliminated; no one wants to assess what is seen as low-quality work. It also goes without saying that this request for assessment will suffer to the extent that students do not see the teacher as a quality person.

Assuming the work has the potential, like calculus, to be seen as high quality, the student should be asked to improve any work that is assessed as low quality. The work should not be accepted until both the student and the teacher agree that it is of substantially better quality. A good grade should be given for the improved work.

To get this process started in a school where it is completely new, it might be reasonable initially to accept work if it has been improved in any obvious way. This is because students who are asked to labor too long on an assignment or test before they have made the shift to quality work will grow tired of it and refuse to extend much effort. By always asking for some improvement, the students will begin to recognize that what is wanted is higher quality work and that even if they did not do it at first, it needs to be done and they can do it. If this is done in a noncoercive, nonadversarial, lead-manager atmosphere, the students will see this as a need-satisfying way to work that they have not experienced before. They will appreciate this way of working and begin to like school much more than when they were boss-managed and accepted as low-quality workers.

While posting and discussing examples of good work will be helpful to students who are trying to learn what quality is, there is no substitute for what students learn when they do a quality job themselves. This is one of the reasons why students work so hard in their extracurricular activities; they know first-hand how good it feels to do something well that is important to them. To an aspiring basketball player, shooting 300 free throws after practice is not busy work. Until students begin to work this hard in class, we will never achieve much quality in our schools.

Exams should be handled slightly differently from class assignments. Tests should be completed by students individually or, if they are working cooperatively, by the student teams. The students should continue to work on the test until all answers are correct or satisfactory. While on other assignments the teacher may settle for some improvement, this should not be the case for tests. The standard should be that no matter how long it takes, all questions must be answered satisfactorily. There should be no such thing as low- or even medium-quality performance on a test: Only high quality should be acceptable.

When the program starts, it may be necessary to give shorter tests, but not necessarily easier ones. No student should proceed to the next test until he or she has correctly completed the last one. Some courses may have to be extended, but anything less than this approach will compromise the move to quality that is the major goal of a lead-managed school.

Since there will be much reworking and improving, especially in the beginning, it would be helpful if the school could develop a core of volunteer tutors to help students both individually and in groups. Tutoring is an obvious solution to many of the problems that will arise. Some schools may decide to put these ideas into place all at once, and others may introduce them one class at a time. My inclination would be to go slowly and introduce them only in classes where both teachers and students accept what has to be done.

But quality goes beyond doing well on tests and assignments. We need to strive for the students setting their own standards for quality, not just doing well according to the teacher. Deming points out that given the encouragement and tools, workers will build better products than boss-managers have ever dreamed possible and will improve them even more as time goes on.

This is obvious when we see the record-breaking performances of athletes in the Olympic games. In many cases, the athletes performed far beyond the expectations of even their coaches. But even if they did not win, what they were proud of was that, as good as they were, they had improved. In other words, the idea of quality had taken hold inside them. This is what we need to try to do with our students: Start very early and talk to them about quality. Give them tools and lots of encouragement. Then stand back and see where they go once the idea of quality education gets inside their heads.

As I write this chapter, I can see people with power, like school board members, saying, "This is a great idea! Let's 'make' students improve the quality of their work." The problem is that we cannot make people do anything well. We have to take the lead-approach and slowly introduce them to quality. If there is any coercion, they will shift the focus from their work to their coercers. To the extent that they do, quality will be lost in the process.

While there is much to be worked out as these ideas are put

into practice, Deming has shown that "working it out" is the easiest part. The hardest part is deciding to do it and getting rid of the adversarial, boss-managed atmosphere that is so destructive to all that we are attempting to do. There is no guarantee that we will achieve quality using what has been suggested here, but there is good evidence that if we do not do something like this, we will never achieve it. The good news is that quality is contagious, and we see this contagion in extracurricular activities. Students do not have to be coerced to put effort into playing basketball, singing in the chorus, or participating in the school play.

If we can achieve quality in our classes, as I believe we can, then academic quality will also become contagious. Many students who work hard now are treated like pariahs by the other students because the "accepted" student attitude in our boss-managed, adversarial schools is to be anti-education. The only way to defeat this destructive attitude is to make quality as much a part of our academics as it is now a part of athletics. Once quality becomes a part of our classes, students will be proud of what they do and this pride will become as contagious as pride anywhere. It is obvious that few students or teachers are proud of what goes on now in too many of our classes.

While we may never be able to define quality in school in any exact way, if both teachers and students work steadily to achieve it through noncoercive self-evaluation, they may reach it even without being able to define it. For those who want to learn more about this complex subject, the ideas related to it are beautifully expressed in Robert Pirsig's definitive work on quality, *Zen and the Art of Motorcycle Maintenance.* [2]

My definition of quality is "whatever we put into our quality world," and unless, through lead-management, many more students than now put schoolwork into this world we will not solve many of the problems we face. What I am suggesting is a huge restructuring of basic educational practice based on control theory and managed by lead-managers. There are, however, many details that must be worked out. In the next chapter, I will take a close look at some of these details.

CHAPTER EIGHT

Grades and Other Basics of a Quality School

"Define a good student." I ask this of small groups of students, usually from junior or senior high school, when I interview them in front of teacher groups. The students answer as anyone else would: works hard; does the best he or she can; has a good attitude; does what the teacher says; does not give the teacher a hard time. Then I ask them to be more specific. "What kind of grades does a good student get?" Even though those selected to be interviewed are almost always good students, they are uncomfortable with this question. They say that grades are not important: What is important is that good students try their best. They usually add, "It's not necessary to get all A's to be a good student." But I keep pushing, "Does a good student get any C's?" And they answer, "Maybe." Then I ask, "Do any of you get C's?" Usually they tell me that they do not, but they continue to insist that C's are acceptable. I ask, "Would your parents accept a C grade?" And they tell me that C's are not welcome in their homes.

The students are trying not to appear conceited because they personally get good grades, but it is obvious, as we carry on the discussion, that good grades are very important both to them and to their parents. From these discussions I also learn that fewer than half the students in their school are good students as they have just defined good students, which means getting A's and B's, no C's. I then ask them, "Do the students who get mostly C's or less ever improve their grades to A's and B's?" The students doubt this ever happens. They tell me that occasionally some C students do well in a class where the teacher conducts discussions or uses cooperative learning, but mostly the C students do not participate in discussions, and if they work at all in cooperative groups, it is to copy from the one or two good students doing the work. If the students were describing a factory, more than half the workers would be receiving minimum wages and doing less than minimal work. Many would even be interfering with the better workers as they tried to work.

I then ask, "Would the poor students like to get good grades?" "Yes," they answer, but add that most of them hate school and won't do the work. When asked why the poor students hate school, they reply that these students do not believe the teachers care about them or what they do. The idea that students who do not work believe that no one in the school cares about them is very strong with all students. When I get an occasional group of poor students to interview, they confirm what the good students have said: They would like to get good grades, but the work is boring and nobody cares, so they don't make the effort.

Finally, I ask both the good and the poor students, "Are the poor students incapable of getting good grades? Are they as a group less capable than the good students?" They assure me that this is rarely the case. They say that if the C and D students worked hard they could do as well as anyone else, and I believe them. We are not talking about inability; we are talking about not working. We are also looking at a situation that both the students and the teachers in a boss-managed school accept: As time goes on, the A and B students will separate from the C, D, and F students, and by high school they will hardly know each other. As control theory clearly explains, once students get low grades they start to take school out of their quality worlds. They do less work and separate from the students who are working.

Even if we are able to make the move to quality schools, grades, the most sacred of all the educational cows, are here to stay. Good students want grades because they represent good pay for good work. Teachers want them because they do not want to lose the power to use grades to coerce: "Do as I say and you'll get a good grade; don't and you'll get a bad grade." As I will shortly explain, a quality school will retain good grades because, if they are fairly earned, their coercive power is not destructive: It is like higher pay for better work. Little will be lost, however, when bad grades are eliminated. If bad grades have any coercive value at all, it disappears when the high and low groups divide. For students who get them after elementary school, they are like beating a dead horse. By the eighth grade, most students and teachers know after a few weeks of school who is going to get a good grade and who a bad grade.

Through a combination of low test scores, failure to hand in assignments, and cutting class, many students know early in the school year they are going to fail a course. When these students are sent to a counselor for misbehavior or no effort, the counselor can do nothing to "motivate" them. Counseling a student in this dead-end situation is like trying to get a condemned man to plan for the future.

In a quality school, there are no bad grades. My guess is that this will be the single most difficult change to make. Teachers, administrators, parents, and politicians will complain that they are being asked to disarm in the middle of a war. Even some students who get good grades may resist. It will take time, patience, and effort to convince teachers to give up the threat of a bad grade, but unless bad grades, with all their potential for coercion, can be totally removed from a school, it will not become a quality school.

Eliminating bad grades does not have to be done quickly. It can and probably should begin slowly with teachers who understand and accept the idea behind this change. Before teachers eliminate low grades in their classes, they should consult parents, explain the reasons for this change, and obtain their agreement to a trial of this approach. If this new way to grade is effective, other teachers will be willing to try. For obvious reasons, in a quality school no attempt would be made by the administration to coerce any teacher into making this change until he or she was ready.

In any school, grades have two major purposes:

1. To give information to students, their parents, and others who may be interested, like colleges, in how well the student is doing.
2. To serve as a substitute for pay.

High grades are a reward for quality work and are very satisfying to students' need for power. In a quality school, however, permanent low grades would be eliminated. A low grade would be treated as a temporary difficulty, a problem to be solved by the student and the teacher working together, with the hope that the student would come to the conclusion that it is worth expending more effort. But besides low grades, any grade, even an A, could be improved at almost any time if the student can demonstrate to the teacher that he or she is now more productive than before. Grades, like pay, should always be tied to increased productivity.

Where a quality school would differ substantially from a traditional school is that only the courses in which students had done quality work would be recorded on their transcripts. The lowest grade that would indicate quality work would be a B; for even better work, A and A+ would be recorded. It is important that a B be at least as good as it is now: What is now a C should not become a B in a quality school. There is no sense doing what we do now, which is to record, with a low grade, the fact that the student has not mastered the material. For example, if a student's transcript in a quality school lists algebra followed by a B, then anyone reading that record will know that the student is competent in this subject. If the grade is A or A+, the student is more than competent: He is skilled. If, in the unlikely case, the student has struggled with algebra for several years and has still not done quality work, there would be no indication of the course on the student's transcript. In a quality school, the record shows what students know, not what they do not know. The record, however, would not show how long it took to master the subject as that could, in some instances, be coercive.

This means that the coercive or punitive C's, D's, and F's that we use so liberally now would be eliminated completely from the permanent transcript. C would be retained, but it would be restricted to temporary use only. As all students would be asked to evaluate all of their work, students who give themselves C's, or are given C's by the teacher, would be put on notice that they have not done a quality job on that test or assignment. This would become a problem that the teacher would like to help the student solve and that the teacher also believes can be solved. Given the warm, supportive environment of the quality school where there is no failure, and where there is almost always the possibility of tutoring, it would be more need-satisfying for students to work to raise their grades than to give up and receive no credit for the course.

Grading should never be on a curve: No student's grade should ever depend on what other students do. Since the purpose of the school is to produce quality work, many students will get high grades. This is not grade inflation: It is representative of what the students have learned. The reasoning behind the elimination of grades below B is the same as the elimination of minimal pay in a successful business. No business that wants to succeed in the long run can afford the "luxury" of low wages because low-paid workers will not expend the effort necessary to make quality products or perform quality services.

A quality product is not an average product or a minimal product. Would you want to be operated on by an average surgeon or eat an average meal in a restaurant? No one wants anything average, so why should we settle in school for the low quality that is now average? Lead-managers manage for quality because they know that less has little value. They are confident they can achieve it, and they are more than willing to pay good wages to the workers who produce that quality.

The space shuttle *Challenger* was a classic example of a C product produced by boss-management. The top managers did not listen to lower managers, and there is some indication that no one at the top listened to the workers. Because of this, the workers did only enough to get by, and a low-quality product was put into space. This is confirmed by the fact that after the disaster more than 200 improvements, many of them major, were made in the design and fabrication of the shuttle.

Even though C or lower is an acceptable grade in much of our society, it should not be an acceptable grade in school. In fact, I doubt if we will improve our society until we make the effort to move to quality schools. Lead-managers do not manage for C work, and they do not see workers as C people. Therefore, every effort is made to see that there are no long-term C students or permanent C work in a quality school. B work, which means competent work, is the lowest acceptable performance.

But what if students work hard, keeping school in their quality worlds, and still do not produce good work? The answer is that in a quality school this would be almost impossible. Anyone, student or not, who works hard at a job he believes he can do will produce good work if given enough time. If a student tells the teacher that he does not believe he can do the job in the class he is in, he would be counseled to move to a class where he believes he can succeed. There is no more sense in trying to make a student do what he believes he cannot do than trying to make a factory worker lift what he cannot budge.

In Garfield High in Los Angeles, all students do not take calculus. But almost all students who take calculus succeed.[1] In a quality school, courses that require a large amount of talent or aptitude would be open to all. Students who had difficulty, even if they worked hard, would be counseled to try to do what they had more aptitude to do, but this would not be a big problem. This is because neither we nor most students have any clear idea what most students can do because too many do not have schoolwork in their quality worlds. I believe there is very little offered in our schools that students could not do if they put it into their quality worlds.

It would be easy to get this quality grading system operational if it were started in the first grade. It would be harder to start it with older students who do not believe they can do quality work because they have never worked hard and have always received low grades. The key with these students is to persuade them to do one piece of quality work in school, and through this another, and then slowly persuade them to begin to put quality schoolwork into their quality worlds. To do this, however, they have to get at least a B. No one will do quality work without good pay.

To get an A in any subject, students would do what is ordinarily A work now. What would be different in a quality school is the grade A +. This grade should be reserved for any student who does work above the quality that ordinarily is given an A. Teachers in each course would set the criteria for this A + work, but I suggest that it be given to students who, on their own, do something significant that is beyond what the teacher or the course required. This means that, using their own ingenuity and creativity, the students demonstrate that they have moved beyond the course requirements. For example, students might complete a voluntary science or computer project, apply what has been learned in the community by helping to solve environmental problems, tutor other students to competency—anything that shows the student went well beyond what is ordinarily required for an A.

This grade would be very valuable for college entrance, and it would help to quell the fears of the parents of the 15 percent of students who do well now. Many of these parents want to maintain low grades so that, in contrast to the others, their children can easily be seen to excel. In many instances only the very intelligent or the very gifted will have a chance to receive the A+ grade, but even they will still have to work hard to earn it. This is another way in which the quality school would differ from today's schools, in which gifted students frequently get A's without doing much work. To get the top grade, A+, in a quality school, even those who were lucky in their genetic endowment would have to work hard. Many capable people do little with their lives because they never learned the value of hard work.

State and District Assessment Tests

The quality school should not concern itself with outside measures of productivity, such as state-mandated achievement tests, because these machine-scored tests do not measure quality. If they have a purpose, it is to pick up the failure of many students to reach the minimal standards of boss-managed schools. The Advanced Placement (AP) calculus test that Escalante's students did so well on is a much better test.[2] Only a portion of this test is machine scored, and it does a fair job of measuring quality learning in this subject.

A quality school would be encouraged to try to involve students in the AP program through which they can earn college credits in high school. The AP tests are so far ahead of the machine-scored assessment tests that there would be little relationship between what goes on in the quality school to prepare students to pass AP exams and what is now done to prepare students for state assessment. Because of this, and also because the state-mandated tests are so far removed from what education is supposed to be, it is possible that lead-managed schools would not do well on them. But they will not do badly either. Basically, there should be no problem with these tests.

For college entrance, the lead-managed school will have special sessions devoted to studying for these noneducational exercises, and students who need good scores on these tests will be encouraged to attend. Students who graduate from a quality school and do well in college would be encouraged to come back and lead the sessions. To prepare for this tutoring, they might take one or more of the special courses now offered by private companies and add what they have learned from the "experts" to what they teach in these cram courses.

Record Keeping, Statistics, and Teacher Training

Deming maintains that the only way to improve quality is to keep statistics so that you know whether the organization is going forward, moving backward, or standing still where quality is concerned. In the lead-managed school a careful record should be kept of each student's progress. While I am not an expert on school record keeping, there is no shortage of people who could do this once they've mastered the concepts of a quality school. For example, if we move to quality in algebra and find that it takes two years for most students to achieve at least the B that indicates competency, this amount of time should be allocated. Right now algebra is given a year, and even our flawed testing system shows that most students do not become competent in that time. Those who do not learn are either given low grades or failed, which persuades many of them to take math out of their quality worlds for life. When they do, we lose them for the technical work our society increasingly needs.

The way we run schools now there is no way to learn if more time is needed to achieve quality. Not only do we not try to teach all students to achieve quality, but there is no record of how long it takes to reach it. There is only a record of how many students have reached A, B, C, D, or F in a year. I cannot see how this data can possibly provide the information we need to tell us how long it takes to learn algebra well given the present way it is taught in most schools. If we tell our math teachers that they are doing an inadequate job and fail to give them the time they need to do an adequate job, then how can they possibly improve?

Statistics should also be kept as to which is the best way to teach. This means keeping a record of how long it takes a group of algebra teachers who use different approaches to teach comparable students to the B level of competence or quality. For example, did the teachers who used cooperative learning do better or worse than the teachers who did not use it? Did the teachers who assigned more homework reach the level of quality quicker than the teachers who assigned less? The purpose of doing this is not to point out who is more or less effective but to learn what the more effective teachers do that others could learn to do.

Deming says, "Institute training on the job." But he also points out firmly that training is worthless unless there is some statistical proof that what people are trained to do works. If we suspect that someone is a great teacher, we need to back that suspicion up with statistical proof. The framework of the grading system suggested for the quality school would make getting this proof much easier than now. From the standpoint of quality, almost all of the money now spent on state and local assessment tests is wasted because it fails to provide the information we need to tell us that one way to teach is that much better than another.

The Need for Role Models

Quality schools need quality teachers. If we are willing to accept the ideas of lead-management, much will be accomplished toward reducing the coercion of teachers that is endemic in the present system, and which significantly reduces their effectiveness. But still much more on-the-job training is needed for what I am convinced (see Chapter Two) is the hardest job there is. To accomplish this we need role models: Nothing less will suffice.

Just as there are stars in every field, there are stars in teaching. But while few star baseball players or virtuoso piano players can teach others to do what they do, it is the essence of star teachers that they could do this superbly given the opportunity. *Stand and Deliver* gives some indication of how star teachers' skills could best be transmitted to others who want to learn: Use the media. Although the movie showed what Escalante did, it did not show how he did it. To show this, we need many hours of high-quality videotapes, made for the express purpose of teaching others to do what worked so well for Escalante. I do not claim that every teacher can learn to do what he did; some of his success is unique to his personality. I am convinced, however, from feedback I have received regarding the effectiveness of counselors I have trained to teach reality therapy, that there is much that can be learned about effective teaching that is not based on personality or unusual aptitude.

Making high-quality videotapes for training is the first suggestion I have made in this book that will cost more money than we spend now, but more than enough money to pay for these needed tapes could be saved by cutting back on expensive mass testing that produces little of value. Thousands of teachers entering the profession each year have not recently seen a great teacher teach and have never in their college preparation even talked about what it is that star teachers do.

There is another reason to videotape great teachers as they teach: The videos could be used to teach directly. Students complain about the boredom of many of their classes, but they never complain of boredom when great teachers are teaching. Done correctly and not overused, videotapes of great teachers could be brought into the classroom and used to teach students. Here again statistics need to be kept on how well this kind of instruction works, and small inexpensive pilot studies could be used to test the process before it is increased in scale.

How would we find the great teachers that we need as models? When I talk to students I caution them not to mention any teacher by name, and they understand why. At times, however, they do slip and mention a teacher, but those they identify are always, in their opinion, great teachers. Just as anyone reading this book knows who the great teachers were who taught him or her, so do students today. Finding great teachers will not be the problem. By far the largest obstacles will be raising the money to make the tapes and getting rid of the professional jealousy that hampers their use.

Homework in a Quality School

Difficult as it may be for both educators and parents to accept, mandatory homework may be the main reason that so many students take schoolwork out of their quality worlds. Even the good students that I interview almost always say homework is what they most dislike about school. Very few claim to do all that is assigned and most admit they do much less. This is supported by the recent Kappan poll in which 79 percent of the elementary school teachers and 85 percent of the high school teachers complained that students do not complete their assignments. This was the teachers' most frequent complaint, substantially larger than discipline infractions (57 percent), the next most frequent complaint.[3] Based on what I have learned from in-depth student interviews, I believe that students fail to complete homework much more often than classwork.

Deming would say that if 80 percent of the workers will not do what they are asked to do, it is the fault of the system. It is neither the fault of teachers, who are doing what the system tells them to do, nor students who are not working. This is a significant statistic proving that the do-what-we-tell-you-to-do-whether-it-is-satisfying-or-not boss-managed system does not work, yet we continue to pay little attention to the system itself. Students who do not do their homework assignments are routinely punished, usually with low grades and threats of failure. By seventh grade, more than half of the students deal with this coercion by taking schoolwork out of their quality world and do less and less classwork. Mandatory homework which is designed to increase the productivity of the system, in practice, severely reduces it.

In a quality school, the lead-teachers would never lose sight of the fact that managing students so that they keep schoolwork in their quality world is the most important priority of the system. Because they know that formal education is over for students who take schoolwork out of their quality world, the focus is always on quality classwork. Students would be given the time to complete their work in class under the direct supervision and support of their teachers and with the help of each other.

The way to solve the problem of students not doing homework is exactly the opposite of what we do now: Reduce compulsory homework drastically and emphasize the importance of classwork. They expect to work in class. If classwork is satisfying, it will become an important part of their quality worlds. They would be taught to evaluate all their work and would always be given a chance to raise their grades by improving it. They would be encouraged to take their work home to do this and most would.

When we attempt to do what does not work, as we are doing now with compulsory homework, both teachers and students lose respect for the system. Coercion is increased and the opportunity for quality is lost. It is unlikely that we will ever figure out how to persuade many students to do the amount of homework mostly assigned now on any consistent basis. Eighty percent of our teachers are not incompetent and they have yet to figure out how to do this.

Besides encouraging them to work voluntarily at home to improve their grades, there may other ways to persuade students to do homework without making it compulsory. A colleague of mine has suggested that homework should be work that can only be done at home rather than an extension of classwork as most of it is now. For example, assignments in which students are asked to interview their parents, watch a specific program on educational television, do research in the community, volunteer for community service, or practice at home or in the community what is learned in school. To promote creativity and initiative, an assignment might be to figure out what could be done at home that would enrich what is being studied in class.

We spend too much effort trying to force students to read and many learn to hate reading. They may still read grudgingly in school but they refuse to read at home. Since reading is so necessary, an effort might be made to promote it at home by trying to convince students that it is satisfying to turn off the television for a while and read. An assignment might be to have each member of a family find something satisfying in a book, newspaper or magazine and read it out loud to the others. Teachers might suggest that there is even much in comics that is educational. For example, "Doonesbury" is excellent for national problems and "Calvin and Hobbes" and "Peanuts" for relationships. Assignments like these could be stepping-stones for more reading. Teachers who have figured out how to persuade students to enjoy reading at home should make this expertise available; we can all use it.

There are many enjoyable games that involve skills of reasoning, decision making, logic, estimating, and geometry that are also educational. Since very few students do homework on weekends, with parental consent, noncompulsory weekend assignments to play Monopoly, chess, checkers, pool, backgammon as well as card games like casino and cribbage might be valuable. All of these are much more educational than watching television or listening to rock music, especially for young children. Given school support, they might even help somewhat in preventing the boredom that leads to drugs.

The Curriculum

For the first ten years of school, most of the curriculum is compulsory. We "know" what students must learn, and we complain because so few of them are learning it as competently as we would like. Actually, there is little wrong with the curriculum. What is wrong is our inability to persuade more than a small percentage of students to learn it well. As in pressuring for homework, if we pressure students to learn what they do not want to learn, and then punish them with low grades when they do not learn it, they counter by taking schoolwork out of their quality worlds, and we lose them as learners.

Instead of telling students what they need to learn and then losing so many of them in the process, we should separate from the bulk of the curriculum the most obviously important parts and ask students if they will accept learning these components well. For example, the popular media consistently reports that only a small percentage of high school graduates can write a good letter. To verify this, at the end of the school year in June 1989, I read the results of this study to an English class at the Apollo School, the school where I consult and where students' academic achievement is low. I asked the students if they would be willing to learn to write three very good letters: one asking for information, another giving information, and the third giving an opinion as in a letter to the editor of the local newspaper. As part of my argument, I said that students should be able to write a very good letter or they should not graduate from high school. I said that I would want students with a diploma from the Apollo School to be able to say that this diploma certifies that they can do certain things well, one of them being to write a good letter. We talked over what a good letter would be, and I said that they should be the judge. Asked if they could recognize a good letter, students thought that they could.

Next we discussed what would constitute a good letter. The students mentioned neatness, good grammar, correct spelling and usage, and correct form, typewritten if possible. I suggested that if students had any doubt as to whether they had written a good letter, they could ask their teacher, who would be helping them and for whom they had great respect. But I also said that if there was any disagreement as to what was a good letter, they could choose any educated adult and I would accept this person's judgment. The students all agreed that this was a worthwhile English project, and the English faculty made this a high priority item for the fall of 1989. By Christmas, some students were already writing high-quality letters, the best work they had done in English in years.

What I am trying to say is that we should explain much more than we do now, as we would in a lead-managed school, about why we teach the things we do. Then we should break down what we teach into recognizable parts. In English, for example, this might be writing a good letter, reading a good book, acting out a skit or a play, and learning basic grammar. Then we should ask students if they agree that these definite and understandable components are worth learning. Finally, are they willing to learn them until they know them well? If we present these understandable components as a learning choice, most students will agree to learn them, as did the Apollo students.

As hard as it may be to accept, we have to sell what we believe is worth learning to those we teach, who may be quite skeptical. A reputable salesman does not try to force you to buy a product: He makes it clear why it is to your advantage to buy what he sells. I don't see why educators consider it beneath their professional dignity to do the same. We make a big mistake when we assume that students do not want to learn and that we must force them. Almost all we teach is needed, and most students have some idea that this is so. But like many of us who may want something, they still enjoy a little sell. Control theory also points out that because of the way we are constructed to function, we all want to feel as if we have some control over what we do. When people try to force us, even if we think it may be for our own good, we tend to rebel.

There is nothing inherently wrong with most of our curriculum. What is wrong is the boss-manager approach we use when we present it to the students. If we cannot figure out how to present what we teach in a way that students will easily see that it is worth making the effort to learn, we should not teach it. More often than not, to try to force learning on the unwilling is to promote ignorance.

CHAPTER NINE

Building a Friendly Workplace

All managers have to deal with absenteeism and low productivity, but teachers are among the few managers who must deal with workers who are disruptive. Disruption, while not common, is extremely difficult to handle, but it is not difficult to prevent, providing the teacher manages so that the disruptive student gets no support from the class. To accomplish this, a lead-teacher avoids doing anything that might lead students to see him or her as an adversary. If they see the teacher as an adversary, they will either continue to disrupt or support a disruption. Even good students who never disrupt may lend tacit support to those who do.

Prevention of disruption was a valuable lesson I learned in the eleven years that I worked in a reform school for delinquent adolescent girls. We succeeded in preventing disruption by establishing an almost totally nonadversarial relationship with the young women there. Those who thought about making trouble rarely started because they knew that they would not get support from the group. They were always looking for this support, and they were used to getting it in other places. What was also very helpful was that we were able to operate with very few rules. Mostly we depended upon creating an atmosphere in which the idea of being courteous prevailed. Courtesy is the core of how a lead-manager deals with workers, which sets an example for everyone.

Courtesy means that you are kind; you listen to what the students have to say; you do not criticize, even when students do something you do not want them to do. There is no putting students down, no sarcasm. It is also important to be careful of your language. Regardless of how profane a student may become, do not respond with profanity. Students do not want you to be profane and they will not respect you if you are.

It is in establishing rules that a major difference between boss-managers and lead-managers becomes apparent. Boss-managers depend on rules; when they are in charge, rules tend to proliferate. Boss-managers accept the cliche that workers do not want to work or that students do not want to learn, and they depend on rules to keep them on task. They do not realize that what workers and students want is satisfying work and that having many rules, with a variety of punishments for breaking them, makes work less satisfying. When rules proliferate, time and effort that should be devoted to work is devoted instead to circumventing the rules. Bosses then figure out more rules because rules are sacred to them and often become more important than the problem the rules were intended to solve.

Lead-managers do not depend on rules. They try to solve problems by managing the operation in a way that makes it apparent to the workers that if they work hard, they will feel good, which means that they will satisfy their needs. The only reason to have a rule is to help this to happen. Lead-managers try to have minimal rules because they know that as soon as they are put in the position of trying to enforce a rule, they risk becoming the adversary of the rule-breaker. Therefore, while lead-managers need to have rules, they try to keep them few and simple. The main effort is to eliminate the unwritten rules, such as "You have to do this" or "You can't do that," that seem to crop up constantly in any work situation.

To establish the rules, the lead-manager holds discussions

with the workers, trying to get all concerned to agree on the rule and the need for it before it is put into effect. In school, a lead-teacher should begin the year with a discussion with each class about what rules the students think are needed to get the work done. This will set the stage for the many discussions about quality that must be an ongoing part of the quality school program, which will be explained in the last chapter. The teacher should emphasize that his goal is to help students to learn. All he wants is a minimal set of rules; he does not want to have to police unnecessary rules.

As the students offer rules, try to get them to see that if they are courteous, in most cases the rule will not be needed. Try to reverse what most see as the teacher's usual role. You are pushing for fewer rules, not more. After you get these rules, tell students that you can always meet again if a situation arises where an additional rule is needed. Then go on to the critical part of the discussion: What should be done when a rule is broken? Students will tell you to punish, as this is the only approach to enforcing rules they know.

Explain carefully that they, not you, are suggesting punishment. You neither believe in it nor want to punish when a rule is broken. Students will begin to get the idea that you are not the usual boss-teacher, and my experience is that they become very interested at this point. Ask them if they think punishment works. Be specific by asking, "Does it work with you?" Although they have just recommended it, most will say that it does not work.

To help students with this dilemma ask, "Do you think the student who breaks the rules usually has some kind of problem?" In all cases they will say, "Yes." Then ask them what is the best approach to a problem. In fact, push them a little further and ask, "What is the only approach to a problem?" Their answer will be, "Solve it." Tell them that this is exactly what you want to do. Then ask, "How do you solve a problem?" or more specifically, "What does each person who is part of the problem have to do?" Here, whatever they say, you should summarize by suggesting that all the people involved have to work on the problem.

Ask students if the people who have the problem can continue to do the same thing that they were doing when the problem occurred. When students say that they can't, try to come up with a typical problem, such as a student who is frequently late for class, and ask how they suggest you and the student solve this problem without punishment. Mostly they will not know what to do: It has never occurred to them that problems like these can be solved without punishment.

Keep insisting, however, and remind them that not only the student, but also the teacher may need to do something different. Ask, "What could I do?" Eventually, they may suggest that you talk to the student and try to make the student feel more welcome in class, or help the student to figure out how to do better, or maybe listen to a personal problem the student is struggling with that has little to do with school. Try to help students to see that your giving time and attention to an area far removed from the presenting problem could be the key to its solution.

See if students agree that if you give a little, the student will give a little also. Point out how different this is from punishment, and ask them if this approach makes sense. This will help you to become more of a leader and much less of a boss.

Once you have a set of rules, write the rules down. Then have all class members sign a paper attesting that they have read the rules and that if they break them, they will try, with your help, to solve the underlying problem. Remind them that the rules are not written in stone: If another rule is needed or any rule does not seem to be working, you are open to their suggestions and you expect that they will also be open to yours.

Lay some groundwork for students to follow the rules by admitting that your class is no different from most classes in that some of the material you will ask them to learn will be boring. But also tell them that when things get boring, you are willing to work with them to try to find a more interesting way to teach the material. What you are doing is preparing students to accept some alternative ways to teach, such as cooperative learning. They will be more willing to try new ways if they are involved with you in figuring them out. Be sure to tell them that they are lucky: Most of what you teach they have to learn only once; you have to teach it "forever."

From the beginning, show interest in students' personal lives and reveal some facts about your life and some experiences you have had that may intrigue them. To avoid subjects that may be too personal, I suggest following a simple rule: Never ask anyone anything about his or her life that you are not prepared to reveal about your own. Most students are not on easy personal terms with adults, in many cases not even their own parents. Sharing small parts of your life, especially little problems and some of your foolishness, will lead students to become closer and more supportive of you. The more they know you and understand some of your struggles, the more they will tend to be on your side. Not knowing another person, especially one who has power over you as a teacher does over a student, makes anyone more likely to cast that person in the role of an adversary or, at least, not as a friend.

Ask for students' help and advice in any way that you can. Don't struggle by yourself with anything that they could conceivably help you with. Nothing gives students more of a sense of power than advising the teacher, and the more they can help you by doing something that you seem unable to do for yourself, the more important they will feel. For example, ask them about how to deal with friends and neighbors, what to buy, where to go, and what to do. It doesn't matter that you may not take their advice, ask anyway. If you do take some advice, try to let the whole class know that you learned something from them.

It may seem that what I have just suggested would take a great deal of time, but it need not. You should try to keep interjecting a few personal asides for a few seconds here and there as you teach. Keep a dialogue going with students about anything: The more you and they talk, even if it is just for a few seconds, the more accepted you will be and the less they will see you as an adversary. Friendly, easy conversation is the most important defense against being seen as a boss. You will convey the message that you want to be followed not because it is good for you, but because it is good for them. By accomplishing this early in the school year, you lay the groundwork for establishing not only that you are not their adversary, but that you are their friend.

In control theory terms, what I have been suggesting in this chapter will enable your students to put you into their quality worlds as a need-satisfying friend. Once there, most of your problems as a teacher will disappear. If you are not able to get into students' quality worlds, it is unlikely that they will do much quality work.

Traditionally, bosses are admonished that they should not be friendly with workers. Where threats and punishment are the main way to "motivate," this is easy advice to follow. Those who give this advice believe in punishment and know that it is hard to punish a friend. They also fear that the weaker friend may try to take advantage of the friendship, and the power of the boss will be compromised.

Empowering the workers is not as easy as it would seem because workers, especially workers who have been boss-managed, are leery of power. They recognize that with it comes increased responsibility. As long as they accept that the manager has all the power, the workers can blame the manager when things go wrong, and they usually do. When the workers have power, they have to work harder or more carefully because now they, along with the manager, are responsible for what is produced.

When lead-managers offer workers more power by stopping punishment, talking over problems, and listening to their solutions, many workers may think at first that they are being manipulated to get them to work harder. But lead-managers use more pay, more personal attention, and more say in what goes on in the workplace as tangible means to convince workers that what they are doing is for their own benefit. Although better grades are the equivalent in school of more pay, more attention and more say-so are perhaps even more important than in industry.

If lead-managers succeed in ridding themselves of the boss image and the quality of the work goes up, then it becomes easy to be friends with those they manage. Everyone shares in the success, cooperation increases, power struggles end, and the whole issue of power melts away. Lead-managers are much different from boss-managers in that they recognize that the manager's main concern should be quality, not power. Lead-managers are well aware that power struggles are the main enemy of quality.

As lead-teachers succeed in shedding the power image and becoming friends with students, more students feel empowered. They work harder and become friendlier with the teacher, and both students and teacher feel better. What finally happens is that the quality of the work becomes very high, everyone feels more powerful, and the craving for power for the sake of power, which is so detrimental to production, becomes unnecessary.

Teachers have an advantage over industrial managers in that friendship between them and good students is traditional and, therefore, more acceptable than friendships in the industrial workplace. So the previous suggestions, equally applicable to school and industry, are easier to accomplish in school. There is a long history of strong friendships, even love, between teacher and student, and much student success is based on this closeness. Annie Sullivan was a loving friend to Helen Keller, and the fictional Mr. Chips was a dear friend to his students.

There is not a person reading these words who has not been befriended by a teacher and who did not benefit from that friendship. My own life was turned around by a teacher in graduate school who asked me what plans I had for the future. This brief conversation was the first time since elementary school that anyone in any school had taken a personal interest in me, and from it I was empowered to try to enter medical school which, because of low grades in undergraduate school, I had thought impossible. Between a teacher and a student, a little friendly interest goes a long way.

Past elementary school, more than half of all students are friends neither with their teacher nor with the students who are doing well in their classes. Not only do they not see the teacher as their friend, but even worse they see the teacher as an adversary. They do have friends in school, but these friends are also allies in their struggle against the unfriendly, boss-managed education they are being offered. This struggle produces the low-quality education that we have.

While these students would be worse off if they had no friends at all, it is unlikely that they will be productive until they believe that they can be friends with their teachers and with the students who now do well in class. These friendships alone may not be enough to get them to work hard, but without them, nothing else suggested in this book will make much difference. Eliminating the adversarial relationships is a good start, but replacing them with friendships is basic to solving our educational problems.

Volunteer "Friends"

I am frequently asked how to deal with the very few students whose behavior is so totally disruptive that it is almost impossible for their teachers to teach effectively. My observation is that, unlike other disruptive students who have friends and are willing to accept friendship from the teacher, these students have almost no friends in school. Driven to desperation by their need for friendship and recognition, they are unpredictably disruptive. Even a competent lead-teacher does not have the time to give them what they need if they are to be reached.

In my opinion, these students need more personal attention in school than it is possible for the staff to give them. They need adults who have the capacity to approach them in such a warm and friendly way that they will be accepted as friends. The best help, and from a practical standpoint the only help, is to use adult volunteer "friends." Senior citizens are especially useful here, and school administrators who are good lead-managers will make it a part of their jobs to reach out to the community and recruit adult "friends" to help with these angry or withdrawn students.

The volunteer "friend" will demonstrate his or her friendship by spending time with the lonely student. What they do together need satisfy only one criterion, that they both enjoy spending this time with each other. Until they are good friends, there should be no other agenda. It should be recognized that unless such students have a friend, they will not function. These students have absorbed a great deal of punishment from a series of bosses in and out of school, and this destructive cycle is best broken by friendship with a successful adult.

What the volunteers do is specifically designed to help the students to satisfy their needs, especially the need to belong and the need for power. As this is accomplished, the students make the crucial discovery that they are happier because of something the school has provided and begin to consider moving the picture of school back into their quality worlds. Unless this occurs, the students will get little benefit from school. The volunteers must spend time with the students on a regular basis. It need be a significant amount of time, usually at least two hours a week. With this much help, most students will begin to work in school, and the volunteers can offer to tutor because these students are usually far behind. Some of them, however, are quite capable. They can do the work and need only the friendly support of the volunteer to get enough need-satisfaction to begin.

Most schools have a tradition of using volunteers to help in a variety of ways, but having volunteers befriend students and serve as mentors to them, as suggested here, is a new idea for many schools.[1] In most cases, the students they help will be difficult to get along with in the beginning. Many will be abrasive, some despondent, and almost all self-destructive. My suggestion is to start with only a few volunteers recruited from interested friends, perhaps no more than three, and give this initial group training and support. As they become skilled and spread the word that they enjoy what they are doing, they will recruit any additional help that may be needed.

Student Peer Counselors

Volunteers should not be limited to adults. Students should also be involved. There are a wide variety of ways in which students can help each other, from tutoring to counseling. One of the best programs is to train student volunteers to act as peer counselors. When a student with a problem is counseled by a trained peer, both are well served. The counselor gains from learning the skills to help others, and the counselee gains from the counseling and also from being exposed to the role model of the successful student who does the counseling.

The student peer counselors should always be available during the same day they are requested, and all students who will accept counseling from their peers should be given this opportunity. Because this takes time away from other things that the student counselor might do, there should always be enough students trained so that no one student will be overloaded with this responsibility. A professional school counselor or administrator should be in charge of the program and should provide regular supervision for the student counselors. Together, they should make decisions as to whether the student being counseled needs more help, more time, or whatever.

It is beyond the scope of this chapter to spell out further how to increase the friendliness of the school. I am sure that experienced teachers could add many ideas to the few I have outlined here. What I am trying to do is to emphasize that in a quality school, no student will be able to say, "No one cares." In fact, it should be hard for any student to say that only a few people care because almost everyone will be friendly and helpful.

The main concern of lead-managers is to provide a workplace in which the workers can satisfy their needs, understanding that all work, including schoolwork, is rarely consistently satisfying. But if the workplace is satisfying, it can usually more than make up for what is lacking in the work itself. What will satisfy an unhappy worker is the observation that the manager is trying to make the workplace satisfying. This is often sufficient to keep the worker going through a difficult time. In temporarily unsatisfying situations, most workers will recognize the limitations that the manager is struggling with. In the case of school, most students will accept that there are subjects that are very difficult to make exciting.

What the students want is a school where it is apparent to all that the staff is constantly trying to make things better. This strong, "We care" message is the foundation of quality education.

CHAPTER TEN

Dealing with Discipline Problems

Several years ago I worked with corporate executives, essentially boss-managers, who were trying to learn better ways to deal with problem employees. They complained about lateness, absenteeism, substandard work, and the inability to work with others, but these problems involved only a few of the people they managed. They never faced the insubordination, total lack of effort, and noncaring attitude that boss-teachers face every day with up to half of their students. While business managers would benefit by changing to lead-management to deal more effectively with problem workers, such a change is essential for teachers.

All managers, lead or boss, find insubordination hard to accept. Both types of managers believe that workers should accept the conditions of the job (or school) and do as they are told, but lead-managers differ greatly from boss-managers in how they deal with the problem of uncooperative workers: They never coerce; they make an effort to talk to workers about their grievances, and they are open to suggestions on how working conditions might be improved.

In industry, a worker who is grossly insubordinate is threatened with discharge. If the worker continues to cause trouble, he is almost certain to be fired. Insubordination is not tolerated. When students are disruptive or nonworking, most teachers also look for a boss approach that is quick and decisive. They want something simple to do that will get the problem quickly under control. Many would love it if they could fire the student, but unfortunately even disruptive students have "tenure" and are almost impossible to get rid of.

When disruption occurs in school, it is usually with students who have had great difficulty satisfying their needs in school. As a result, they have very few pictures of school, schoolwork, or teachers in their quality worlds. When these students sit in class, at any moment the difference between whatever it is they may want and what they have may become extreme. Pushed by this difference, their attitude is an angry, confrontational one: "I don't care what you do, I am not going to sit down and pay attention." What is so hard for boss-teachers to face is that there is nothing they can do at that tense moment that will be effective.

Kicking disruptive students out of class, keeping them after school in detention, or suspending them may control the immediate situation, but it does not deal with the basic problem: how to get them involved in quality learning. In the quality school, lead-teachers must learn how to handle a disruptive student in a way that is not punitive yet gets the situation under control and, at the same time, opens the student's mind to the option of beginning to work in class.

Among the first thoughts that cross most teachers' minds is to call the student's home, but this rarely works the way it is intended. Boss-teachers who do this want the parent to punish the child for what he or she has done in class, and too many parents, also boss-managers, are more than willing to do so. Students do not like to be punished in any case, and in this case the student correctly sees the school as the cause of the trouble he or she now has at home. This common practice thus tends to compound many more problems than it solves.

Lead-teachers try very hard to deal with a disruptive student without notifying the parents. In fact, I believe that, as a general rule, the school should notify parents only to tell them positive things about their child. As much as possible, discipline problems should be dealt with when they occur without involving parents. This says to the disruptive student, "We believe you are capable of working out your problems without getting your parents involved."

This message also strongly says, "We want to solve the problem, not punish you, and we are not looking for a way to get your parents to punish you," which is what many students believe is the main reason teachers contact parents. Calling in the parents is also an admission that the school cannot handle its own problems, an admission that managers should not make.

Sometimes, however, parents are called to discuss problems that have nothing to do with discipline. The student may be having trouble making friends, for example. When a conference with parents is necessary, the student should be present and the lead-teacher should make clear that the student is not doing anything wrong and that the purpose of the conference is not to get the student punished at home. The goal is to involve the parents in a nonpunitive plan to help their child do better in school.

Good advice for parents who are called in to school for any reason is for one or both to spend more time doing things with the child that both the child and the parents enjoy. It is especially important that the parent who is with the child the least, usually the father, spend this quality time. Some students disrupt in school hoping that the parent they do not see enough of will get involved, because even negative attention from this parent is better than the small amount of attention they now receive. If there is no father or male in the home, as is often the case, then the school should encourage the mother to have a male relative or friend spend some time with the student.

Dealing Effectively with Disruptive Students

Suppose that you have begun to convert from boss-managing to lead-managing. You have stopped punishing, you are doing your best to model and facilitate in an effort to improve classroom conditions, and you have worked out a set of rules with your students that they have agreed to follow. You have the needs of your students in mind and are trying to run your class in a way that is satisfying for all.

There are, however, still occasional problems with students who, while not grossly insubordinate, refuse to settle down to work as quickly and quietly as you would like. You know that these students are not lonely and that they are capable of doing good work, but today one of them is choosing to ignore the rules enough so that you must deal with him. Although the class is not supportive, they are watching and you have the distinct impression that they are casting you back into the boss-manager role you are trying so hard to get away from. Unlike boss-managers, lead-managers should be able to deal with any disruptive students effectively.

In what follows in this chapter, it is assumed that for the first several years, as it changes from boss-management to lead-management, the quality school will have a time-out room to which a disruptive student can be sent. Without such a room, disruptive students cannot usually be counseled successfully. As I am well aware that teachers with classes of more than thirty students have little time to deal with problems, none of the following suggestions takes more than twenty seconds of class time. But no matter how busy you may be, these few seconds are well spent. To do less is to make the problem, whatever it may be, more difficult to solve.

The lead-teacher is aware that he has no magic, no quick fix to solve problems. He must communicate to the student clearly that not only does he have no magic, but he needs no magic. The lead-teacher communicates this by dealing with all infractions in essentially the same matter-of-fact way. Because it is always the same, the student will get the message that his particular insubordination is no big deal and that the teacher has confidence in what he, the teacher, is doing. It also tells the student that his disruption is his problem, not the teacher's: the teacher knows what to do.

The lead-manager teacher should always say something like the following to the disruptive student:

> It looks like you have a problem. How could I help you solve it? If you'll just calm down, as soon as I have the time, I'll talk it over with you and I think we can work something out. As long as you're doing what you're doing now, we can't work anything out.

Tailor what I suggest to your own style: I am sure that many of you could say it in fewer words. You could also add gestures, a shrug of your shoulders, or an extension of your hands to take the place of many words. However you do it, you are making it clear that you will not help the student to work out the problem until he cools off. A lead-teacher will do this calmly. There is no reason to get angry or be put on the defensive by one disruptive student. If most of the class is satisfied, any disruption will be only a little brush fire, never a big blaze.

If the teacher can joke a little while asking the student to calm down, so much the better. A joke cuts the tension and works best when it is at the teacher's expense or exaggerates the problem. The fact that the teacher had the confidence to make this kind of joke is a show of strength, never weakness. Although the teacher can put himself down a little, he should never put the student down. Perhaps the teacher could say in a mock serious tone:

> Wow, you're upset. I must be doing something really terrible. Calm down, and as soon as I can, we'll get together and maybe you can help me work things out.

Said with a smile and an appropriate gesture, this may break the tension and "allow" the student to sit down because he knows he has made his point. Getting the immediate situation under control is the way to begin dealing with any disruption.

If the student will not calm down after this reasonable request, there is no good way to deal with him in class. Some ways are better than others however, including never getting into an argument or even a long discussion with an angry student about the merits of his case. Above all, do not threaten. Just do what has been suggested and if the student will not calm down in the twenty seconds that I suggest should be allotted, ask him to leave the class. (What should be done with the student when he leaves the class will be covered in detail shortly.) Keep in mind that the vast majority of disruptive students who do not have the tacit or active support of their classmates, if dealt with as I have suggested, will calm down in twenty seconds. There is nothing better that can be done at that tense moment; anything else will usually be worse.

All the students, including the one who has just disrupted, should hear the message that lead-managers do not threaten. They recognize that there are problems and try to solve them, but they cannot solve them by themselves. They need the cooperation of the student. If the student will not cooperate and must be asked to leave the room, the teacher should say something like this:

> Since you won't calm down, I have to ask you to leave. I hope we can get together later and work this out, but

if you are not willing to settle down, it's better that you leave now.

This way the door is kept open, and there are no threats or hassles. The disruptive student is looking for someone to blame in order to justify keeping his grievance alive. But it's hard to stay angry at a teacher who is saying, both in words and demeanor:

I want to help you work this out. I am not looking to punish you for what you have just done. If there is a problem, let's solve it.

Teachers who are used to the boss approach may find it difficult to accept that there is nothing effective that can be done immediately. The teacher can only set the stage for solving the problem later when both are calm. The ultimate goal is to get the disruptive student to start working. Even if a threat gets the student to quiet down, it does not get him to think about changing what he is doing in school.

Only when teachers stop looking for what has never existed—quick fixes—will they begin to accept that the only good solutions to discipline problems are systematic and long-term. Long-term solutions to problems, no matter how serious, must be developed while the student is not disruptive. Problems can never be solved in the heat of anger, so the lead-teacher focuses first on calming the immediate situation.

If the student calms down in class, you need to find a time to talk to him. This may be in class, between classes, before or after school, or any time you can spare a few minutes. If you need more than five minutes, you will have to arrange a special time. A minute or two should be enough to deal with most cases, however, except those that are so severe that you need to involve a counselor or an administrator. When you have the time, what you say should always be about the same as the following:

> What were you doing when the problem started? Was this against the rules? Can we work it out so that it doesn't happen again? If this situation comes up in the future, let's work out what you could do and what I could do so we don't have this problem again.

In this way you are solving the problem by giving the attention that the student wants and may also need. If you are wise, you will try to give him a little extra attention in the ongoing dialogue that I have suggested be a part of what you do regularly when you teach. But because you are now running a need-satisfying class, most of the time you will not have to work anything out. Once the student calms down, he'll probably agree that it won't happen again.

The vast majority of disruptive students you will have to deal with will not have big problems. Once they cool off, they usually do not want to go through a lengthy discussion about their temporary foolishness. But if a student is having trouble with another student, you may have to talk to one or both students to work out a way that they can get along better. You would handle this situation the same way:

> What were you [first student] doing? What were you [second student] doing? How could each of you [address each student] do something different that would prevent this from happening again?

Do not spend time trying to find out whose fault it is. Just tell the students involved that each has a problem to solve and that they can work on it separately or together, depending on which they prefer. Tell them that your goal is to help them to get along better and to do well in school. You are not looking for whose fault it is, just for a solution.

Obviously, the student or students may not be as cooperative as I have described, but this should not change your approach. No matter what students do, stick to getting the facts on the table: What was done was against the rules. You should insist that students focus on what they can do to prevent this problem in the future. It doesn't matter if the students do not come up with an exact plan; what matters is that you insist that there's a way to solve the problem. And if the disruptive students see you as a leader who cares, not as a boss who punishes, they will usually figure out a way to follow the rules.

Students will soon discover that you have given them every chance. If they want to stay in class, they have no choice but to follow the rules, at least until you talk things over. And if your students are satisfied most of the time, they'll want to stay. If a student calms down and seems satisfied, keep in mind that he may still have a problem that could be helped by talking to him, but this is not the time to attempt to do this. Wait a while, maybe a few days. Try to find a time when the student has enjoyed a little success in class, and then ask him if he would like to have a chat about how he is doing. If he opens up to you, just listen. Compliment him on doing better in class, tell him that you have enjoyed your little talk, and suggest that the two of you get together again for a talk. The student will probably agree to this suggestion. If you follow through, it is unlikely that you will have much trouble with him in the future. While this may sound like a lot of work, teachers who do it report that it is very pleasant and gives a real sense of satisfaction to their jobs.

Too often managers tend to manage by the "leave-well-enough-alone" philosophy, but "well enough" will not be good enough unless there is an ongoing effort to make the workplace satisfying for everyone. Therefore, the lead-manager is constantly trying to see that small problems are solved before they become large ones. Taking a little time to listen to a student who is a potential troublemaker is part of being a good lead-teacher.

What this accomplishes is that students, who see you always trying to make the classroom a better place to learn, try to solve many of their own problems and often help each other. They recognize that a little effort on their part is necessary if they are to keep the good situation that they have. If students do not see that you are making this effort, they will let you take over when problems occur; after all, "you're the boss." Don't be the boss: Talk to your students and be a problem solver, and fewer problems will occur.

Dealing with Students Who Are Asked to Leave the Class

Whether it happens early in elementary school or in the last part of high school, the first time a student disrupts enough to be asked to leave the class is a crucial point in that student's school career. If this situation is dealt with well, it may be the last time he disrupts to this extent, but once it becomes a chronic problem where he is kicked out of class over and over, it becomes almost impossible to solve.

Whether it is an administrator or a counselor who deals with the student who is sent from class, the lead-manager approach should be continued. Concede that there is a problem, maybe even be a big one, but you will try to help the student solve it. There should be no threats or punishment, no semblance of the usual boss-manager approach that the student may expect. If, however, the student has been exposed to a lead-managed school, he will not expect punishment and will already be amenable to the problem-solving approach that is the only one that will work in the long run. Just because it did not work in the classroom does not mean that it will not work. If it is used consistently both in and out of class, it will work eventually, in one place or another.

Do not be misled into thinking that because the problem-solving lead-manager approach is nonpunitive, it is soft. It is really the toughest approach of all because the student has to take some responsibility for solving the problem instead of letting the boss do it all. This approach can involve restricting the student to a "time-out" room, a restriction that should be continued until he is willing to start working on the problem. A time-out room is just a room in the school run by someone who has experience dealing with students who have been asked to leave class. If the school is lead-managed, no matter how large the school, there will rarely be more than a few students in the room.

In the lead-managed Apollo School where I consult, there are almost no disruptive students and no need for a time-out room. When a problem occurs, the student is always ready to work to solve it. As a school begins the move to becoming a quality school, the need for a time-out room begins to diminish, so what I am talking about here is only temporary. When the transition to a quality school is complete—this should take no more than four years—there should be no discipline problems serious enough to require a time-out room.

It usually does not take more than an hour or two to get a solution started, but the student should remain in the time-out room even if it takes much longer. The student may protest that it is unfair and that you are punishing him by keeping him there, but you have to point out that it is his choice not to begin to work to solve the problem. As soon as he starts working on a solution, he can go back to class.

You should also point out that in the time-out room he not only has a chance to do his schoolwork, but he may even get some help so that he can keep up with the class. He is always treated with courtesy and offered counseling. The student's parents should not be involved unless he starts to fall behind in his classwork. He should be constantly reminded that no one wants him to stay in restriction: Everyone wants him to begin to work on the problem and will help in any way possible. The student should be told over and over, and as kindly as possible, that it is his choice to be there and that only he can make a better choice.

In the time-out room the only rule is that the students sit quietly. They are encouraged to do their work, but if they just want to sit, that is their privilege. If the person running the time-out room judges this to be beneficial, students may be allowed to work together as long as they are not just socializing. The teacher or counselor running this room may also involve the students in a discussion of how they can solve their problems, but this is optional. The main thing is that this room be seen as an opportunity to solve a problem, not as punishment, and that the person in charge is a friend trying to help, not a boss trying to throw his weight around.

When counseling in the time-out room, the counselor should be prepared to deal with the following common complaints:

1. The teacher doesn't like me.
2. The class is boring.
3. I don't need this class for anything that I want to do with my life.

While the whole staff should constantly work to make the school a better place, this is not the time to apologize for what the student thinks is wrong with the school. Agree with him if he says the teacher does not like him and that the class may be boring. Point out that the teacher is not a saint and that no one likes a person who makes trouble. If he finds the class boring, is being in the time-out room better? Don't argue about whether or not he needs what is taught in the class, but ask whether he needs this particular class to graduate. If this is acceptable policy in your school, you might tell him, "If you are willing to do enough work to get to the point where you are in good standing in this class, I will consider changing you to a different class, but I will not change you as long as you are doing poor work." Some schools have a no-change policy to prevent too much student movement, and for these schools this suggestion would not apply.

The purpose of doing this is to show the student that slacking off is his choice, but it is not a way to escape from responsibility. If he starts to work, it is likely that he will find the class less boring than when he was not working and also that the teacher may begin to like him. After that, this class may seem as good as any other class he might move to. Besides, in this class he does not have to start over.

The important thing is not to argue with the student. You will not convince him, and he will enjoy the fact that you are arguing for a lost cause. Your position should not be based on how good you think any class or teacher is or how bad the student may think one or both of these may be. It should be based on the fact that this is the best school that you can offer him right now and that everyone is working to make it better. If he continues to argue that the school has shortcomings, you should ask, "What are you doing to make it better?"

As you counsel, be warm and friendly. Do not make the student's problem into a big deal. Imply or say flatly that what he is struggling with is solvable but that he has to do something different in order to solve it. To make this point, go through what he did in class to get removed. Ask him if what he did was against the rules, which of course it was, and then tell him that he should be prepared to stay in the time-out room until he works out a better way: There is no other choice. Remind the student that the length of stay is up to him. It is not that hard to work out a plan to get back to class, and you don't want him to spend a long time in the room.

Be sure to point out to him (if it is true, and it should be true if the school has switched to lead-management) that he has little support from the class for what he did to get removed and even less for the time he is spending in this time-out room. Ask him to ask his friends if they think it is smart to stay in this room instead of trying to make a plan to get out. The point you are trying to make is that a class led by a lead-teacher will not support a disruptive student by giving him a great deal of attention. This lack of support is crucial to the success of this program.

As you work out a plan for the student to do something better, make sure he understands that it is not that hard to follow the rules because almost all the students (in a lead-managed school) do. Then take the further step of trying to work out a way to get the student and the teacher on better terms. Tell him that the plan will work best if the teacher who asked him to leave is able to see that he is doing something tangible to be a better student. If he is willing to try, ask the teacher to make some sort of a small, special effort to express appreciation that the student is trying.

Try to get the student back to class as soon as possible, but do not rush him back so quickly that he does not have time to realize that he should be thinking of something better to do. Also keep in mind that the student should stay out of class long enough so that the teacher does not think he went through a revolving door. The amount of time the student stays in this room should not be related to the degree of disturbance, but to his willingness to try to find a way to correct what he did wrong in class.

What I have just described should be the only disciplinary

approach used in a quality school. Do the same thing over and over. Use the time-out room for all problems of disruption. Do not use this room for problems that do not involve disruption, such as not working in class. These are educational, not discipline, problems and can be solved only by counseling, usually by the lead-teacher herself. Taking the nondisruptive, nonworker out of any class only makes the problem worse. He, more than anyone, needs to be in class. The argument that his nonwork will be contagious is not valid. Students do not avoid work because of what others do; they avoid it when they fail to find it satisfying.

Obviously the person in charge of the time-out room should have training and time to work with students. This is a job for a school counselor, but, at present, few school counselors can take the time to sit in a room with only a few students. This may be another job for volunteers; in some schools it has been handled competently by parents or senior citizens.[1]

Keep in mind that all of the ideas suggested in this chapter and the previous one will work well only if the students see their school as a place where they can satisfy their needs. This is always the goal of lead-management.

CHAPTER ELEVEN

Creating the Quality School

In July 1989, I was approached by the superintendent of a small (grades 9 to 12) school district in central California who told me that he had read some material on the quality school, had visited the Johnson City Schools, and wanted to move his school in that direction. Whether or not this school follows through and becomes a quality school, what we worked out could serve as a start-up model for any school that wants to move in this direction.

We began with a meeting in which he and his top administrators, following the Johnson City model, agreed to gradually involve all of the staff in control theory and reality therapy training. This would start with the top managers taking a week's training during the school year. For reasons I will shortly explain, I do not believe that any school will be able to complete the move to a quality school until all the administrators and a majority of the teachers have at least two one-week training sessions in these basic concepts.

The superintendent, however, asked me if it would be possible to begin the program in September before anyone began formal training. He felt, and I agreed, that if they had to wait until everyone was trained in the theory and practice, a process that takes several years, they might lose interest long before much was accomplished. As important as it is, the formal training is not the first thing to do when an administrator decides to try to move to a lead-managed, quality school.

What the person in charge has to do is present the ideas in the first chapter of this book to teachers and show them that he is serious by beginning to use lead-management when he makes this presentation. Teachers will not be interested unless they see immediately that they, as well as their students, are to get the benefit of this new way to manage. Starting in that meeting and continuing unchanged throughout the whole process, the message from the top to the staff must be, "How can we help you much more than we have helped you in the past?"

In schools where the present management is considering making this move, the managers are very likely to be on good terms with the teachers. Still it would be unusual for the teachers to see management, friendly as it may be, as a direct source of help. There is a big difference between a benevolent boss and an actively helping and facilitating leader, and the best way to make this difference clear is to ask at this first meeting for suggestions from the teachers as to how management could help them to teach more effectively.

The teachers will be wary of this new approach, as most low-level managers are when the boss tells them that things are going to be better. The first thought that will go through their minds will probably be: "This is another half-baked scheme that isn't going to work. It's going to make a lot more work for us, and we have too much already." It isn't necessary to address this attitude, but it is necessary to know that it is there as it will tend to limit the suggestions the teachers will offer. It may be that very few will be offered, but all of them should be carefully written down. This initial reluctance to go on record is also to avoid being seen by the boss as a complainer and will dissipate when the teachers find as the program develops that their job is actually better. Skeptical as they will be, asking them what they want that they do not have is a very good way to start.

If I were running this meeting, I would address the universal complaint of good teachers that boss-managers rarely address: Teachers are locked into the classroom, and administrators and other out-of-classroom personnel have no appreciation for how little free time a teacher has during the day for research, preparation, and counseling students. I would also address the corollary complaint, which is that once a teacher moves to an out-of-classroom job, whether it is as a consultant, counselor, or administrator, he or she tends to forget how locked in teachers are.

A very effective way to reduce the initial skepticism is to present a way in which lead-management would begin immediately to deal with both these real issues. As the teachers agree that they would like more out-of-class time, the administrator running this first meeting should suggest getting together with a committee of teachers to work out how this and other problems could be solved. He might add that one way this could be accomplished would be for out-of-classroom personnel to spend more time in class relieving teachers so that they are less locked-in. This offer to work out problems through committees, which always include people who have the power to solve the problems, is the heart of lead-management.

The specifics of the plan would have to be worked out in committee, but I recommend that the wide gap between those who teach and the administrators and consultants who do not be drastically narrowed in a quality school. All out-of-classroom personnel, even including the superintendent, should teach on a regular basis at least one hour a week and up to several hours a day when possible. In most schools, there are enough able teachers not teaching now so that in time, with the additional help of volunteers and student assistants, it might not be unrealistic for all teachers to have an extra hour each day of classroom free time in addition to what they have now. This would show that the out-of-classroom personnel appreciate what teachers do and would lead to a better feeling between the two groups, which is a goal of a lead-management.

After this initial meeting in which the administration declares its desire to move to a quality school, the teachers should be asked if they would be willing to spend more time after school begins in staff meetings for the purpose of learning more about what constitutes a quality school. There is enough material in this book to get any interested teacher well acquainted with these ideas even before formal training begins. (The sooner it can begin, however, the better.)

Assuming that there is initial interest, the first three chapters of this book should be made available on a chapter-by chapter-basis to all faculty and discussed in meetings led by an administrator familiar with the whole book. After the staff has gone carefully through these three chapters, teachers would have enough information to make a preliminary decision as to whether they wanted to get involved in a specific program aimed at moving the school to a quality school. The administration would already have shown their good faith by forming the committee working on utilizing out-of-classroom personnel in the classroom, and this should encourage teachers to choose to get involved.

If at least half the faculty were interested after reviewing and discussing all the implications in the first three chapters, there would be sufficient numbers to move further. If not, I do not think it would be worth making the effort, and the school should wait until there are enough models around so that the value of these ideas is obvious.

Once this preliminary commitment is made, I suggest that all interested teachers agree to spend the first school year going through the rest of the book systematically to understand the ideas well enough to test them in their classes during this first year. Uncommitted teachers would be encouraged to attend these meetings but, following lead-management, attendance would be optional. By the end of the school year, the administration would be ready for the second week of training, and teachers who could work it into their schedules would take the first week.

Assuming there was interest at the initial meeting, the first step would be for the administration to write a purpose for the school because, if an organization is to achieve quality, Deming insists that top management begin by clearly and succinctly defining the organization's purpose. After this is done, the administration would need to consult with the teachers who were interested after reading and discussing the first three chapters to find out if they accept this statement of purpose. While quality schools may differ slightly in what they see as their purpose, I doubt if any school that does not agree to the following will be able to make the move to quality:

> All students should achieve a level of competence in all courses they attempt that both they and their teachers agree is quality education.

This purpose is stated in very general terms because, as Deming explains, to be specific here is not desirable. To set precise standards or goals for what is to be accomplished is to risk limiting the productivity to that standard. For example, if both faculty and students agree that one of the tasks of a quality school is to teach all the students to write a quality letter, there should never be an exact definition of what this is. No matter how well students write, they may still be able to do better. To quote Deming, "Improve constantly and forever the system of production and service."[1]

If either the teacher or the student decides that a submitted letter is not quality, the student should work until both decide it is. If they have trouble deciding, they should get another opinion. In a quality school, however, it is accepted that quality can be recognized and that people can usually agree that it is present. But it is also accepted that it need not be defined and that, good as it may become, it can always be improved.

Training in Control Theory

Once the purpose is set, the part of the staff that agrees to this purpose and wants to start the move to a quality school needs to become highly conversant with the concepts of control theory and reality therapy. Although this may take several years, the experience of the Johnson City schools, the best quality school models around, confirms the importance of this training. Teachers will not move to lead-management unless they are more than just acquainted with the control theory that explains the needs, the quality world, and the way we behave. They must know it well enough so that they use it in their lives, and this takes time and at least two weeks of formal training. To attempt to move a school to the point where all the students are involved in quality work without this training would be more difficult than learning to fly an airplane from an instruction manual.

It takes a working knowledge of control theory for teachers to accept that the students in their classes who are not working hard have not yet figured out how to satisfy their needs in these classes. Without enough training to use control theory in their lives, teachers will tend to continue to believe that they can make students work. Training is necessary because even the smallest amount of this coercive, boss attitude will taint the atmosphere and prevent any school from becoming a quality school.

Training in reality therapy, the method of counseling I have been teaching for years that is based completely on control theory, is also necessary. Teachers who take this training learn how to talk to students, especially to the nonworking students, without using coercion. For most teachers, the complete elimination of coercion is a new experience, and if they do not learn how to do it, they will fail to become lead-teachers. In this context, reality therapy is far more than a method of counseling; it is a noncoercive method of talking to people that managers need to learn to be successful. As managers grow skilled in this noncoercive way to deal with workers, they will be able to persuade workers to begin to take responsibility for what they do and, at the same time, prevent them from believing that they are being pushed by a manager to do what they do not want to do.

Extensive training in a combination of reality therapy and control theory is available, and most of the staff of the Johnson City schools have had some or all of the training offered.[2] The administration at Johnson City has had complete training and uses what they have learned to manage teachers as well as students. In Johnson City, no one bosses anyone and lead-management flourishes. As I write this book, the Johnson City schools have also begun a project to train all students in the ideas of control theory, having discovered that the more students know about how they function, the better they tend to behave.

I also have feedback from many teachers in districts other than Johnson City who have become skilled in the use of reality therapy and control theory and have taught these skills to students. They have discovered that students have no difficulty learning these ideas. They catch on quickly to the fact that they have needs they must satisfy and that they choose the behaviors they use to satisfy them. Once they do, they stop blaming others for their problems and start working on making better choices in their own lives. Students become especially intrigued with the idea that they have quality worlds inside their heads and see the value of working with their teachers to keep schoolwork in these worlds. In a quality school a systematic effort would be made, starting in the first grade with the concept of the needs, to teach all students control theory and how to use it in their lives.

While every concept in this book is based on the ideas of control theory and reality therapy, neither a book nor a training course can tell a school exactly how to implement these ideas. For example, when and how should a school break with the traditional system of grades and move to the system suggested in Chapter Eight? This is something that each school has to work out for itself. Teachers would have to decide when this was a good move to make and how to make it. Students and parents would have to be involved and a school board persuaded that it was in the best interests of the students.

During the first year, when many small changes would start to take place, I do not think it would be a good idea to involve the students in much discussion about what was happening. Like teachers, students are quite skeptical when "great changes" are announced, and this skepticism would hamper the process. For example, the two most important practices of a quality school are the elimination of coercion and student self-evaluation. As I will discuss next, both should be started as soon as the decision is made to begin, but neither need be announced as being part of a "big deal" process that is now getting started. If these practices work well, and students and teachers support them, they will speak adequately for themselves. Then, because they have been accepted, they can be mentioned and their vital role in a quality school explained.

Student Self-Evaluation

While most teachers and administrators will require training if they are to manage students without coercion, little or no special training is needed to persuade students that it is to their benefit to evaluate their work. As covered extensively in Chapter Seven, we all know quality when we see it, but students in a quality school need to be alerted to look for it much more than they do now. Teachers should begin by talking to students in a general way about the subject of quality. They might use a course that all students take, like social studies or history, so that all are exposed to a similar discussion. Each teacher must figure out for herself the best way to do this, but I suggest spending part of several periods on the subject. After this introduction, all teachers involved in the process should spend a few minutes each day talking about quality so that students get the idea that evaluating the quality of what they do, both in and out of school, is now a high-priority goal.

Ask students to look for quality in how they dress, how they wear their hair, the language they choose to express themselves, the music and the movies they like, what they watch on television, what is advertised, and what they buy. After they develop an appreciation of quality in these areas of their lives, move into a discussion of what it takes to be seen as a quality person. Ask them to use history and current events for examples of quality people, and try to get them to see that they judge some people as having much more quality than others. Ask them to tell you why they made these judgments, and then discuss with them what may be some of the criteria for human quality. As you talk to each other informally at lunch and at breaks, share what you have learned in these quality discussions and help each other to become more skillful in this new area of teaching and awareness.

Once students are acutely aware of what quality is, ask them to think about quality as it applies to school. Is there quality in the subjects they take and in the assignments they are asked to do? If they do not see quality in the subjects they take, or if they see it in the subjects but not in the assignments that are given in these subjects, ask how more quality could be injected into what they do in school. Try to explain how to find quality, for example, in math, science, English, and history. This is not an easy task; you will have to do it in small segments as you continue teaching, but there is no hurry. Go slowly and students will remain interested. It takes time for this new idea to gel. You are aiming to have students see the quality of what you ask them to do. If they cannot see this, they will never do the high-level work that is the core of a quality school.

As you do this, ask students to take the next necessary step, which is to begin to judge some of what they do in school for quality. Use classroom assignments rather than homework, as many students do not do their homework. See if they would be willing to evaluate in writing the quality of one of their assignments. Discuss what to write on the top of the paper to indicate the evaluation. For example, it could be a grade, a number, or the words "high quality," "average quality" or "low quality." After you have agreed on a designation, ask students to try evaluating their work.

Make sure the first time you do this that what you assign is clear-cut enough so that judging the quality is easy. For example, assign them to write a paragraph describing their favorite television show and then judge what they wrote for quality before turning it in. Tell students that you are very serious about this process and that you are going to begin to keep two records of the quality of what they do: your evaluation and theirs. Tell them that you will do this as soon as you are convinced that they are making a serious effort to judge the quality of all they do. This means that their grades on future assignments (not tests), will be based on both your judgment and their judgment of their work.

During the second part of the first year of the quality school program, have students begin to evaluate every aspect of the school in which they are involved. For example, regardless of

how anyone else evaluates what they do, what is their evaluation of their participation in extracurricular activities? How
do they judge their effort to keep the school clean, help other
students, help teachers, spread the idea that their school is a
good place to learn, and any other aspect of school that you
or they can think of?

You are trying to get students to judge the quality of the life
they are choosing to lead. They are used to judging the quality
of others and having others judge them. It is judging themselves that will be new, and this judgment is vital. Unless
students begin to do this on a regular basis, it will be very
difficult to move to a quality school.

Try to teach students this important lesson: The success or
the failure of our lives is greatly dependent on our willingness
to judge the quality of what we do and then to improve it if
we find it wanting. But during the first year do not focus on
what students could do to improve their lives. Until coercion
can be eliminated from the school, they may see your asking
them to improve as coercive. If they ask whether you are
interested in their improving the quality of what they do, tell
them that your main interest is that they judge their performance; improving it is up to them. Actually, you may never
have to focus on improvement because, driven by our need for
power, once we become aware of a shortcoming, we cannot
help trying to improve. If all the teachers who have made the
commitment to a quality school do what is suggested here for
at least a semester, they will be well on their way to a quality
school.

This should not be difficult to do. You are not asking students to do anything that takes a great deal of time or effort.
Once they get used to doing this, it is amazingly easy to make
these judgments. It may not be easy for your students to live
with their evaluations if they are low, but that is not your
problem. It is their problem, which is the purpose of doing

this. As a lead-manager, however, you will offer help if students want to improve, which most of them will want to do. The more they want to improve, the less you will feel that you must push them. The urge to coerce will thus be greatly reduced by this self-evaluation plan. There will also be less work for you when your students get involved in these evaluations and do better work. It should also be fun. There is grist for many good discussions and laughs as you struggle with students in this new direction.

Involving All the Students in Quality Learning

In any school there are students who not only do not do quality work, but in fact do no work at all. We now try to rectify this problem, by setting up special programs to "fix" these low performers, many of whom are diagnosed as having a mental or emotional handicap, although research fails to confirm this diagnosis.[3] By introducing more need-satisfying classes, we should be able to persuade most of these students to start doing much more in school and to gain the confidence to attempt to do quality work. Keep in mind that these will be the students who will be most resistant to evaluating their work, who will be immune to coercive discipline, and for whom quality schoolwork is a foreign idea.

Identifying these students should be easy; it is well known who is working and who is not. Once they have been identified, they must be persuaded to start working much harder than most do now. To do this, a teacher, counselor, or administrator should follow up the quality discussions the students are exposed to in class with a personal interview or even a series of short personal interviews about quality. Using no threat, ask each student the following question: "We believe you can do more than you are doing: What do you think about doing something of quality in school?"

Many will try to convince you that they are satisfied with the way things are now. They say this because they do not believe that they could do much better in this school, and they do not want to expend energy in what, to them, is a lost cause. For many, the whole idea of doing quality work is overwhelming. They have no recent experience of doing well in school, and the question does not make much sense to them.

The key here is to begin to focus quickly; quality school-work is too abstract a concept for these students to follow. Ask, "Is there any part of any of your classes that you consider valuable enough to work hard and do quality work?" Gently and with encouragement, the teacher, counselor, administrator, peer counselor, or volunteer must keep asking this question over and over in a variety of ways until the student agrees to do a very small amount of what he or she considers quality work. Here the teacher has to figure out how to exhibit persistent interest that the student will see as caring rather than nagging or pressuring. To be more persuasive, the teacher should offer to help the student to get started or arrange to get a tutor involved.

Someone must persist in this even if it means going to the students' homes and talking about it in front of their parents or whoever is there. For these students the point must be made that we care and are going to show that caring actively and in ways that we have not shown it before. For home visits, I suggest that the school put together "quality teams" made up of students who are doing some quality work, along with a staff member or volunteer. The teams might wear T-shirts incribed with the words, "I am a member of the Hudson High Quality Team."

When they find that people from the school will not give up, that quality teams come right to their homes or wherever they can find them, students will be impressed. They cannot help thinking that the school cares and has confidence in them, that they are being given a choice they have never been offered before, and that the question is not coercive. To help them to see the value of working, it may be a good idea to talk to them about whether they want to graduate. Argue gently that graduation is worthwhile and that they can go further in life if they get involved in the quality that the school is now talking about.

If you are persistent, students will eventually say that they are interested in doing something that they judge has quality. Then a plan has to be made with the teacher of the subject in which they want to do quality work. Anything of quality should be acceptable, no matter how little, because what is needed to get nonworkers started is for them to do one piece of quality work. It is a beginning. After they have done one assignment well, they will feel some of the power that goes with quality, and it will be easier to help them plan to do more and start evaluating all of their work.

If these students start to succeed, ask them to join a quality team that visits other students. When the low-achievers, who tend to know each other, see a former low-achiever on a quality team, it will be very persuasive.

Beginning to Eliminate Coercion and Criticism

Even before anyone takes the formal training in control theory and reality therapy that will focus on dealing with students and teachers without coercion, the staff should start eliminating coercion from all they do. For dealing with students, use the examples in Chapters Nine and Ten. When students break a rule or fail to exert effort, tell them that you will work with them to help them figure out how to solve what is obviously a problem. Where rules are concerned, emphasize that you will no longer threaten or punish, but you will not be able to keep a student in class who is not willing to work with you to follow the rules.

Ask your students to help you by pointing out when they think you are threatening or when you criticize them personally. When they point out a slip, ask what you could have said or done instead. Not only will they be amazingly sensitive in this area, but they will also be creative in suggesting alternatives. Most students know what teachers should say instead of the coercive remarks we tend to use, but they never tell us because we usually never ask.

Tell students that you want to be their friend, not their adversary, and then make a point of showing this in all you do. Let them know that you want to help them do what both you and they agree is quality work, but you need their help. You cannot teach the way they would like if they are not willing to get actively involved in the process.

Cooperative Learning

When the superintendent approached me for help, he told me that cooperative learning was already a significant component of the school program because he was well aware that this is a very need-satisfying way to teach and learn. This method has been covered extensively in *Control Theory in the Classroom* and need not be repeated here, except to say that it is hard to visualize any quality school that is not deeply involved in this method of instruction. A quality school would make training in this method available to all interested teachers. In fact, I recognize now what I failed to see when I wrote *Control Theory in the Classroom*, which is that cooperative learning has been slow to catch on because it is so difficult for boss-managers to give students the control over their work that is inherent in this method of instruction. In a lead-managed quality school, cooperative learning should flourish.

Governing the Quality School

Lead-management should extend to student and parent participation in the government of a quality school. While there should be elections for half the students who serve on the student-faculty-parent association that should govern the school, the other half should be selected differently. All students who want to serve on this body, or on a separate student council that gives recommendations to this body, should put their names in a hat, and the ones drawn should be selected. This would give the less popular students a chance to have a say in the running of the school that they would never get if they had to be elected. The meetings of the governing body should be open to all who are interested, and anyone should have a chance to speak. At least once a semester a town meeting, open to all, should be held to discuss school concerns. All major changes in the way the school was governed should be voted upon at this meeting.

Name Tags

An effort should be made to increase the number of people in the school who know each other by name. People who call each other by name work together much better and become friends much faster. To accomplish this, the faculty might agree that they, and all adults in the school on school business, will wear name tags. This would set an example and encourage students to do the same. The name tags could be creative, standard, or both. To encourage students to wear them, prizes could be given for the most creative tags. A student without a name tag would be asked to put one on, and teachers should have a supply of temporary tags to hand out to students who need them.

While it should not be compulsory to wear a name tag,

every effort should be made to persuade all to do so. No teacher would then have to talk to a student without knowing his or her name. This simple procedure, more than anything else that can be done, would reduce discipline problems. The students should be encouraged to wear their name tags in the community, and some businesses might be persuaded to give discounts to students wearing their name tags.

Bonuses for Success

When the quality of the work increases, as it will in a lead-managed school, it will be because the workers and the managers are working together much better than before. They should be compensated for this effort. The fairest way to do this is to award a financial bonus to the whole school for any obvious increase in quality, but this bonus should be totally excluded from all salary negotiations. While I cannot give an exact formula for this bonus, it seems fair to compare past and present records and relate the award to how close the school comes to reaching the following quality school goals:

1. Students do not leave school; the dropout rate is essentially zero.
2. Student attendance is almost perfect; tardiness and absence disappear.
3. Teacher absenteeism goes significantly below the average for the state.
4. There are no discipline problems that are not quickly and easily solved.
5. The records show that all students have achieved competence or beyond in what are considered hard courses, like math and science, and substantial numbers of students took courses at what would be considered college level. These numbers should be far more than what is achieved

in comparable boss-managed schools.
6. There are few or no diagnoses of learning disabilities.
7. There is significantly less student delinquency in the community the school serves as reported by the police and juvenile agencies.

To the extent that there are significant improvements since the school began the move to quality and a bonus is awarded, I suggest that 75 percent of the money be divided equally among the faculty and 25 percent be used for the direct benefit of students. Even the faculty who did not actively participate in the program should share in the bonus as it is unlikely that any faculty member would remain completely uninvolved if the school began to reach these goals.

As the goals are reached, the community the school serves would save a substantial amount of money, and a representative of the teachers should work with the community financial officer to accurately assess the actual amount of this saving. The bonus should be paid out of this sum. If all the goals listed above were reached, both the sum and the bonus to the teachers should be substantial. The student bonus should be used to improve the school plant and equipment, send students on trips, award scholarships, and pay students who tutor other students a small fee. These are only suggestions; the student-faculty-parent governing body would make the actual decisions.

Summary

None of the ideas in this book is beyond the capability of any school in the country right now if the leadership is willing to do the work to make the move. Just as there is nothing wrong with American workers, there is nothing wrong with our students. Deming is right; it is the way we manage them that must be changed. By the end of the first year, if most of coercion has been removed from the school and most of the students are evaluating what they do in school, the move to quality will be well underway. Much hard work will remain, however, as the staff gets involved in the training. The ideas in this book are only the basics. Much more will be added and refined by each school as the staff is trained and the payoff for the move to quality becomes more and more apparent.

Nothing we can do will improve the quality of life in any community more than quality schools. Young people who are involved in quality education do not engage in self-destructive activities and are an asset to the community. And since most industries can now be located almost anywhere, good schools are a major incentive for an industry to move to a community. There is no more effective and economical way to improve the economy of a community than for it to become known for excellent schools.

I look forward to an increasing number of quality schools and ultimately a Quality School Association that maintains the standards, helps other schools to make the move to quality, and sends out committees to evaluate schools that believe they are ready for the official designation, Quality School. My vision is a quality flag flying below the American flag on the flagpoles of an increasing number of schools. I invite you to share that vision.

PART TWO

Introduction

Since this book was initially published in the spring of 1990, well over 1,000 school principals have inquired about what they need to do if their schools are to become Quality Schools. Over sixty-five school staffs, both elementary and secondary, have signed contracts to work with me and my staff towards becoming Quality Schools. To help them, I have offered to answer any questions that arise as they move toward this goal. As many schools asked questions, it became apparent that most were similar and that my answers could be of use to everyone.

To make these answers available, I wrote what I called "reference bulletins" and sent them not only to all the contract schools but to many other schools who had been keeping in touch with us because they were thinking seriously about signing the contract. The feedback has been very good. I have been told that this new information greatly focuses and clarifies the material in the original book.

By agreeing to include them in this new edition, Hugh Van Dusen, my editor at HarperCollins, has given me the rare opportunity to respond to what I know are the specific needs of many readers. Although the bulletins were written in response to questions, answering them has helped me to think through the whole Quality School process and figure out what I believe is the most sensible order in which to arrange them here. As usually happens when we learn more about a subject, what is learned last is best shared first and that is mostly what I have done. I have left in the dates they were written as I believe some readers would be interested in how my thinking has evolved.

I am continuing to write these bulletins. For information on how to get on the mailing list, write or call the Institute for Reality Therapy. (See author's note in the beginning of the book for the address.) If, after reading the book, you have a question, please send it to me. I will answer all inquiries and I am sure that some of my answers will be in the form of a new bulletin. Don't think you are imposing when you write. If we are to improve education, I need your thoughtful questions and comments.

CHAPTER TWELVE

Defining the Educational Terms We Talk About
BULLETIN #11, 3-25-91

While I stated in the earlier chapters of the present book that the solution to the problem of students not working in school is better management of both students and teachers, I did not define the three terms that are central to this problem: education, teaching, and managing. I fell into the same trap that most of us who are trying to solve this problem do: I talked about these terms as if we all agree on what they are. It took me until now to realize that we don't agree at all. Ask ten teachers to define education and get ready for almost ten definitions. It is, also, almost the same for teaching and managing.

In fact, most of the people who work in the field do not even think about defining these terms. What I want to discuss here is that we need both to define these terms and to agree on the definitions if we are to get more students working in school. It is, I believe, our failure to do this that has, as much as anything else, made this problem so hard to solve.

Suggestions for improving education are published daily in the popular press as well as in scholarly books and journals. However, none of these suggestions include a definition of education. Articles about teaching or managing also fail to define these terms. There is no way to improve a process (or a system like education) unless there is widespread agreement on exactly what it is we are trying to improve.

In this bulletin, I will offer definitions for education, teaching, and managing that are based on control theory. I do not claim that these are the only possible definitions. However, I do claim that if those of you who are already a part of the Quality School Consortium, as well as those of you who are thinking about joining, can agree on what I suggest here, this agreement will help you move your school to a Quality School. Let us begin with education:

> Education is the process through which we discover that learning adds quality[1] to our lives.

It is vital that this process start early in a student's school career. Until this happens, students will have little incentive to learn anything more than they already know. If you are trying to teach something to your students, this definition will immediately tell you if you are on the right track. If they are learning a great deal, you can be certain that what they are learning is adding quality to their lives. If they are having difficulty learning, you can be equally certain that what you are trying to teach them is not adding quality to their lives.

By itself, however, this definition does not tell you what to do if you want to learn or teach. It is like the definition of nutrition. You can describe food, but knowing what it is does not tell you how to fill your stomach or feed anyone else. If you run a school, however, this definition is valuable because it will tell you why some students are learning a lot more than others. If, however, we want more students to learn, we need to look at the definitions of two closely related processes: teaching and managing.

> Teaching is the process of imparting knowledge through a variety of techniques, like explaining and modeling, to people who want to acquire this

knowledge because they believe that, either now or later, it will add quality to their lives.

For example, I was impressed by a TV clip during the recent Persian Gulf War that illustrated this definition perfectly. It showed soldiers listening intently to an expert who was teaching them how to avoid getting killed by Iraqi land mines. It was obvious that this teacher was highly successful. His "students" were paying very close attention to what he was explaining. Public school teachers rarely achieve this level of success. Unlike these soldiers, less than half the students who go to public school want to learn what their teachers teach, so, as I will soon explain, it is much more accurate to call what teachers do managing rather than teaching.

Unfortunately, most teachers do not see themselves as managers: They cling to the incorrect idea that they are teachers even though they fail to teach the large numbers of students who do not believe that what they are asked to learn adds quality to their lives. Frustrated because so many students refuse to learn, almost all teachers and administrators believe that coercion is a necessary part of teaching, and that with enough coercion, students can be made to want to learn what they are taught. They refuse to believe what they see with their own eyes every day in every school: The coercion they employ does not work because it always reduces the quality of the lives of the students who are coerced. Therefore, if we are to solve the problem of not enough students learning in school, we have to accept that a major part of what we do is managing and then learn how to manage without coercion.

The following definition of managing is based on control theory because this theory is vitally concerned with the quality of our lives:

> Managing is the process of convincing people that working hard and doing a quality job of what the manager (teacher, in the case of the schools) asks them to do will add quality to their lives and, usually, to the lives of others.

As you can see, this definition is considerably different from the definition of teaching. It is also obvious that managing is a much more difficult task. Our failing in both school and industry is that, according to the definition above, we have not learned how to manage successfully. This is because very few managers define managing as I have here. The vast majority define it as the art of making people do what they are told to do, whether or not it adds quality to their lives. Furthermore, they are more than willing to include coercion as a way to make them do it.

Only if we are willing to accept the fact that people learn or do anything else that they choose to do because they believe that, sooner or later, it will add quality to their lives, will we begin to treat students and teachers much differently than we do now. To manage or teach successfully, we constantly need to keep the following axiom in mind: Coercion does not increase the quality of anyone's life. It is my hope that the schools in the Quality School Consortium will provide the noncoercive models so urgently needed if these ideas are to spread.

CHAPTER THIRTEEN

Creating a Quality Organization
BULLETIN #18, 1-1-92

This is meant to be a useful guide for the leaders of a school, or any other organization, private, public, profit or nonprofit, to follow as they try to move to quality.

The leaders of any organization that wants to achieve quality should begin by agreeing on an initial working definition of what it is. Based on many years of study of control theory and the work of W. Edwards Deming, I suggest that the following five conditions be a part of whatever definition is used to get started.

1. Quality is always a product of warm, caring human relationships.
2. Quality is always useful in some way—for example, personally, as in learning a desired skill; economically, as Deming's work in Japan; biologically, as Pasteur's discovery of microorganisms; socially and politically, as exemplified by the Constitution of the United States; or intellectually, as shown by the works of great people such as Einstein or Shakespeare. Characteristic of quality is that it is never destructive either to individuals or to society.
3. Quality is the best that everyone in the organization,

working both separately and together, can achieve at any particular time. A quality organization never settles for less.

4. Quality can always be improved no matter how good it is at any time. A quality organization is always alert for ways to improve what it does and how it does it.

5. Quality always feels good, and the greater the quality, the longer the good feeling lasts. (Following the first condition, however, that it is never destructive, no matter how good it feels, it is never quality to abuse people, property, or addicting drugs.)

If the organization's leaders have the goal of producing quality products or services and they agree to include the above five conditions in the startup definition, then success in reaching quality will depend on how well these conditions can be put into practice. To accomplish this, the following four procedures are vital to the process.

I. CONTINUING EDUCATION

There can be no quality without continuing education aimed at increasing the quality of the work and lives of the workers. But for that education to be effective, everyone involved must agree that what they are asked to learn is useful and enjoyable either immediately or a little later. When education satisfies these criteria, it always adds quality to the lives of everyone the organization touches.

II. LEAD-MANAGING AS TAUGHT BY DEMING AND OTHERS

Those who manage in an organization at all levels must lead, not boss, which means to focus on:

A. Emphasizing quality in all they ask everyone to do,

and never asking anyone to do anything that is not useful or is less than the best they can do.

B. Establishing a fair, friendly workplace, giving all who work a fair share of the profits, doing away with all coercion, and accepting (as explained by control theory) that, in such a workplace, the natural desire for quality need be the only motivator.

C. Teaching everyone to evaluate his or her own work because quality can only be achieved through self-evaluation. A lead-manager would help establish the criteria for this evaluation. While external evaluation may lead to good work, it will never lead to quality work because it sends the clear message, "We do not trust you to do quality work." In a quality organization, managers trust the educated workers at all levels to evaluate their own work and it is this trust that leads to quality.

III. UNDERSTANDING AND USING CONTROL THEORY, A NEW THEORY OF HOW THE BRAIN WORKS, AS TAUGHT BY GLASSER AND HIS ASSOCIATES

Glasser explains that we should give up stimulus-response theory because it is based on the false idea that we are externally motivated, an idea that leads to the coercive bossing that makes quality unobtainable. We should follow control theory, which explains:

A. That all of our behavior is internally motivated and is always our best effort to satisfy basic needs built into our genetic structure. These needs are love, power, fun, freedom, and survival. Whatever we discover that is highly satisfying to one or more of these basic needs, we define as quality. Therefore a quality organization is always a need-satisfying organization.

B. That it is not possible to coerce those we manage

into doing quality work because coercion is never need-satisfying. Unless the work and workplace are need-satisfying, there can be no quality.

C. That we are forced by the way our brain works (control theory) to evaluate all we choose to do to determine if it is satisfying to our needs. Therefore, quality, and the happiness that accompanies it, can only be achieved through this process. The main difference between happy and unhappy people is that happy people mostly evaluate their own behavior and constantly attempt to improve what they do. Unhappy people, on the other hand, mostly evaluate the behavior of others and spend their time criticizing, complaining, and judging in an attempt to coerce them into "improving" what they do. A quality organization, therefore, will consist of many more happy than unhappy people.

IV. TREATING ALL THOSE WHO WORK IN THE ORGANIZATION AS PROFESSIONALS ASSUMING THAT, ONCE THEY LEARN TO DO THEIR WORK, THEY USUALLY KNOW AS MUCH OR MORE ABOUT HOW TO DO IT WELL AS ANYONE ELSE—AS PROFESSIONALS, HOWEVER, THEY ARE ALWAYS OPEN TO LEARNING TO DO IT BETTER

This will occur most often if the leaders of the organization believe in education, practice lead-management, and base what they do on control theory. Treating people as professionals is best accomplished through:

A. Discussing with those they manage what needs to be done and continuing this discussion until everyone agrees that what is asked of them is useful and, therefore, has the potential for quality.

B. Explaining why they ask the people they manage to do what they ask of them and continuing this discussion until the reason for it is understood by all who are asked to do it.

C. Show, model, or suggest but never tell an educated worker, or even a student, how to do the work, unless the worker, or student, asks for this help. Professionals, like teachers, need to know what needs to be done and why it needs to be done, but they want the option of figuring out how best to do it. Offering them training to improve what they do and explaining why this way may be better often leads to more quality. However, insisting that they follow what they have been taught to the level of how to do it is coercive and, therefore, always destructive to quality.

CHAPTER FOURTEEN

Quality Schoolteachers Are Treated as Professionals
BULLETIN #9, 12-20-90

Professionals are people who know how to do quality work in their chosen fields. This means that they do not believe they need anyone to tell them what to do on the job. They are also open to learning more about how to practice their profession and are always attempting to improve what they do. Finally, true professionals are always willing, and usually eager, to share their expertise with others in their field. It would follow, then, that any professional would have continuous improvement as an important goal.

Professionals treat other professionals professionally: They respect the professional judgment of their colleagues. They accept that there is no one way to teach or not to teach. This means that a teacher who did not want to participate in a Quality School Program in her school would not be coerced to do this. At the same time, the nonparticipating teacher would be expected not to criticize the effort of those who want to move in this direction.

In a Quality School, the administration makes a continuing effort to treat all teachers as professionals, which means that they are never to be told what to do in their classrooms. It is assumed that they will teach the appropriate curriculum for their grade level or subject but the details of what they teach, the time they spend on various parts of their curriculum, the tests they give, the grades they assign, the way they maintain interest and order in their class are all left to their professional judgment.

To help the teachers achieve the professional goal of continuous improvement, all Quality Schools would offer ongoing training as an option, not only from outside experts but from the talent that is indigenous to every staff. To make progress, teachers would be encouraged by the administration of a Quality School to try out new ideas even if it means departing from accepted ways. It would be expected that they would develop a rationale for what they ask students to do that is new, and also help evaluate whether this departure is effective or not.

Because many schools do not treat teachers as professionals, teachers who are told how and what to teach or are boss-managed in other ways are reluctant to try new ideas. Some believe they are forbidden to try new ideas. This is because if something does not work well or something unforeseen happens, as it often will, instead of helping and encouraging teachers to work out the problems, boss-administrators or bosses on the staff criticize what happens. This is unfortunate because, unlike medicine, where new ideas can cause injury or death, in education little harm can be done by a careful departure from accepted practice.

Because they have been boss-managed almost all of their lives, many teachers are insecure, and this is often shown by their unwillingness to try out new ideas. Consequently, administrators need to be aware of the fact that the lead-managers do much more than allow new ideas in their schools: They figure out a variety of ways to encourage their teachers to get actively involved in new ways to teach, such as cooperative learning. They go into classes and help or they free up teachers who know how to do this well by taking their classes while they go and help a teacher who is trying to get started. The number one priority of the administrators in a Quality School is, "How can we encourage, help, and support our teachers both professionally and personally to try out new ideas?"

Perhaps the most unprofessional practice that almost all school administrators are forced to do by state law is to evaluate their teachers annually. No matter how skillfully it is done and no matter how competent the teacher, teachers fear evaluations. This fear inhibits creativity all year long and is a legal obstacle to the necessary move from boss-management to lead-management that is the crux of a Quality School.

The administrator of a Quality School must evaluate teachers differently from what most do now by interpreting state law as a lead-manager. To do this, he or she would ask teachers to evaluate their own progress as follows:

The teachers would be asked by the administrators to explain what they believe are their strongest points. They should be encouraged to take their time and feel free to explain why they believe that what they have explained works so well. They should then be asked by the administrators what help they could use to do even a better job of what they are doing so well. Finally they should be asked if they would be willing to help other teachers who might be interested in learning to do what they do so well.

Next they should be asked to tell the administrator about one area in which they believe they could improve and what help they think they need to make this improvement. They should be asked if they would accept help from a teacher who was strong in that area. The teacher and the administrator should begin, in this conference, to set the stage for the teacher getting some help to improve.

Their actual evaluations should be based on how willing they are to participate in this self-evaluative process, to work toward helping others, and to accept help for themselves. It would be almost impossible for a teacher to get an unsatisfactory evaluation unless he or she refused to cooperate.

There is nothing destructive about this kind of evaluation. It does not provoke fear or anger, both of which are common to the ordinary methods of evaluation that are now in use. It will always lead to higher-quality teaching—the goal of a Quality School.

CHAPTER FIFTEEN

What Is a Quality School?
BULLETIN #15, 07-17-91

The purpose of this bulletin is to try to help teachers and administrators to conceptualize a Quality School. While there will be more to such a school than is written here, all of the ten points in this bulletin will be very much a part of what goes on in a Quality School. The purpose of a Quality School will be to educate children according to the following definition of education: Education is the process through which we discover that learning adds quality to our lives. (To define quality, it is necessary to understand the control theory concept of the Quality World. See Chapter Five.)

As most of you know, as yet there are no designated quality schools. When we get to the point of starting to designate a school as a Quality School, we will ask both teachers and students about their school. If we get the answers written below, I believe what goes on in the school will have satisfied the above definition and the school will be ready to receive the designation "Quality School." Although each school has to do much on its own, my purpose is to help a staff to achieve the ten points in this bulletin. It is also strongly suggested that all of the staff read the following of my books: *Control Theory in the Classroom, Schools Without Failure, Reality Therapy,* and *Control Theory.* More reference bulletins will be coming in the coming school year.

A school is a Quality School when all students who are asked to describe their school will say:

1. I like school; I look forward to going each day.
2. I am learning things at this school that I believe are good for me.

    Older students who have gone to schools other than Quality Schools will also say, "I am doing better school work than I have ever done at school before. Some of it I would call quality work."

All teachers would say:

1. I like working in this friendly school: No one coerces me, and I do not have to coerce anyone else.
2. I am treated like a professional; I am encouraged to teach the curriculum the way I believe is best for my students.
3. I am pleased with the new way of evaluating students.
4. I no longer even think about discipline problems: They have disappeared from my classes.

To help students and teachers arrive at a point where they say what is stated above, the following practices will be in place:

1. Staff and students are friends. Neither need fear threats or punishment. Coercion does not exist. Together they will make all the rules and then sign that they accept these rules. Signs will be posted in all classes and in the office saying, "All problems will be solved by the staff and students talking with each other without anyone threatening or hurting anyone else." Regular meetings

will be held with all of the staff, students, and interested parents to figure out the best ways to conduct all school business.

2. There will be no nonsense taught or tested for. Teachers will be required to explain how what they teach can be used in their students' lives either now or later. Special training will be given to teachers who have difficulty explaining this to their students.

3. From K through 12th grade, there is an emphasis on the skills of speaking, writing, calculating, and problem solving, both as individuals and in groups, as these are the skills that have the greatest payoff in life. All students will work on these skills in all classes so that well before graduation they are able to speak, write, calculate, and solve problems in a way that they and their teachers agree is quality. Teachers will be encouraged to add additional skills as they see fit. (In the higher grades, calculating becomes mathematics.)

4. Subjects such as history, social studies, health, science, and foreign language are taught the way the teachers of these subjects think is best. They will be under no pressure to cover ground or prepare students for tests like the SAT. A special course in preparing students for such tests will be an optional elective. If teachers follow the above suggestion, students will do very well and, in fact, better than they presently do on such tests.

5. All students will be asked to evaluate all of their work for quality. Starting in kindergarten, teachers will teach students how to do this.

6. All tests will be open book. There will be no requirement to memorize facts. All questions will be written or oral and will query how the information that has been covered can be used in people's lives. No objective tests (such as multiple choice) will be allowed. Demonstra-

tions of competency such as a student writing a letter to a newspaper and getting it published, doing a project (as in science), or working in the community with what has been learned in school will supplement tests whenever possible.

7. As long as students want to work to improve, any grade can be raised. Students will be encouraged to keep working to the point where they and their teacher's evaluation of what they have done reaches the level of quality. B will be considered a competent grade and to get credit for a course, the student will have to do at least B work. Once students accept the idea of quality work, at least one bit of quality academic work, such as a quality report, will also be required in order to get credit for the course. Summer school will be offered to students who need credit for courses in which they have not achieved a B as well as to students who want to raise any grade to a higher one.

8. A corps of good students will be trained to serve as tutors for any student who needs one-on-one tutoring in any subject. Students who need individual help will get it from a student tutor as soon as they ask or when a teacher believes they need it. No student will be allowed to sit in class not knowing how to do the work and not being offered help. The students who act as tutors will get credit that they can use to raise their own grades immediately or later in the courses they tutor. This is one way to get an A + grade and will be an important incentive to join this program.

9. There will be no busywork and, therefore, no compulsory homework in a Quality School. Students who want to get credit and cannot make a "B" with what they have done in class will be counseled by their teacher as to what they need to do at home to get credit. Most

students will also assign homework to themselves to learn more, to prepare for tests and to improve their grades beyond what they can achieve if they only do class work.

10. All teachers and all students will be taught control theory. All teachers will be taught how to counsel students using reality therapy. Students who want to act as counselors and help other students who will accept their help will also be taught the reality therapy method of counseling.

If you have trouble understanding or agreeing with what I have stated in these ten points, think of something that you have learned on your own as an adult, such as skiing, contract bridge, a foreign language, or photography, or what you learned as you prepared for a trip and while you actually traveled. You will see that without being aware of it, as you have learned, you have carefully followed many of these points. Therefore, what I am suggesting is not radical—it is the natural way we learn as we attempt to increase the quality of our lives. Why should we not do the same in school?

CHAPTER SIXTEEN

Some Further Thoughts on Noncoercive Discipline
BULLETIN #4, 4-20-90

It is proving to be difficult for the teachers and administrators in schools enrolled in the Quality School Training Program to understand the actual process of dealing nonpunitively with students who don't obey rules. Further, the fact that a lead-managed Quality School has little need for the many rules that almost all boss-managed schools have used for years is far from an easy concept to accept. Therefore, to move to managing students with few rules and no punishment is difficult because it requires most of those who manage to reject what they have believed all their lives. But what is the hardest of all to accept is my claim that the many rules and sanctions that are inherent in boss-managing are the cause of almost all the discipline problems that teachers complain so much about.

The only rules that work in school (or anyplace else) are those that are accepted by the people they govern, and the only reason people accept a rule is because they believe it is more to their benefit than to their detriment to do so. When a rule is not accepted, it is frequently broken, and when this happens, all a boss-managed society seems able to do to try to get people to obey the rule is to punish the offender. This punishment, however, rarely works. The rule breakers continue to break the rule they are punished for and show little respect for most of the other rules they are asked to obey. Schools have no shortage of students who have been punished over and over for years and who continue to break many of the school rules.

In a community, a rule is called a law; and an example of a law that is frequently broken is the law against drunk driving. Partly it does not work because drinking is accepted by the vast majority of those who drive, and many drinkers, who are otherwise law-abiding people, drive without realizing how much they are impaired by alcohol. Mostly, however, it does not work because punishment (the main way we try to enforce the law) has not significantly reduced the practice. I am not suggesting that we get rid of this law any more than I am suggesting that we get rid of all school rules; but I am suggesting that a preventive rather than a punitive approach would not only be more effective in school, it would be more effective in reducing the number of people who drink and drive.

For example, if lead-managers were given the problem of reducing drunk driving, they would replace almost all punishment with: 1) increased law enforcement so that more offenders would be picked up before they got into accidents, 2) vastly increased treatment and much closer supervision of offenders, 3) devices to disable the cars of offenders so an intoxicated driver could not start the car, and 4) ways to mark the cars of all offenders so that everyone would be easily alerted to the fact that this car might be in the hands of a drunk driver. Much of what I suggest could be paid for with the money saved by eliminating the expense of prosecution and incarceration of offenders plus a substantial increase in the taxes on alcoholic beverages. Spending millions of dollars to prosecute and incarcerate these offenders (most of whom are good citizens when sober) has proven to be a waste of time and money.

Laws against drunk driving are examples of rules that we may need, but they are also examples of rules that punitive boss-managers—our legal system is almost 100 percent boss-managed—have not figured out how to enforce. In school, we have almost no rules that are as needed as the laws against drunk driving, but even with the much less necessary rules that we do have, school boss-managers seem equally unable to figure out how to enforce them.

Let's take a typical school rule: Unless you are excused, you must attend school and go to class on time. Most people would agree that we need this rule. Still, in many high schools, 20 percent or more students are absent each day; of those who show up, many are tardy for one or more classes and significant numbers come to school but fail to attend all their classes. If you understand control theory, you would know that in our boss-managed system, many students do not have school, teachers, or schoolwork in their quality worlds. And the more we punish students for breaking rules, the less they will have school, teachers, and schoolwork in their quality worlds. Therefore, what we do to improve schools actually makes them worse.

Typically, this attendance rule is enforced by detention, suspension, and the threat of failing any subject in which a student misses more than a prescribed number of classes. Some schools fail a student for missing as few as three classes, some allow up to a dozen, but few who use this procedure allow anyone who has more than a dozen unexcused absences in any class to pass. Some schools, usually in "good" neighborhoods, report that sanctions like these seem to work. It is no secret, however, why in certain schools these seem to work. They work when students come from homes where school is respected and where it would shame their family if they failed a course. With these students, however, almost any approach would work well, but the lead-managed, problem-solving approach I am going to suggest will work much better than what we are doing now.

In schools where most students do not come from school-supportive homes, these boss-managed approaches persuade most students to remove school, schoolwork, and teachers from their quality worlds beginning as early as elementary school. As this occurs, they pay less attention to the rules and they are punished even more. As this happens the staff and students begin to spiral apart and by middle school almost all the students and staff have become adversaries. Once this occurs, all improvement in that school becomes impossible.

Right now there is no shortage of threats and punishments in all schools, but in schools where most of the students do not come from "good" homes, this approach destroys whatever chance that school has to educate most of its students. High school students in these schools feel especially unwelcome, and many (up to half in some large city schools) quickly join the dropout group, which is substantial, no matter whose figures you believe. Considering that dropouts are a huge drain on the economy, it would seem wise to give up bossing and to look closely at what can be accomplished through a nonpunitive approach like we use at the Apollo School, where dropouts have been very much reduced.

When I ask students why they cut school, come late, or do not go to class, they give three reasons: 1) it is too hard to succeed, 2) it is boring, and 3) the teachers (or the important people) do not care. Of these three reasons, "no one cares" seems to be the most important, and it is obvious that punishment only increases the problem. All you have to do is look into your own life and you will find that whenever you did not do as you were "supposed" to do, the same reasons applied. Further, as much as you believe in punishment, you will also find that it rarely motivated you, and when it seemed to work, it was much more because someone cared than because you were punished.

You will also find that you do not always believe that punishment is either the only solution or the best solution to the problems that arise when a rule is broken. Let me give an example of someone who breaks a rule but whom you would not punish. Suppose you're a strict, "enforce-the-rules" schoolteacher and you get a call from a department store that your seventy-two-year-old mother has been picked up for shoplifting. They don't want to call the police, but they are holding her until you come. You go and tell them that you will take care of the situation and they let you take her home. She tearfully admits to the shoplifting but says that her life has been boring and the shoplifting gives her some excitement. She has been (and still is) a healthy, competent woman, but she is retired from her long career as a head bookkeeper. Her husband of forty-five years has been dead for three years, her children are busy and not as attentive as she would like, and her life is not satisfying. In terms of the basic needs, she has a lot of freedom but not enough love, power, or fun. She shows you a closet full of things, some quite valuable, that she has stolen over the past several years. While she is tearful, you have the impression that she is somewhat proud of her late-blooming crime career and has less determination to stop than you would like.

Are her reasons for doing what she did much different from the reasons students skip school or class? She found it too hard to satisfy her needs by doing lawful things like joining a volunteer group or learning to play cards. She was bored and she did not think her family cared that much about her anymore. Remember, it is not that you did not care, it is that she does not perceive your caring. In fact, you are showing more caring and concern right now than you have in quite a while.

But the pressing question that you have to answer is, "What are you going to do?" Should what you do be any different from what you would do if a student in your senior English class had an unexcused absence today for the thirteenth time—one over the limit of the twelve allowed for passing? The work itself is satisfactory, but you decide to fail him even though you know that by enforcing this rule he will not be able to graduate with his class.

It is doubtful that in your mother's case you would fault the law against shoplifting, even though she may continue to shoplift and the next time get arrested. You talk to a lawyer and she tells you that the only defense if she is arrested would be to hire a psychiatrist to say that she is mentally ill and that because of this illness the law should not apply to her. You, she, the lawyer, and the psychiatrist all know that she is no more mentally ill than the boy who cut thirteen classes, even though he did tell you he was upset because his girlfriend rejected him and he skipped those classes to be with her while he was trying to persuade her to change her mind.

While you might not argue for changing the rule against shoplifting even to help your nominally good-citizen mother, suppose it were your son who was being denied graduation, and the school offered to waive the rule and let him graduate on the teacher's recommendation because he was a good student. What would you tell them to do? My guess is that you would accept the school's offer and take a chance on his not "learning his lesson."

To go back to your mother, however, suppose she tells you that she will not shoplift any more and asks for both forgiveness and forbearance. Should you just drop the whole issue, or should you do something more? If you drop it, she will still not do much about her unsatisfactory life. Without the excitement of shoplifting, she will be more bored and more lonely than ever. If you think carefully about this, you will do something to persuade her to get more involved in satisfying activities, and you will also make more of an effort to spend "quality" time with her on a regular basis. If you do not do something like this, it is likely that the next time you hear from a store it will be to tell you that they have called the police.

But you have another choice. You can punish her as you are

punishing the boy who cut thirteen of your classes. You can make her take all the things in the closet back to the stores she took them from, and if the stores decide to prosecute, you can let her face the consequences and go with a public defender. This is pretty rough, but it would be consistent with your boss-manager approach to education.

Isn't it also pretty rough to deny a passing student the right to graduate because of attendance problems? Your student's crime, unlike your mother's, hurt no one seriously but himself. He did do enough to pass the course, so if you passed him you would not be turning an illiterate with a diploma loose on an unsuspecting public. You also find out that he has good attendance on his twenty-hour-a-week job, so you can't argue that flunking him will teach him the lesson he needs to know to hold a job.

Still, in the real world that you are very much a part of, the student is much more likely to be punished than is the seventy-two-year-old shoplifter. Students who hurt few people except themselves are much less likely to be offered mercy than adults who hurt others but have a record of previous good citizenship.

I am not advocating less mercy for adults; I am advocating more mercy for students. In a Quality School we do not like the idea of vengeance—not allowing a capable student to graduate is vengeance—and we do not complain if we are not "backed up" by administrative punishment. We recognize that students who do poorly in school hurt themselves far more than they hurt anyone else and that they need our help to do better. What we try to do from the start in kindergarten and to the end at graduation is run a nonpunitive, warm, and friendly school where there is no reason for the staff and the students ever to become adversaries. We are much more concerned with establishing a loving, flexible atmosphere than a rigid, threatening one. We keep rules to a minimum. We only need rules to protect others. We do not need rules to protect people from themselves. This means that we do not even need rules as basic as: "Do not run in the halls." This does not mean that we do not tell children who are running to slow down, but rather when we do, we tell them why we want them to walk. When we ask them to slow down they listen because in the atmosphere we have created almost all the students have placed us into their quality world. We never threaten or punish. We let children know from the start that we want to help them to get along, to like school and to gain the satisfaction that is inherent in doing quality work. If students do not do what any teacher thinks they should do, we look at this as a problem that not only can be solved but also will be solved in a way that is satisfactory to all concerned.

Since a Quality School staff practices democracy, they do not waste time preaching it. When a student has a problem of any sort (even with a teacher), she or he is not immediately thought to be wrong, as is mostly the case in boss-managed schools. Instead, the student is listened to with respect and given a chance to work out the problem just the same as if she/he were a staffperson. In a Quality School, people are more important than rules.

For example, a student disrupts a class in a Quality School and is sent to the office. Since we have few specific rules, he/she will have broken only the general rule of courtesy—the most important rule of any quality workplace. In the office, the student knows that there will be no punishment or threats; there never are. He/she also knows that no one is going to spend time looking for whose fault it was. The only thing that will be looked for is how the problem can be solved so that it does not happen again. The student is also encouraged to work on the problem, because he/she knows that there are no general solutions like "twelve absences and you fail." All problems are considered individually on their own merit and all solutions are based on what is best for both the student and the school in this specific situation.

In a Quality School, it is likely that the counselor or administrator will start by asking the student if he/she was unhappy in class when he/she disrupted it. Because there is no threat or punishment, the student will say yes. The counselor will then say, "What can we work out so that you will be happier in that class? If we can work out a way for you to be happier, I think we can solve the problem." If the student continues to disrupt and refuses to work on the problem, the time-out room will be invoked as described in Chapter Ten. But from our experience at the Apollo School, there is no need for a time-out room once we stop using coercion and move, as above, to problem-solving with students who are not our adversaries. The few discipline problems we have at Apollo we solve in this way. There will never be many problems because they cannot flourish in a noncoercive environment where the only important rule is courtesy.

The hardest part will be to make the commitment to begin the move to noncoercive lead-management. Until a staff begins to experience the benefit of this approach to quality work, they cannot appreciate its usefulness. All I can do is what I have attempted here: present a logical argument for making this move. Then it is up to the principal to demonstrate what he/she means by dealing with all students without coercion and by leading, not bossing, the staff. It will take a few years to get rid of coercion, but we are not short of time. Schools have been the way they are for hundreds of years. The four to five years it takes to move to a Quality School is nothing compared to where we have been for so long and where we will continue to be, as long as we practice coercion.

CHAPTER SEVENTEEN

Additional Thoughts on Self-Evaluation
BULLETIN #19, 4-20-92

A Quality School is based on three concepts: 1) focus on quality, 2) eliminate coercion, and 3) persuade students to evaluate their own work. Experience so far has shown that self-evaluation is the most difficult for teachers to put into practice. Recently, while interviewing six very thoughtful junior and senior high school students about improving the quality of their schoolwork, I brought this subject up. This bulletin is the result of that informative discussion.

The students immediately saw the value of evaluating their work but they were unsure as to what they should actually do and kept asking me to tell them. As I tried to answer this reasonable request, I became slowly aware that I had not thought enough about this whole process. I began by saying what I have said before in this situation, "Do anything that makes sense to you. If you want, just put a grade like A, B, C on your work." As soon as I said this, I could see that they became uneasy and I realized that self-evaluation is a much more complicated process than I had previously realized.

They told me that if all they did was put a grade on their work it would have little value. Other students have told me the same thing, but somehow these students were able to make it clear that if all that was wanted was a grade, most students would take a quick look and then write down a good grade whether they deserved it or not. When I questioned whether or not this was honest, they told me that they didn't see it as a question of honesty. If what we were talking about was quality work, grades, which meant much more to parents and teachers than to them, had little to do with achieving it. If quality was what was wanted, that kind of an evaluation would be a waste of time, and wasted time is neither honest or dishonest. Since many other students had told me the same thing, there is no doubt in my mind that this is correct.

To try to learn more, I asked them what they thought they should do. Initially, they got off the subject of self-evaluation and onto evaluation itself, saying that the only evaluation that has any real value is a detailed explanation of what the teacher thinks they did. A written evaluation should point out both strengths and weaknesses and do it so that they could understand why one part was strong and another weak.

If, however, the teacher takes the time to explain personally what she meant when she wrote what she did on their papers, this teaches them the most. Compared to doing this, a written grade or a brief comment means very little. By doing this, the teacher also convinces them that she really looked over what they did and is willing to tell them in detail what she thinks. This sends the message that she cares, a message that group after group of students tells me that they do not hear enough. And the reason they don't hear it enough is obvious: There are not enough teachers.

As I began to catch on to how to solve this problem, they began to catch on with me. First one and then almost all of them said that what they wanted from their teachers is what they should do more of themselves. But they need a teacher to get them started, to teach them what they need to learn to do this. What they were saying is that they can't evaluate themselves accurately and in depth until they are taught how to do it. Right now they get a grade or a few written comments but often have no accurate idea of where the grade came from or what the comments mean. Even if their grades were good, most students concentrate much more on getting through than on learning what was covered. They go from assignment to assignment with little improvement and not much conviction that they have learned anything worthwhile.

To support the point of this bulletin, I admit that I have conducted many similar discussions, but this is the first time I have evaluated in depth what it is I am actually asking students to do when I suggest that it is important that they evaluate their own work. It is now apparent to me that if the goal is quality, it can only be achieved through a detailed and accurate self-evaluation of the subject in question, an evaluation as important as the work itself. There should be no time limit, no pushing ahead until the evaluation of what has been covered is complete. Contrary to conventional wisdom, how much we cover is not important, all that is important is what students learn. And without detailed self-evaluation followed by more learning based on that evaluation, little of permanent value will be learned and the purpose of education—to improve the quality of our lives—will be defeated.

What this makes clear is that in our present schools we teach too much too fast. One test or paper that has been thoroughly evaluated by the student with the help of the teacher and then improved is worth more than twenty tests or papers that have been graded and/or evaluated briefly and then, as they mostly do now, put aside. Please introspect into your own life and you will see that whenever you did something of quality, you spent a great deal of time evaluating the whole process. Based on this evaluation, you slowly but significantly improved what you did. Your students need to be taught that process and encouraged by you to use it.

I would be very interested in having teachers who are willing to try what is suggested here send me some samples of the work that has resulted from this process. I don't think there is another way to achieve quality in school, or anywhere else, and I believe we have not begun to scratch the surface of what we could accomplish if we made a serious effort to move in this direction.

CHAPTER EIGHTEEN

How to Introduce Students to Quality
BULLETIN #2, 4-15-90

From the feedback I am getting, teachers (especially at the secondary level) are finding it difficult to get students interested in talking about quality in their academic classes; and if they persist, the students grow quickly bored. A major source of this difficulty may be that most students have never done quality classwork and find it difficult to relate to the concept of quality in a classroom setting.

I think that when you begin to discuss quality it would be better not to attempt to talk about it directly or to try to go deeply into the concept in the first few discussions. Quality schoolwork is a new idea for most students, and their first instinct will be to resist what they fear may be another way to coerce them into working harder. I also would not bring up this idea until you have established a comfortable way to talk with your students by spending a few minutes each day in some sort of casual discussion about anything that you know would interest them. No matter what you teach, bring up a current event, movie, TV program, or ask them what they have done lately that is interesting and talk about it for a few minutes. Let the nontalkers know that you are interested in what they have to say, but don't push them too hard. An example of what might interest students here in California could be the massive antismoking campaign that the state has just started. Teachers would be wise to dialogue with their students about the effectiveness of the advertisements and ask for their suggestions.

If you have established a dialogue with your class on a variety of subjects, then when you begin the important discussion of quality, they will not think it is anything special that they have to be wary of, and it is unlikely that they will find it boring. Still, when you begin, it is a good idea to use the synonyms for quality rather than the word itself. Ask them what in their lives right now is good, valuable, or enjoyable. Or ask, "What is good for you?" or "What do you like to do?" or "What do you usually work hard at doing and do well?" All of these terms or concepts are understandable to students of all ages, and if you do this over a number of days and do not persist too long on any one day, you may be able to pique their interest. If they ask you what you are driving at with your questions, tell them that you are very interested in their opinion of what adds quality to their lives. This way, you introduce the word but you do not emphasize it because, by itself, it is a new concept that students have to get used to thinking about.

To go beyond discussion, you might do a quality assignment in any class using advertising material like the ads in catalogues or slick magazines. For example, as a classroom assignment, group the students into pairs or threesomes and give each group a slick magazine or a catalogue. Ask parents to send this material to school; ask other teachers to save them for you. Save the catalogues that seem to come in the mail all the time or get a hold of some old Sears catalogues. Then ask the groups to go through the magazine for ten minutes and pick out something that they agree is very good and that they would like to have. Then ask each group to show the class what they picked out and tell the class why they selected that item. As they talk, write down some of the words they use, even slang words like "boss" or "rad." Don't take too long to do this assignment, and when you are finished, leave the words on the board.

Then as various ideas or subjects come up in your regular classroom teaching, ask the class if these ideas are appropriate to one or more of the quality words listed on the board. When they agree that something is, write it on the board and keep it on a separate list of specific classroom occurrences that are related to the quality words. Try to hold an occasional discussion about why these classroom happenings are better than others; for example, why one story in English was better then other stories, why one set of math problems was better than most math problems, or why one science idea seemed so much more interesting than other science ideas.

Take your time. There is no need to hurry. In a Quality School, the idea of quality will slowly become part of the school as students start to think about quality and then begin to evaluate their work for quality. As they improve, and also as they begin to appreciate that they can improve, they will begin to experience a degree of control over what they do in school that most of them have never had before. In a traditional school, even the good students do not have a strong sense of control over what happens in school. In a Quality School, this sense of control—the idea, "I can do quality work and I enjoy doing it"—is a vital component of the process. This is a process that has to start with an appreciation of quality followed by the new idea that quality can become a part of what they do in the classroom.

CHAPTER NINETEEN

Making the Connection
BULLETIN #3, 4-15-90

Recently, in a psychology class that I was visiting at the Apollo School, someone asked a class member if she had passed the GED test she had just taken. She said, "Gee, today's the day they said they would have the results in the office," and ran to find out what had happened. When she came back, she was elated because she had passed. She had no interest in whether she had done well or barely passed and it was also apparent that, in her mind, there was no connection between the schoolwork that she had done to pass and anything she had learned that was useful in her life. All that was important to her was that, by passing, she had jumped a required hurdle; the hurdle itself was unimportant.

This incident is a graphic example of the major flaw in our schools, a flaw that I believe can only be corrected by making quality a part of every student's education. Unless we can convince students that what we ask them to do in school has quality or is "useful" to them, they fail to make the connection between what they do and its value to them. Most students and many workers do not make this vital connection and put forth just enough effort to avoid punishment or job loss. If we do not address this and teach them in a way so that they can easily make this connection, we will have neither quality schools nor a quality society.

As I move from class to class, I frequently ask students to

tell me why they are doing what they are doing. Mostly they shrug their shoulders and say, "to get credit" or "for the teacher." Frequently they say, "I don't know." I can hardly remember a student volunteering that he/she expected to learn something useful from what he or she was doing. As long as we persist in the boss-management approach to teaching—"learn it because we tell you to"—this present "fact of life" will not change.

While this topic is covered in detail in Chapters Five and Seven, I did not use the "connection" idea to explain it as I am trying to do here. I think this idea clarifies the problem, so I thought I would use this bulletin to bring this concept to your attention. Whenever a lead-manager asks anyone to do anything, she/he tries hard to explain how what is being asked can benefit the person or people asked to do it. Lead-managers should do this before the work starts and continue to point this out as the work progresses. After the work is finished, the lead-manager should talk to the students to find out if they have made the connection between what they have done and its benefit to them.

If we are to get more students interested enough to begin to do quality work—especially in math and science—we also must realize that no matter how much we explain that the work is beneficial, if we ask students to regurgitate memorized facts, give us right answers without indicating how they arrived at them, make correct choices on multiple-choice questions, or distinguish true from false, they will never make this connection strongly enough so that they will see the value of working hard. For students, these standard methods of evaluation become extraneous hurdles to jump. They never connect students to what they think has quality for them. It may be helpful to try to measure what they have learned, but we have to be careful that the measurement itself does not block our attempt to persuade them that there is a connection between what we are asking them to learn and its value to them.

What we need is to develop methods of evaluation that actually increase the connection. For example, it is not enough to tell students that writing a good letter is important. It is also not enough that they write a good letter for their teacher. We must teach them that the better the letter they write, the more likely it is that they will get a satisfying answer or result. It is getting a good answer or a good result that is the real evaluation. All other evaluations are more make-believe than real. And it is this real evaluation that makes the connection between doing the work to write a thoughtful letter and bene- fiting from that work. One letter published in a newspaper, one nonform answer from a politician or from an inquiry to a store or business, will make this connection more solidly than ten good grades from a teacher on an unsent letter. Even a thoughtful answer from a relative or friend with whom they have not had recent contact will go a long way toward making this necessary connection.

In a Quality School, all teachers make a constant effort to teach so that what students are asked to do is connected to the real world in a way that has value to them. If students do a good job on an oral or written test, the teacher asks them to take the test home and show their parents what they did and tell them why what they did had value to them. It is when they show and tell what they did to someone they respect and who cares for them that they make the connection. If they do not have someone at home, the school should provide a group of volunteers who will listen to them explain that what they did was good. Most students have a parent who would be inter- ested and supportive of their child's good work. Many parents, however, do not support the school because the only time they hear from the school is when their child is doing badly.

This is also why cooperative learning is so valuable. Work- ing together is one of the easiest and most satisfying ways to make this necessary connection. It is hard to make it by one-self, and most students work by themselves in school. I am not so naïve as to believe that this connection can be made on all work all the time. But I think it has to be made much more than it is now. If it is made once a week in each academic subject, there will be an almost infinite increase over how many times it is being made now in most schools.

CHAPTER TWENTY

Some Further Thoughts on Self-Evaluation
BULLETIN #7, 8-15-90

Of the three cornerstones of a Quality School—1) focusing on and supporting quality, 2) eliminating coercion, and 3) moving from total teacher evaluation to the acceptance of student self-evaluation—student self-evaluation will be the hardest for teachers to implement. Coercion will be hard to get rid of, but since we understand it, at least we know what it is that we have to eliminate. While it will be difficult to achieve quality, we also have a good idea of what it is, so we are on familiar ground. But when it comes to accepting student self-evaluation as being just as important as teacher evaluation, we are on unfamiliar ground. Since the evaluation of students has always been done exclusively by the teacher, it is really a new idea.

In almost all schools, it is taken for granted that teachers' evaluations are important to students and that poor evaluations will "stimulate" students into working harder to get better evaluations. It is also assumed that students are not capable of evaluating themselves accurately; only teachers possess this expertise. In practice, however, the students who get good evaluations and who care about what the teacher thinks of their work tend to work hard for a good evaluation. Students who get poor evaluations (and in most schools this is a majority of all students) usually don't care enough about what teachers think of their work to try to improve it. When they are given low grades, they blame teachers and hate schoolwork. As long as we persist in teaching this way, schools will not improve.

W. Edwards Deming states that of all the things we do that are destructive to quality work as we attempt to manage workers, evaluating them is the most destructive of all. This is because it is almost impossible consistently to evaluate a worker (or a student) in a way that he or she thinks is fair. Because of this, the evaluation is often seen by the worker as criticism. Control theory points out that criticism is always destructive to the criticized person. There is no such thing as constructive criticism. Deming suggests strongly that we stop evaluating workers and instead ask them to evaluate their own work. If after this self-evaluation they want to improve, a lead-manager asks how he or she can help.

Control theory explains that it is impossible to evaluate anything that you value without trying to improve it. So if we assign quality work and persuade workers (and students) to evaluate it, they will try to improve and be anxious for any help we can give them.

In the workplace, self-evaluation is much easier to implement than in school. Unlike students who are continually learning new skills or new knowledge, most workers know a lot about what they are asked to do even before they do it. Even when the work itself is complicated and difficult to learn, the worker usually has a basic understanding of what he or she is asked to do. For example, a cabinetmaker may begin by just learning how to glue, but has some idea of what a finished piece of furniture should look like. Workers also tend to work in a finite area; cabinet makers don't work with metal or plastic and they perform many of the same procedures over and over so that they can't help knowing a lot about what they are doing. Because of all they know about what they are doing, it is almost impossible for workers to be unable to make an accurate evaluation of the quality of their work.

In school, and especially in academic subjects, students are continually moving to new areas where they may know little or nothing about what they are asked to do. Unlike industrial workers, I doubt if one percent of the math students in the whole country have any understanding of the math they are going to study on the day they start the subject. Then as they take the course, the teacher tells them to move on to a new area before many of them are competent in what they are presently doing. Ready to move or not, few students will question the teacher's judgment, and the ones who are not competent pay little or no attention to the fact that they do not know what they are doing. When we talk about self-evaluation in school, we are talking about something that must be taught; in the way we teach now, it does not happen.

If what we want is quality schoolwork, we will have to do two things that we are not doing now: 1) We have to assign schoolwork that the students accept as quality, and 2) we have to teach them to evaluate their own progress. In fact, the only way to achieve quality in anything we do is to evaluate our progress as we do it. This is because inherent to the process of self-evaluation is getting deeply involved in what you are evaluating. Without this involvement there is no quality.

Suppose, for example, that you were given the task of evaluating a teacher whom you knew nothing about. By the time you finished, you would know a lot about both that teacher and the subject she teaches because without that knowledge you would say, "I can't evaluate her; I don't know anything about her or what she does."

What we ourselves do is usually more important than anything else in our lives. When we evaluate ourselves and our own progress, we learn much more than if we evaluate someone else or try to find out what someone else thinks of us. For example, suppose you decided to evaluate your ability to swim. You could not do this without getting into the water and learning a lot about swimming. Unless you knew something about your actual progress in the water, you could not come close to rating yourself with any accuracy. Contrast this with asking someone else to watch you swim and evaluating this same ability. Suppose the person told you that you were a good swimmer. How much would you actually know about your true ability? The truth is that you might know very little and, if you had to swim for any distance, you might drown. And as you were drowning, you might say to yourself, "I should have found out for myself. I was foolish to listen to her."

In a Quality School, starting in kindergarten and continuing to graduation, students would be taught not only how to evaluate their own work, but also that evaluating it accurately is the most important part of their education. The lead-teachers in Quality Schools would take the time to teach students how to evaluate the quality of their work on both assignments and tests. As they learned to do this and then did it consistently, the need for many formal tests would begin to disappear. Everything they did in a Quality School would become a test of their ability, and if they wanted to improve, as most would, the lead-teacher would be on hand to help.

Suppose you were teaching long division. In a regular school you would teach and test. There would be no attempt to get any students involved in self-evaluation of their progress. Even though most would have learned how to add, subtract, and multiply (all easier math processes than long division), many less would learn long division. But in a regular school, if the ability to do long division were all that were lacking, all the students would move on and many would graduate not knowing long division. None of these students would put math into their quality world; their interest in math would end with this failure to master long division.

Students learning long division would have already learned how to evaluate their work and would be used to using this knowledge to evaluate the math being taught. As in all schoolwork, they would evaluate for neatness and legibility, but in math they would evaluate the process itself by learning to ask themselves as they worked on problems, "Do I know what I am doing to get the answer?" and specifically, "Do I know when and where I would use long division?" Students who could not answer these key self-evaluation questions with a "yes" would be asked to keep working until they could. Here would be a natural place for cooperative learning with students in small groups asking and answering these questions of each other. Answering these questions affirmatively would also be the goal of the one-on-one tutoring that would be integral to a Quality School.

Students would not be told when to move to a new area of study but would be asked, from their own evaluation of their progress, when they were ready. When they said they were ready, they would take the test or tests that tells both them and their teacher that they have mastered the material. Students might move much slower than now, but they would have confidence in what they are doing. They move along briskly in our existing schools but too few know what they are doing when they move. What is most important is that once students learn something well, no matter what it is, they tend to put that knowledge into their quality world. Persuading students to put schoolwork into their quality world is the ultimate goal of a Quality School.

Therefore, teaching in a Quality School would be far different from the standard approach in which the teacher decides when to test and what grade to give the student. In a Quality School as in a regular school, the teacher would teach the subject but, in addition, the emphasis would be as much or more on:

1. Teaching students how to evaluate what they are learning.
2. Asking students to use the ability to evaluate their own work.
3. Testing only when the students, based on their self-evaluation, are ready for the test.
4. Awarding the student at least a B and perhaps an A or A+, depending on both the student's and teacher's evaluation of the work done.

I am sure that students will be taught many different ways to evaluate their schoolwork. English, for example, might be evaluated differently from math, history, or science. What would help would be more educational research on how to teach students to evaluate the wide variety of work they are asked to learn in school. Until this research is available, however, the Quality Schools will have to do this for themselves. As we get together in our consortium meetings, sharing this new knowledge will be an integral part of each meeting. Eventually university researchers will contribute, but in the beginning this will be another problem for the consortium and its individual schools to tackle.

CHAPTER TWENTY-ONE

Avoiding Nonsense in a Quality School
BULLETIN #5, 6-10-90

In the May 27, 1990, issue of the *Los Angeles Times* (page E14), there was a wire service article by Mary Corey, a writer for the *Baltimore Sun,* entitled "An Epidemic of College Cheating." She describes how an estimated 40 percent of all college students cheat on exams. She is trying to make an issue out of the fact that so many college students cheat, but to me, the issue is not that they cheat, but why they cheat. What needs to be examined is the tests: Specifically, what is being tested that makes cheating not only possible but, for many students, even desirable?

The students she talked with did not feel guilty, which leads me to conclude that they view cheating on tests about the same as they view watching a hamburger commercial on television. We don't expect the hamburgers in the commercials to look like the ones they serve in restaurants, but no one calls the commercials "cheating." It is the same with many tests. Just as the commercials are natural to advertising, the tests are natural to college: No one believes that either has anything to do with what is important in the real world.

What this cheating should be telling us is not that students are living in an ethical vacuum, but that much of what is tested for in college is evaluated by the students and considered nonsense. Since there is no virtue in learning nonsense, there is no sin in cheating: It is just a way to avoid useless work.

While Corey's report confines itself to college, we all know that the problem of testing "nonsense" starts long before college. Any test that can be scored by a machine, or depends on memorizing something that is only useful in schools, is likely to measure nonsense.

Before going further, let me use control theory to explain how education has gotten so involved with nonsense. As explained in Chapter Five of this book, and in more detail in Chapter Three of my 1984 book *Control Theory* (where I used the term "the pictures in our heads" rather than "quality world"), the most important part of our lives is the extremely need-fulfilling information that we decide to put into our quality worlds. More than anything else we have learned, it is this information we call *sensible* and will be motivated to work very hard to acquire—whatever it is. For example, most children will put both the skills of reading and a warm and caring reading teacher into their quality worlds. Given these sensible motivations, they will make a strong effort to learn to read, and most will succeed.

However, even if we do not believe that what we are told to learn, and the person who tells us to learn, is need-satisfying enough to put into our quality worlds, we do not immediately label it nonsense. It may not be essential right now, but we keep an open mind as to its ultimate value to us. If we are able to remember it, fine; if we can't and later find that we need it, we know we can easily look it up. But when a teacher, especially a teacher whom students do not regard as a need-satisfying person, attempts to coerce them into working hard to retain something that they do not believe is essential, the nonessential becomes nonsense.

For example, when my oldest son was in the eleventh grade, he was told by his history teacher that an important question on the final exam would be to write down all the presidents in the order that they were elected. "Fail this," she told the class, "and you risk failing the final." Knowing the presidents in or out of the order they were elected is nonessential until you are threatened with failure for not knowing them; then the nonessential becomes nonsense. There is not a student in the country who would store information like this in his or her quality world, yet education is filled with teachers who try to coerce students into memorizing it.

When my son asked me what he should do, I was of little help; I just laughed and told him I was trying to forget some of the presidents and wished him luck. It is, however, exactly this kind of nonsense testing that leads to cheating. I don't know if he cheated, but if he did and got away with it, as Mary Corey says many students do, he saved himself a lot of work. I was not afraid that he would learn that crime pays, because he, like most students and many teachers, would not consider what he did criminal behavior. But if he were caught and severely punished, he might take history out of his quality world, hardly the goal of those who put history into the curriculum.

In a noncoercive Quality School, there would be little chance that students would convert the nonessential into nonsense, because there would be no coercion to learn the nonessential. A teacher who was interested in teaching "sensibly" about the presidents would discuss with the class the contribution that many of the presidents made to the welfare of the country. She might tell the students that their final test would be to select one president whom they thought had made a significant contribution and describe what he did. If the students wanted to take notes at home and bring them to class to help them write the answer, this would not only be allowed, it would be encouraged. The purpose of a history test in a Quality School would not be the parroting of briefly remembered nonessential knowledge; it would be to think "sensibly" about the past and put some of this sense down on paper.

I can see teachers reading this suggestion and saying that students would get help from their parents or would go to the library and look up what others said about what this or that president had done and then copy these notes on the test. It is not that doing all that work to learn something sensible about a president and then copying it on a test would be bad educationally. It would, in fact, be good; infinitely better than writing down all their names and the dates of their election. The students who were willing to do it would learn a great deal, especially as they summarized the information for the test.

But a thoughtful teacher could flesh out the basic question to check whether or not the students had a working knowledge of what they wrote or were just copying something thought out by someone else. One way to do this would be to ask the students a few more questions like:

1. What was so significant about this president that you chose him?
2. Where did you get the information that led you to select him?
3. Who did you talk this answer over with as you prepared for the test? Why did you talk to these people?
4. Do you think that you will use this information in your life as you get old enough to vote? Give some reasons for your answers.
5. For what purpose other than voting for president might you use this information?

Any high school student who could give a good answer to these questions in addition to a good answer to the basic question would learn a lot of history. It is also obvious that there would be no easy way to cheat. There is too much information and too many personal opinions called for to make copying the easy way out. And if they went to the library and came well-prepared, they would not want to copy from someone else. Once students find out that sensible questions like these are going to be asked, almost all the incentives to cheat, as well as the opportunities, would disappear.

I can also hear teachers saying, "This is too hard for high school students." It would be if this were done every week; but if this were all that was asked on a unit test, it would not be. It is aimed at being sensible enough so that students would put it into their quality worlds. The only purpose of the education offered in a Quality School would be to increase the amount of knowledge that students thought sensible enough to put into their quality worlds. Test questions like this would be an important step in this direction.

But teachers who are used to covering a lot of factual material might complain that it did not cover enough ground. My answer to this is that I believe that every student who took this test would come away with some sense of history. When we try to coerce them into parroting facts, they come away with less than they started with. From having either a good opinion or no opinion of history, they learn to hate it. When we test nonsense, the students don't break even educationally . . . they lose.

Therefore, the "Is it nonsense?" test of all that is taught in a Quality School is, "Will the students choose to put it into their quality worlds?" If they won't, and we attempt to coerce them into doing it, then what we ask becomes nonsense and we should not have asked it in the first place. But how is a teacher to know what students are willing to put into their quality worlds? To answer this question, a teacher must ask him/herself whether or not what he or she is teaching and testing for is in his or her quality world. If it is, then there is a good chance the students will accept it into theirs.

However, if the teacher is asked to teach material that is not in her quality world, then she is being forced to teach nonsense. This is so hard to hide that most students immediately become aware of it. In a Quality School, no teacher would be asked to teach nonsense. Teachers would be treated as professionals and given the option to test sensibly. Except for the state-mandated achievement tests, no teacher would be coerced into teaching nonsense. Teachers would encourage their students to do their best on the state tests, but they would also be allowed to tell students, "What counts is what I teach, not what the state is trying to assess."

If teachers teach in a need-satisfying, noncoercive way, as lead-teachers would do in a Quality School, then most of their students will put both the teachers and what they teach into their quality worlds. It is not that any of our present curriculum is nonsense; it is that we make it into nonsense by how we teach and test. This would not happen in a Quality School.

CHAPTER TWENTY-TWO

The Quality School Curriculum
BULLETIN #8, 11-25-90

Recently I had a chance to talk to a high school staff that has been working hard for the last six months to change its school into a Quality School. They believed they were much less coercive than in the past, but complained that many of their students were still not working hard and that a few continued to be disruptive. They admitted that things were better but asked me if maybe they should inject a little coercion back into their managing to "stimulate" the students to work harder. I assured them that the answer to their complaints was not to use more but even less coercion; but, at the same time, I realized that in their teaching they had not yet addressed a vital component of a Quality School . . . the curriculum. To complete the move from coercive boss-managing to noncoercive lead-managing, they have to change the curriculum they teach.

This was made even clearer to me during the break, when I talked to a few teachers individually. They said that they had already made many of the changes suggested in this bulletin and were not having the problems with students that most of the staff was. I strongly believe that until almost all the teachers do change their curriculum, they will be unable to get rid of the coercion that is causing too many of their students to continue to be their adversaries.

In Chapter One, I briefly cite the research of Professor

Linda McNeil of Rice University to support my claim that boss-management is destructive to the quality of the curriculum. From feedback I am getting, it seems that the schools which are trying to become Quality Schools have not paid enough attention to this important point. This is partly my fault. When I wrote *The Quality School,* I did not realize how vital it is for teachers to make sure that they teach quality, and I did not sufficiently explain what this is. To correct this shortcoming, I will expand on what I wrote earlier, and I strongly encourage the staffs of all the schools who want to move to quality to spend a great deal of time discussing this bulletin.

It is necessary to face the fact that a majority of students, even good ones, believe that much of the present academic curriculum is not worth the effort it takes to learn it. No matter how well the teachers manage them, if students will not put what they are asked to do in their classes into their quality worlds, they will not work hard enough to learn it. The answer is not to try to make them work harder, it is to increase the quality of what we ask them to learn.

Faced with students who refuse to make much effort, even teachers who are trying to become lead-managers give a lot of low grades, a practice so traditional that they fail to perceive it as coercive. Students then deal with their low grades by rebelling and working less. The teachers, in turn, resent this attitude. They believe that because they are making the effort to be less coercive, the students should be appreciative and work harder. The teachers fail to see that what the students are rebelling against is not them and their efforts to become lead-managers but a curriculum that lacks quality. Therefore, if we want to create Quality Schools, we must stop all coercion, not just some, and a way to do this is to create a quality curriculum.

Before I describe a quality curriculum, let me use a simple

nonschool example to try to explain what is nonquality about the curriculum we have now. Suppose you got a job in a factory making both black and brown shoes. You were well-managed and did quality work. But soon you became aware that all the brown shoes you made were sold for scrap; only the black shoes went into retail stores. How long would you continue to work hard on the brown shoes? As you slacked off, however, you were told that this was not acceptable and you would lose pay or be fired if you did not buckle down and do just as good a job on the brown as on the black. You were told that what happened to the brown shoes was none of your business; you were just to work hard. Wouldn't it be almost impossible to do as you were told?

As silly as this example may seem, students in schools (and even in colleges and graduate schools) are asked to learn innumerable facts that both they and their teachers know are of no use to anyone except to pass tests. I call this throwaway information, because, after they do the work to learn it, that is just what the students will do. Dates and places in history, parts of organisms and organs in biology, and formulas in mathematics, chemistry, and physics are all examples of what I mean.

When the newspapers publish the periodic studies of widespread cheating in schools and call it a symptom of our moral disintegration, what they call "cheating" is mostly the ways students have devised to avoid the work of memorizing throwaway knowledge. And although students, faculty, and most of the informed public are all aware that there is no value to much of what students are asked to remember, no one seems upset about it—except the honest students who are penalized, of course. I am not condoning cheating. What I am saying is that as long as we have a curriculum that holds students responsible for throwaway information, there will be cheating and few will care.

As I describe in Chapter Twenty-One this throwaway knowledge could also be called "nonsense." While it is not nonsense to ask students to be aware of formulas, dates, and places and to know where to find them if they need them, it becomes nonsense when we ask students to memorize this information and to lower their grades if they fail to do this precisely. Whether it is called throwaway knowledge or nonsense, this kind of memorized information would never be a part of the curriculum of a Quality School.

This means that there would never be test questions that called for bare facts such as those written in a book or stored in the memory of a computer in a Quality School. Students would never be asked to commit this portion of the curriculum to memory. All available information on what is being studied could always be on hand, not only during class but during all tests. No student would ever suffer academically because he or she forgot some fact or formula. Where facts, formulas, and other information is concerned, the only way that this kind of information would be tested for would be to ask, not what, but where, why, when, and how this information is of use in the real world.

While a complete definition of quality is elusive, it certainly would include "useful in the real world." "Useful" does not have to mean practical or utilitarian; it can be aesthetic, spiritual, or whatever is meaningful to the user, but it is never nonsense.

When the questions where, why, when, and how are asked on a test in a Quality School, the answers to them would never be as restrictive as they are now in what are called "objective" tests requiring multiple-choice, true/false, or short factual answers. If, for example, a multiple-choice test were used to ask where, why, when, and how, the student would not be restricted to those choices. There would always be a place for a student to write out a better answer if he/she believed that the restriction of the available choices made the answer less accurate than what he/she believed.

For example, a multiple-choice test question in history might be the following: George Washington is called "the father of his country" for the following reasons: (and four reasons would be listed). Which do you think is the best reason? The student could answer as he/she thought best or could write in another reason and explain why it is better than the listed choices.

SKILLS, NOT FACTS OR INFORMATION, WOULD BE EMPHASIZED

In a Quality School there would rarely be a question as narrow as the example above. This is because there would be a constant attempt to relate all that is taught to the lives of the students. Therefore, if a "why, when, where, and how this information could be used" question were asked, the question would always be followed up with a further question, which would be, "How can you (or anyone else) use this information in your life now and/or in the future?" This query, however, would never come out of the clear blue sky. It would have been emphasized in lectures, in class discussions, through cooperative learning groups, and possibly in homework assignments in which students were asked to discuss with parents or other adults how this information might be useful in the real world.

The purpose of this necessary followup would be to point out strongly that in a Quality School the curriculum emphasizes skills, not facts or information that have no use in the lives of those who are taught them. I define a skill as the ability to use knowledge. If this were emphasized in every academic subject in the Quality School, there would be no rebellion. Students would get equal credit for explaining either why or why not what was taught was of use to them. This would encourage them to think, not to parrot the ideas of others.

To continue the George Washington example, a teacher in

a Quality School could ask a student who said that he/she thought that George Washington's refusal to be crowned king makes him a good candidate for father of this republic, "How could you use this information in your life now or later?" The student might say that he/she prefers to live in a republic; he/she would not like to live in a country where a king made all the laws. The student's answer could be more complicated than this brief example, but what the student would have thought over would be how this decision by George Washington affects his/her life today.

Without memorizing any facts, students taught this way would learn more history in a few weeks than they now learn in years. And more importantly, they would learn to like history. Too many students tell me that they hate history. That is an educational disaster. I hope that what they are really saying is that they hate the history curriculum, not history.

BEYOND HAVING SKILLS, STUDENTS WOULD ALSO BE ASKED TO DEMONSTRATE THAT THEY CAN USE WHAT THEY HAVE LEARNED

Another important element in the curriculum of a Quality School would be for the students to demonstrate how what they have learned can be used in their lives now and/or later. If they could do this, the teacher would know that the student has really learned something. Almost all students would have no difficulty accepting that reading, writing, and arithmetic are useful skills, but in a Quality School, they would be asked to demonstrate that they can use them. For example, students would not be asked to learn the multiplication tables as if this knowledge were separate from their being able to demonstrate that they know where, why, and when to use this skill in their lives.

To do this they would be given problems to solve and show how multiplication was used in the solution. The problems might use several different processes, such as addition and subtraction, and they could show where each was used. What they would learn is not only how to multiply but, much more important, when, where, and why they use multiplication in their lives. Once they know how to multiply, the actual mathematical process (the multiplication itself) could be done on a small calculator or by referral to tables.

In a Quality School, once the process itself is mastered, students would be encouraged to use a calculator. To do math processes involving large numbers over and over is boring and nonessential. Today, most students spend a lot of time memorizing times tables. They learn the how in great detail but fail to demonstrate the skill of when, where, and why to multiply. I will admit that tables and the calculators do not teach the how, but they are what people in the real world use to get answers, a fact finally recognized by the Educational Testing Service, which is going to allow the use of calculators on the Scholastic Achievement Test (SAT) from now on.

Teachers in a Quality School, however, would teach the how by asking students to demonstrate that they can do the calculations without a calculator. They would be told that as soon as they can demonstrate this ability by hand, they can use the calculator. For most students this would be more than enough incentive to learn how, knowing that they would not be stuck with working one long, boring problem after another.

In a Quality School, there would be a great deal of emphasis on the skill of writing and much less on the skill of reading. This is because anyone who can write well can read well, but many who can read well can hardly write. From the first grade, students would be asked to write: first words, then sentences, paragraphs, and finally articles, stories, and letters. An extremely good project is to have each middle school student write a book or keep a journal. Any student who did this would leave middle school with an education even if that were all she or he did.

To do this by hand would be onerous, but on a computer this same process is highly enjoyable. In a Quality School, all teachers would be encouraged to learn word-processing skills and teach them to their students. These skills could and should be used in all classes. Computers could be made more available in schools than they presently are. Funds can be easily raised to buy the few that would be needed. If students were encouraged to write, we would see fewer students diagnosed as having language learning disabilities.

At the Apollo High School where I consult, the seniors were asked if they would accept writing a good letter on a computer as a necessary requirement for graduation. They accepted it, and almost all of them learned how to do it. One way they demonstrated that their letter was good was to send it and get an answer. They were thrilled to receive the answer and we used this as a criterion for satisfying the requirement. This also shows that demonstrating the use of what is learned in a real-life situation is among the best ways to teach.

Testing in a Quality School

As much as demonstrating is the best way to show that something worthwhile has been learned, this is not always easy or even possible. There must be tests, but as already stated, the tests in a Quality School would always show the acquisition of skills, never the acquisition of facts or information alone.

Let me use a science example to explain what would be considered a good way to test in a Quality School. Science is mostly the discovery of why and how things work, but where and when they work is also important. Too much science is taught as what works, such as *these are the parts of a cell.*

Students all over America are busy memorizing the parts of a cell, usually by copying and labeling a cell drawn in a textbook. They are then tested to see if they can do this from memory—a wonderful example of throwaway information taught by coercion. Teaching and testing like this is worse than no science at all, because many students learn to hate science. Hating something as valuable as science is worse than just not knowing it.

In a Quality School, the students would be taught that all living organisms are made up of cells and some basics of how a cell works. To show them that this is useful knowledge, the teacher might introduce them to the subject of cancer to show them that, unlike a normal cell, a cancer cell fails to cooperate in the normal way and in so doing can kill the host in which it grows. All students know about cancer and all would consider this useful knowledge.

The test in a Quality School might be to describe the workings of a cell or some part of a cell with their book open and available. They would then also be asked how they could use this information in their lives now and/or later and, to do this, would be encouraged to describe the difference between a normal cell and a cancer cell. They would be taught that one way they could use this information might be to avoid too much sun, as excessive sunlight can turn a normal cell into a cancer cell. For most students this information would be of use, because all students have some fear of cancer.

I can sense some concern that what I suggest would not prepare students for tests like the SAT that mostly ask for throwaway information, like the parts of a cell. My answer to this concern is that with my system they would be better prepared because in the process of explaining how something works, a person is more likely to remember what it is than if he/she had just learned what it is. Even if less ground were covered, as would likely be the case when we move from facts to skills, a little covered well would still be better preparation than a lot covered poorly, even for nonsense tests.

HOW THE QUALITY SCHOOL RELATES TO OUTCOME-BASED EDUCATION (OBE)

We should never forget that people, not curriculum, are the desired outcome of both Outcome-Based Education and a Quality School. What we want are students who have the skills to become active contributors to their society, enthusiastic about what they have learned and aware of how learning can be of use to them in the future.

What is missing in many of the explanations of Outcome-Based Education is that the curriculum changes I suggest here will increase the number of students who fit the outcome we desire. If the outcomes are facts and information, then even if we can persuade most students to memorize them, we will not get the students we want. To be able to convince a factory worker to make quality brown shoes when he knows they will be thrown away is of no benefit either to the worker or to the society in which he lives.

Therefore, the practical question that must be used to test the effectiveness of OBE is: Will the students accept the outcomes that the teachers want? If we accept control theory, the answer is obvious. When the outcomes the teachers want are in the quality worlds of their students, they will accept them. In my experience, skills will be accepted as quality in almost all cases; facts and information will rarely be accepted.

Assuming that skills are taught following OBE, the teacher still has to explain clearly what she will ask on tests. Sample questions should be given to the students, and the use of all books, notes, and materials should be acceptable. Even if a student copies the workings of a cell from a book at the time of the test, the student will still have to answer the question of how this information can be used in his/her life and how he/she might demonstrate the use of this skill if given a chance to do so by the teacher. If a student can answer these questions, he/she will know the material whether or not it has been copied.

Tests, and especially optional retests for students who wanted to improve their grades, could be taken at home with questions such as, "Explain the workings of a cell to an adult at home and write down at least one question that was asked by that person and how you answered it." All the facts would be available in the text; it is the skill to use them that would be tested. The main thing to understand here is that after a school stops testing for facts and begins to test for skills, it will not be long before it is clear to everyone that skills are the outcomes that have value; facts and information have none.

In most schools, the teacher covers a body of material and the students have to guess what is going to be on the test. Some teachers even test for material that was not covered. In a Quality School this would not happen. There would be no limitation on input, and the teacher would not ask his/her students to figure out what part of this input will be on the test, as now occurs in too many of our classrooms. There would be no hands raised asking the age-old question, "Is this going to be on the test?"

Since it is always skills that are tested for, it would be very likely that the teacher would make the test available to the students before teaching the unit so that as they went through the material in class, they would know that these are the skills that need to be learned. But another feature of a Quality School test would be to ask the students if they could figure out any other skills that they have learned from the study of this material besides what the teachers ask. This is part of the open-endedness that is always a part of all testing and discussion in a Quality School. These questions would be implicit in all tests: "What can you contribute?" "What is your opinion?"

"What might I (the teacher) have missed?" "Can you give a better use or explanation?"

Keep in mind that in a Quality School, students as well as teachers would evaluate their tests. If they were dissatisfied with either their own or the teacher's evaluation, they could continue to work on the test and improve. Following Deming, the idea is to constantly improve usable skills. In a Quality School, this opportunity is always open.

As I look over this bulletin, I see that there is a lot of material to be mulled over and discussed. There is, however, nothing here or in any other of my suggestions that requires any teacher to change anything that he or she does. If what is suggested appeals to you, implement it at your pace. We believe in lead-management; there is no pressure on you to hurry. You might want to begin by discussing these ideas with your students. In a Quality School, the students should be made aware of everything that you are trying to do. If it makes sense to them, as I think it will, they will help you to put it into practice.

CHAPTER TWENTY-THREE

Evaluating Students in a Quality School
BULLETIN #12, 4-20-91

I am a great believer in the golden rule. I love it when others apply it to me, and I try to use it whenever I can. If we were to apply it to education, it would go as follows: Teach unto others as you would want them to teach unto you. It is easy to see what we would all want if we were students: to be treated kindly, courteously, warmly, and supportively. I am sure we would also want our teachers to explain how we could use what they ask us to learn in our lives and to do a lot more than lecture. We would certainly want our teachers to be sensitive to our needs and to make learning fun.

But assuming all of the above were in place, we would still not be satisfied that they were teaching the way we wanted to be taught unless we were able to succeed. That would mean that our teachers were able to teach ("manage" is always implied when I use "teach") so that we learned as much as we wanted to learn and, usually, as much as most of the other students. From the student's standpoint, the golden rule could be stated as, "Teach me so that I can learn as much as you would like to learn if you were I." This is where the way we teach falls short of what most students want. Very early in their school careers, many students who are capable of learning more and who would like to learn more still do not succeed in learning nearly as much as they would like to learn, even though they are taught by teachers who do many of the good things that are suggested in the first paragraph.

This is because almost all teachers, good and bad, embrace the *traditional* method of evaluating students' progress, a method of evaluation that no more than half of the students in the best schools have the strength to handle successfully. The difference between good teachers, who do as suggested in the first paragraph, and others, who do much less than suggested, is that more of the students of good teachers can deal with this destructive method successfully but still no more than half.

An accurate description of our present method of evaluation is: I, the teacher, will punish you unless you can show me on my, or our, test that you know what I have just taught. If students do not succeed in showing this to their teachers on a test that either the teacher or the school selects, they are punished with one or more of the following: given a low or failing grade, put in a low-track class, put in a special class, or eventually flunked. As these punishments pile up, which they do for well over half of the students, the punished students lack the strength to keep trying. They conclude that they are fighting a losing battle, and they stop trying to learn.

It is obvious that this method rewards only the students who accept it—those who are willing to work hard, do their work on time, and learn just what the teacher asks them to learn, often in the exact form that the teacher or the test demands. It is a system that separates those who accept it from those who don't or won't. The latter group amounts to many more than half of all students. Even with good teachers, this method of evaluation ensures that schools will not do what they are supposed to do. If you try to convince students that this system is for their benefit, you will fail.

Obviously, this is not a method of evaluation that a Quality School can use. As I describe herein, the Quality School system is based on all students doing competent work plus some work that is quality work. It is never punitive. All students have a chance to learn; learning is not geared rigidly to time; objective tests are never used; and tests may be dispensed with completely if alternative means of evaluation (including student self-evaluation) are used. Examples of alternative evaluations involve demonstrating competence, such as: doing a science project, writing a poem, measuring space in a building, interviewing for historical research, or showing the teacher (or a representative of the teacher) that they can practice what they have just learned.

When tests are used, as they will be, they are never tests of memorization or rote retention. They may be any of the following: 1) tests of written or oral opinion, 2) written or oral evaluation of data or other material, or 3) problem-solving. Students are encouraged to bring all notes, books, and other written material to all tests and to ask the teacher for assistance in getting their thoughts clear even during the test. No test is final. All students will be taught to evaluate what they have done, and all students, including those who have done A or very high-quality work, will be given opportunities to improve what they have done and to raise their grades.

While this is easy to write down, it may still be hard, for a teacher who wants to do away with the traditional system, to visualize how this would work in practice in a typical academic class. To clarify what I mean by the Quality School system, let me take an example from the math program taught by Marvin Remster at the Apollo School.

Students are flocking to math at Apollo. The way it is being taught has led students to tell others that in this class they are not only learning as much as anyone else but a lot more than they had ever learned before in math. When I talk to students, most of them tell me that they hated math in previous schools because they felt stupid and were usually behind the class. Their experience was that most of what they did was wrong and they either failed or got very low grades. It was like being at bat against a pitcher who was so tough that they never got a base hit.

At Apollo, they use the textbooks that they tell me they like, and they start at the place in the book where they feel competent. For some, this is pretty close to the beginning; for a very few, it is as far along as algebra. They sit at tables, and no effort is made to stop them from talking to each other as they work. The atmosphere is like being on a job: Do the work but at the same time enjoy the company of those with whom you are working.

After students demonstrate that they can do one typical calculation by hand, like long division, they are encouraged to use the calculators available at each table. Some use them, but many do not. The ones who don't use calculators say that they like to do the calculations manually. It is obvious that in this no-pressure, nonpunitive situation, they get satisfaction from working out the answers by hand. They go through the problems in the book doing the odd numbered problems for which there are answers in the back. If they get stuck they ask for help from students at the table. If they still don't understand how to do the problem, they call Marvin,[1] who is always circulating from table to table.

To check their progress is easy. They tell Marvin when they have mastered the principles involved in the series of problems on which they have been working and then show him how they can do one or two of the problems. As soon as he is satisfied that they have mastered what has to be done, they go on to the next series. If a few of them are having the same difficulty, he gets them together and explains what is needed. If an important principle is involved, he will explain it to the whole class. There is no pressure to move quickly. They go as far and as fast as they can and they get credit for what they do. Grades are available for those who want them; but mastery, not grades, is what is important.

There are no discipline problems. Some work harder than others but all get credit for what they do. They can go as far as they wish or do as many as they have time for. For Apollo, the classes are large—some are over twenty-five students. But there could even be more because much of the time they help each other. Without pressure, they don't rush to get help from the teacher. They tell me they like to try to figure out what to do on their own or with each other.

There is no drudgery. The work does not seem boring to them, because succeeding and learning is a satisfying new experience. Since Marvin has no interest in comparing them with each other, they have little interest in this either. They like the fact that their success is based on what they are able to do, but they are more than willing to help each other if they are asked. As more of them succeed at arithmetic and pre-algebra, a large number are asking for algebra. This subject may take more teaching, but since the measure of their success will be the same—demonstrate competence and move ahead—there should be no more problems with algebra than with what they are doing now.

Marvin also runs a store in the class. He buys food items at wholesale and sells them at a small markup. The students work out the math for the food operation and keep the books. As long as they are neat (which has never been a problem), the students can eat in class. If they are hungry, they can also earn some money for food by working to clean up the little mess that might be a natural part of eating in class. The money they earn is from the profits and they can also borrow small sums if they are short. What Marvin's approach has created is classes in which the students are relaxed and usually happy to do their math. There is no tension because there is no antagonism between Marvin and any student about anything.

If a couple of students want to talk quietly, Marvin does not tell them they can't. If they do not disrupt, they can talk for the whole period—but they don't. If that is what they wanted to do they would not come to class at all. Student attendance, however, is high, because they want to learn. What they need to do is clearly understood by them and they see that success is always possible.

As described, this individualized learning works well for math. It would have to be modified for other subjects, such as English, science, or history, but the same principles would apply: no failure, move at your own pace, evaluate your own work, strive for quality, demonstrate competence when you are ready, work together if it helps, get credit for what is accomplished, and don't worry about what others are accomplishing because you are not being compared with them.

I believe that Marvin is teaching the way almost all of us would choose to be taught if we were given that choice. What is going on here is education. Students are working because they have discovered that competence in math is adding quality to their lives. It is not so much that the math itself is adding that much quality: It is coming from the confidence they are gaining in their ability to use their brains. Gaining confidence in what our brain can do for us is the essence of achieving quality and a key goal of a Quality School.

It also leads students to want to learn, making it possible for teachers to teach them—a much easier job than managing them, as teachers had to do in the schools they attended previously. Keep in mind that as much as a Quality School is based on lead-management, as soon as lead-managing is in place, then much of what was formerly managing becomes teaching.[2]

CHAPTER TWENTY-FOUR

Tutoring in a Quality School
BULLETIN #6, 6-25-90

On June 12, 1990, a "Frontline" program on PBS showed how difficult it was for excellent schoolteachers to do their best in a small town where there was little support for education. One of the problems they struggled with was how to keep a fifth-grade girl, who seemed to lack almost all math skills, interested in school. Her classroom was team-taught by two dedicated teachers who decided that one of them would spend at least 100 hours tutoring her in math throughout the school year. The result was successful, and the teacher who did this one-on-one tutoring said that without this intensive work, the child would have failed and likely given up on school that year. To do what they did, the other team teacher agreed to teach the combined class of over fifty students by himself while his partner tutored. This girl, however, is going to need more tutoring, and the odds are against the possibility of her getting this kind of personal attention from future teachers.

As I watched, it seemed to me that this tutoring could have begun earlier and could be continued as long as needed if it had been done by student volunteers either from her own class or other classes. Even a younger student could have done it, as it was mostly simple arithmetic; she was mostly shown being drilled on her times tables. Her teacher could have supervised a student tutor (perhaps even several) in a fraction of the time she spent in tutoring herself.

There is no doubt that there are many students in every grade, K through 12, who would benefit greatly from one-on-one tutoring and there are plenty of students in every school who, given the right circumstances, would very much enjoy tutoring them. In a Quality School, a committee of the staff would be encouraged to meet to figure out how to set up a one-on-one tutoring program in the school. Not only would this group provide tutors for the students who were slipping behind, but they would tutor any student, even those doing high-level work, who wanted some special help from someone skilled enough to provide it. For example, there could be computer tutors who would help students learn to use a computer. This could go on not only in school but, under the direction of the program supervisor, out of school. I suggest starting the program on a one-on-one basis; however, some tutors would have the skill to tutor small groups of students who needed help in the same area. This would become the equivalent of a good teacher assistant (TA) program in a college. The strong message of the tutoring program to all students in a Quality School would be, "When either you or your teacher thinks that you need help, good help is always available."

It would be prestigious to be a part of the tutoring program in a Quality School. I would suggest that in middle or high school, the program be a part of a credit course called Academic Leadership, which would be led by a skilled teacher. This class might meet regularly once or twice a week so that the student tutors could not only get instruction from the teacher but also give each other instruction as they shared successful experiences and materials that they would be encouraged to develop. The tutoring program would be open to any student willing to try it. There would be a training period under the supervision of the program director that would probably involve watching an accomplished student tutor and then tutoring under this student's supervision. The goal in all cases would be to persuade the tutored students to begin to do some of what they and their tutors would call quality work.

At the end of the year, in the usual award ceremony, certificates would be awarded to all tutors. Awards would also be given to students who were tutored and had made significant progress, and these awards would be presented by their student tutor. This would help all students to see that there was nothing demeaning about accepting help from each other . . . it was the "cool" thing to do. Although the program should be under the direction of a teacher, it is also a place to involve adult volunteers who could assist with the organization and supervision of the program. Adult volunteers could also tutor as part of the same program and might be trained to do this by experienced students and experienced adult volunteers. For significant educational work with students, there are plenty of volunteers in any school district. What turns volunteers off is menial work or work that does not involve students. In a Quality School, volunteers would never be asked to do anything that they did not think was a needed addition to the education offered by the school.

Since there is great satisfaction in tutoring, I do not believe that there would be any shortage of student tutors; but I also think that there should be some specific compensation offered for their time and effort. To do this, I suggest that a careful numerical progress record be kept on all students who were tutored. If a tutored student raised his or her math score 15 points in a month, the tutor should be given a tutoring bonus of 15 points in his or her math score. If the tutor were an A math student, these bonus points could be used to earn the A+ grade that is the top grade in the Quality School. If the tutor was not an A student, then it would be at the discretion of the teacher what bonus points could still be used to raise the grade. The only time the teacher would not allow the points to be used to raise a grade would be if the tutoring was at a level far below where the class was working. Getting bonus points for high-level tutoring would encourage students in the same class to help each other.

The bonus points could also be used to determine the level of the honor's award in tutoring . . . an award that would be helpful in getting a job or into a good college. Perhaps a local foundation or business group could also be persuaded to give scholarships to students who got a high honors award in tutoring. Giving this compensation and making the tutoring prestigious would make it more acceptable to parents who worry about their child taking time away from his or her schoolwork. These parents should also be made aware of the fact that the best way to learn is to teach someone else; anyone who tutors is getting as much benefit as the student being tutored or more. These are only suggestions. It would be up to each program group to work out what is best for that school.

It is also important to keep in mind that one of the biggest problems in school right now is the gap between the high- and low-achieving groups of students. If many low achievers were successfully tutored they would gain more confidence and more acceptance and this gap would begin to close. Even if they did not reach the achievement levels of their tutors, they would become friends with students whom they do not even know now. This would do a great deal for the morale of the whole school.

As members of the staffs of Quality Schools begin to get together and share ideas, elements of what makes a tutoring program successful would certainly be high on the list of what is shared. I can see both teachers and students visiting other Quality Schools to demonstrate what works well for them. It is hard to learn to do something unless you are shown how. Schools have worked in isolation for too long. In the beginning, the first schools in the consortium of Quality Schools will have to work out many of these ideas on their own from my book. But soon, we will begin to get together, and, as we share, all that seems so hard to do now will become much easier.

CHAPTER TWENTY-FIVE

Homework

BULLETIN #13, 4-30-91

Having heard that Mr. Sherlock Holmes was back in practice, about six months ago, I sent a copy of the original edition of *The Quality School* to his Baker Street address. Having always admired his ability to cut through the fog and go right to the core of a problem, I wanted his opinion on whether it would be possible to create a Quality School. Basically, were there any serious flaws in my ideas? I told him to take his time but, if he did notice something that I should know, to please give me a call. To my surprise the phone rang the other day and he was on the line. With his permission, I recorded the conversation. With minor editing, the following is what we said:

GLASSER: Hello, Glasser speaking.

HOLMES: Holmes here, is this a good time to talk?

GLASSER: Thank you, thank you very much for calling. This is a perfect time to talk. Please keep a record of the phone charges and I also expect to pay your usual fee. I can't tell you how excited I am to be talking to you.

HOLMES: Well, I read the book. What you say is quite clear, but I'm not sure I agree with your idea that all children should succeed in school. That's curiously American. I can't picture my Baker Street irregulars even going to school. But I suppose times have changed and maybe you are on to something.

GLASSER: But how about the concept, the quality ideas of Deming and the control theory that backs them up?

HOLMES: Oh, control theory makes perfect sense. Everyone knows that if Pavlov had used a cat, he would still be waiting for it to salivate. But Deming's ideas, that quality is what we all want, I don't know. I've worked with some people who had some very peculiar concepts of quality. Still, the world has changed a lot since Watson and I went to school. Maybe it is time to make some changes in the way we run our schools.

GLASSER: Please, don't keep me in suspense. I'm anxious to hear what you think. Will it work? If we could run a school with no coercion, with total emphasis on quality and where the students evaluated their own work, do you think that they could all get involved in learning?

HOLMES: Oh, no doubt about that; it would work. I think it would even work for the lads who ran errands for me today. They go, but they tell me that they hate school; their interest is strictly in the streets. I'll admit that before reading your book it never occurred to me that they could ever like school. But look, I'm sorry to disappoint you but it's not going to happen because there's a serious omission. Sort of like the case I had years ago—remember the one where the crucial clue was that the dog didn't bark. Well, there is a dog in the book that should be barking, but he's quiet. Unless you can get him to bark, and then get the people who run the schools to pay attention to what he's barking about, there will never be a Quality School.

GLASSER: What dog, what should he be barking about?

HOLMES: Well, you see, sir, your whole case rises or falls on doing something that has almost never been done—running a school with no coercion, breaking down the adversarial relationship that normally exists between the students who are forced to go to school and the masters who are frustrated because so many of the "students" refuse to learn. But how can you get rid of the coercion that is endemic in almost every school unless you get rid of the main reason that it exists? Unless you do this, all your ideas, good as they may be, will come to naught. You see, I've made a few calls to some schools around here and asked them if they would consider what needs to be done and they thought I was daft. I can tell that you were thinking about recommending what needs to be done when you wrote the book, but you lost your nerve. Do you know what I am talking about?

GLASSER: I'm not sure; is it complicated?

HOLMES: To the contrary, it is elementary, my dear Doctor, elementary. I am talking about homework. Homework is the root of almost all the coercion that goes on in a school. It's even what separates the good students from the bad, and this adds to the trouble. It's as simple as that. Unless you get rid of compulsory homework, you'll not be very likely to get a Quality School.

GLASSER: But homework is a part of every school. What school is going to give up compulsory homework?

HOLMES: My point exactly, so why talk further? If you don't want to give up on homework, there's not much I or anyone else can do for you. Besides, it galls me to labor the obvious; I thought you knew this much about me when you sent me the book.

GLASSER: No, please don't hang up. If I'm to tackle this sacred cow, I'll need some help. It's not as elementary to me as it is to you. Tell me what's so obviously wrong with homework that we have to get rid of it. I need your ability to think clearly; I need your help. I can't help thinking that anything that has been around as long as homework can be that bad.

HOLMES: If you want to run a Quality School, it is that bad. Homework will kill a Quality School before it gets started every time. But look, if you are serious about Quality Schools, I'll be more than happy to explain.

GLASSER: I've never been more serious about anything.

HOLMES: Keep in mind that I think your thesis is accurate and I give you credit for thinking about something that never occurred to me. I'd even like to see a Quality School in this part of London, but as long as we have compulsory homework, I never will. To begin, let's face a fact: No student likes to do compulsory homework. Those who do it do so because they have the foresight to know that if they want to make something of themselves, that is the price they have to pay. But outside of the few students who go to fancy schools like Eton and Harrow, how many students are willing to pay that price? Look in your own book, the answer is on the first page—fewer than 50 percent.

And when students don't do their homework, even the warmest and least coercive teachers believe that they have no choice but to punish. As soon as that punishment starts, out goes your basic thesis. Believe me, the struggle to make students do homework leads to more coercion than anything else we do. Even the best students, the ones who do their homework, see the pressure and resent the fact that their teacher will turn against them if they stop doing it. You can't have compulsory homework if you want a Quality School.

GLASSER: But couldn't we learn to teach in a way that would persuade students to do it? Don't you think this would be possible?

HOLMES: Well, if I've learned anything in 150 years, it

is that anything is possible; but it's unlikely. Compulsion of any kind, including homework, is like a small rotten apple. Give it time and it will spoil a barrel of anything. For example, if teachers assign homework, it is only right that they should evaluate it. Take the time to give each child some feedback as to how he did. If a teacher is not willing to take the time to do this, the child will mostly look at the homework as busywork, and busywork is always punitive. But even if they did grade it, they would still have to fight with the students who didn't do it, an effort that takes time and energy desperately needed elsewhere.

Homework is counterproductive for both students and teachers, directly in the sense that students hate it and indirectly in that it prevents teachers from planning exciting instruction. It leads to more students hating school than anything else we do. It is, in my hardly humble opinion, the leading cause of students dropping out of school. And even for those who stay, because it is universal and starts early in elementary school, it is the leading cause of the adversarial relationship between students and teachers which, in turn, is the leading cause of low-quality school work.

After I read your book, I visited the school in this neighborhood where my lads attend. Teacher after teacher complained that one thing that makes their jobs so hard is trying to teach a class of over thirty students when many of them are at a different place in their learning. This is mostly because so many students do not do the homework or do it inadequately. In too many classes, the work is so tied to how well the students do their homework, at best an unpredictable and irregular process, that there is no way to keep a class together.

Homework is also the leading cause of friction between parents and students, especially in the homes of parents who want their children to do well in school. Almost all schools call parents and tell them to get after their children to do their homework. It is an additional cause of tension in homes where there is too much parent-child tension already.

There is also the indirect effect in that schools also call parents because their children are out of order in school. But most of this disorder is due to the students resisting the teacher's pressure to do better or more schoolwork. And much of this teacher pressure is caused by the friction that arises when students do not do homework or do inadequate homework. Parents who do not know how to deal with their children noncoercively—who, here in England, are far too many—become angry and frustrated when they are told that their children are doing badly. They realize that they cannot make their children do what they do not want to do. Ultimately, homework assignments that are not done create a three-way adversarial system: Children, teachers, and parents all become adversaries, each blaming the other for what they cannot make the other do.

GLASSER: Is it really that bad?

HOLMES: It's worse. Teachers keep assigning homework even when they are certain that a substantial group of students cannot possibly do it well or even at all. Many students tell me that if they do not understand their homework assignment, they have no one to explain it to them. Children in crowded homes may not have the place or the time to do the homework. They may have to help out with younger children, cook, do housework, or work at a job to support family needs or their own. In this situation, students feel trapped. They learn to dread school and to hate learning because they know that they will be both punished and put down for what they cannot do or do not have the time, strength, or opportunity to do.

Besides, homework is the main enemy of quality. If it is done at all, even good students tend to do just enough to get by. And teachers, tired of wrangling, tend to accept low-quality work. Students are well aware that teachers do not put much value on most homework (they just check it off), so they do it as quickly as possible. They work with the radio or television on and learn that doing a good job is not important—all that counts is getting it done. But, anytime anything less than quality is acceptable anyplace in an organization, all standards are lowered. Your man Deming explains that point clearly.

If the teacher tries to set a high standard, she runs the risk of being criticized by the rest of the teachers or even by parents for being unrealistic. Face the fact, Doctor, what is realistic in most schools is hardly what any of us would call quality. Getting into the habit of doing quality work is almost impossible where homework is concerned, even for good students. And bad habits, once acquired, are hard to shed.

If you define education as the process of students becoming aware of the fact that learning adds quality to their lives, homework denigrates the whole process. From the student's point of view, homework reduces the quality of their lives, and as they hate it, they learn to hate learning. Before I read your book, I never thought of the teacher as a manager whose purpose is to persuade students to produce quality work. Obviously there can be no quality when workers hate the job, the manager, or both. Teaching is hard enough—we do not need compulsory homework to make it harder.

GLASSER: When I sent you the book, I never expected you to tell me what you have just told me. If I accept your premise, I have the problem of telling teachers that they have to throw out what is almost as sacred to school as scripture is to church. How do you suggest I do this?

HOLMES: You're right, this indeed is not an elementary problem. Go slowly and certainly don't just blurt out, "No more compulsory homework!" We both know that would be a disaster. I suggest you start by sharing what I have said here with anyone who will listen. I'm not an educator, but the word of Sherlock Holmes may still carry a little—how do you "Yanks" say it—clout. But, following your control theory, what you need to do is to suggest what needs to be done in its place. Keep in mind that for a conscientious teacher, homework is a lot of work for very little payoff. They may not resist as much as you fear.

When teachers, students, and parents are free from the problems caused by homework (as I have just described), they will then have the time to concentrate on quality classwork, which is the essence of what a school should be. Once the management problems caused by homework are eliminated, teachers could (and should) use the time to plan a good lesson each day that would include all kinds of learning, both individual and cooperative. And they should enlist their students in planning these lessons too. Like adults in the world of work, children (in my experience) do not resent doing sensible, well-planned work, and they appreciate the chance to do some of the planning. They accept that they are in school to work, and if the work is seen as useful, they are more than willing to do it. As students get more involved in quality work and as they evaluate and get the chance to improve what they do, they will find that they do not have enough time in class to do as much quality work as they want to do. What they will do then is take it home to improve it. At home, they may work alone, with friends, or ask their parents for help, but since it is now all voluntary, there is peace and satisfaction instead of tension and fighting. If home is not a good place to work, they will ask their teacher to help them find a better place. I would suggest that a Quality School should be kept open at night—staffed by adult and student volunteer tutors—to help students who want to improve. What I like so much about this program is that it seems to be such good preparation for adult life. All of us who want to improve the quality of our lives often take work home. What we resent is being coerced to work at home. In this respect, we are the same as students. Most of us don't like to do it even if we are paid.

You may not be aware of it, but my investigation revealed that homework is often the refuge of teachers who do not want to make the effort to plan interesting and exciting lessons. Once compulsory homework is eliminated, these teachers will be deprived of the excuse that they often give for not putting more effort into their teaching. That excuse is that students are "lazy" and "uninterested" because they don't do their homework. It is these same teachers who will tell you that without homework, they cannot possibly cover the curriculum. But covering the curriculum and learning to do quality work are vastly different. As you point out so clearly, we don't need to cover the curriculum; we need to learn to do quality work, and we won't do it until we get quality lessons in a noncoercive environment.

GLASSER: I'm still holding on to the idea of homework. Is there nothing that could be assigned that would have educational value and lead to quality?

HOLMES: Yes . . . there is. I often sit down with my young Baker Street chaps and explain things to them that school does not teach. Young minds want to learn. They want to talk to adults and ask questions. But they don't want to do at home what they can see is more easily and better done in school. What I suggest is that teachers who insist on homework should at least assign work that cannot be done in school. It still would not be compulsory, and could be fun, as it brings children and their parents closer together.

GLASSER: What do you mean?

HOLMES: For example, ask a child to watch an educational program on television and then to talk it over for a few minutes afterwards with an adult in the home. Ask the child to interview an adult about something that the adult obviously knows and which is interesting to the child. Ask them to visit places in the community or to do a project like earning some money and then report to the class how they did it. There is much that a student could and would do at home that could not be done in school. This would serve to teach the child that learning is not at all restricted to school—it is all around them all the time.

But, look, difficult as it is for me to admit, nothing I have suggested has value just because I have suggested it. Even Scotland Yard has rejected many of my ideas, and in the area of crime, I do know what I'm talking about. All I hope is that some headmasters will encourage their teachers to try the no-compulsory-homework, better-classwork path that I have outlined here. But teachers need support and encouragement to try it. It will have to be planned and then evaluated.

Parents will have to be made a part of this experiment and encouraged to do educational things on their own with their children that both they and their children enjoy. They need to read this bulletin and have a chance to ask questions and, perhaps, have the right to have their children assigned homework even if it is not compulsory for the others. But they should not have the right to insist that the teachers punish their children for not doing it. I have been in the business of catching criminals for a long time and have seen them punished. If punishment worked, I would have been out of business a long time ago.

If any of your schools try what I suggest, keep data. See if the quality of work that students do rises when they are treated the way I suggest. But, please, whatever happens, keep me posted on the progress of the Quality School.

CHAPTER TWENTY-SIX

The Value of Knowing How We Relate to Each Other
BULLETIN #1, 2-15-90

In some combination of the four following ways, we relate to each other socially or at work as: 1) friends, 2) counselors to counselees, 3) teachers to students, and 4) managers to workers or lower-level managers. Often, especially when we believe we are teaching and counseling, we are actually relating much more as managers than as teachers or counselors. Until teachers and counselors become much more aware of how they are actually relating to those they counsel or teach and learn to manage much better than they do now, they will not be effective in much of what they do. To understand why so many of us lack this necessary awareness, we will examine these four relationships individually in some detail. Then, to learn to manage better, we need to look at how each of them is adversely affected by coercion.

Friendship (from casual acquaintance to intimate love)

Friendship is based on the ability of both parties to find mutually satisfying common ground. Each attempts to help the other find satisfaction in what they do together. A good friend often finds satisfaction in doing what she knows her friend will enjoy even if she does not enjoy this as much as her friend does. Good friends continually look for ways to reciprocate, but they do not make reciprocation a condition of friendship. In fact, successful friends have few if any conditions for friendship.

Successful friendships are always based on "What can we do for each other?" and somewhat based on "What can I do for you?" Friendships based on "What can you do for me?" are rarely successful for very long, because the unsatisfied party usually becomes coercive: This coercion destroys the friendship. There is no coercion in a long, successful friendship. We should keep in mind that if coercion destroys friendship (the most common and necessary of all human relationships), how could it possibly be an effective tool in counseling, teaching, and managing?

Counseling

Counseling is based upon what I, the counselor, can persuade you, the counselee, to do that you believe makes your life better. I will advise, make suggestions, or try to persuade you to evaluate what you are doing so that you can then decide to make a change that will lead you to a more satisfying life. As I define counseling, the counselor has no preconceived agenda for the counselee to follow. It should make no difference to the counselor what the counselee chooses to do (assuming it is legal and not destructive). All I, the counselor, am trying to do is help you do better than you are doing now in whatever area you decide you want to improve.

For example, if you come for counseling and say you are unhappy in your job, the counselor will try to help you find happiness on this job or in another job, become self-employed, get retrained, or retire. The counselor has no agenda except to help you find employment (or retirement) that satisfies you better than what you have. Good counseling is almost always based on a growing friendship between the two parties. Since the counselor never has a specific agenda of his or her own and attempts to become friends with the counselee, there is no coercion in the counseling.

Teaching

In its purest form, teaching is based on what I, the teacher, can teach you, the student, that you want to learn. The teacher claims that he/she has specific teaching skills and has, as an agenda, the desire to teach the subject. For example, he/she may teach algebra, tennis, or surgery, but does not claim to have the skill, or even the desire, to manage, which means to persuade you to learn what he/she teaches. Although pure teaching, as described here, is a very common human relationship, it is not common in public schools. For example, only a few students who enroll in algebra have a strong desire to learn what is taught; therefore, most who "teach" algebra are not able to teach in the sense that teaching is defined here. If this is what they attempt to do (and many math teachers do attempt to teach without managing effectively), the majority of their students learn little algebra. On the other hand, almost all who teach subjects like tennis and surgery, where most of their students want very much to learn what is taught, can teach successfully without managing. There is no reason for teachers who teach (as teaching is defined here) to use coercion.

Managing

As I define it, successful managing is the art of persuading subordinates to do what the manager wants them to do and to do it well even when, initially, they may not want to do it. The manager, like the teacher, always has an agenda. To be successful, the manager must be able to persuade the people he/she manages that doing what he/she asks them to do and doing it well is to their benefit. When managers have difficulty persuading the people they manage—for example, principals persuading teachers to stop coercing students—they may be tempted to use some sort of coercion themselves in the form of reward, punishment, or both.

When they use coercion, however, the workers always become more resistant than before, because now they not only continue to resist the work but increasingly resist the coercion of the manager. Unless principals resist this temptation and model noncoercive lead-management as they work with teachers, the teachers will increase their resistance to what the principal is asking them to do. The more coercion any manager uses, especially punishment, the more the people they manage will become their adversaries and the more the quality of the work will suffer.

Probably the workplace where managers (teachers and principals) use the most coercion and where more low-quality work is done than in any other workplace is the public schools. This is because students, who are the workers of our schools, are more resistant to doing what they are asked than are workers in any other workplace. Therefore, successful managers do not coerce, because they find it to be counterproductive. They figure out how to manage so that when workers work hard and do quality work, they also succeed in satisfying their basic needs. (How this is done in school is described in detail in Part One.)

Problems Associated with Managing

What we fail to realize is that when people have problems getting along with each other, the problems are mostly due either to faulty managing or to attempting to manage people who do not want to be managed. For example, when friends (or loved ones) have difficulties, it is usually because one will not do what the other wants him/her to do. The friend who is dissatisfied then attempts to manage the other and usually does so by trying to coerce the person into doing what he/she wants. When this happens, the friends become adversaries and the friendship falters or fails. The only way to salvage a failing friendship is for the dissatisfied friend to stop all attempts at coercion and try to find some common ground (new or old) that is satisfying to both. Anything else usually fails. Many friendships (and even more love relationships) fail because, while one or both is attempting to coerce the other, it is almost impossible to find the common ground that is needed to maintain the friendship.

Most counselors manage as much as or more than they counsel. For example, when a student is sent to a counselor for some school problem, the counselor always has an agenda, which is to manage the client so that she/he stops causing that problem. To the extent that the counselor adds coercion to the managing, she/he will mostly fail. A coerced client will rarely work to find a need-satisfying, alternative way to behave that is necessary if the problem is to be solved, because almost all the client's effort is devoted to resisting the coercion. Except for counselors who see voluntary clients (mostly in private practice), almost all counselors have an agenda and spend a great deal of their time managing their clients so that they will follow this agenda. This means that counselors have to develop the skills to manage without coercion or the counseling will fail. Of these skills, making friends may be the most important one.

While public school instructors are labeled teachers and tend to think of themselves as teachers, they are, with few exceptions, much more managers than teachers. Like all teachers, they have an agenda; but unlike many private skill-teachers or college teachers whose students share the same agenda, it is unusual for public school students to have the same agenda as their teacher. When they don't have the same agenda, the teacher can't teach them; no one can teach a student who does not want to learn what the teacher is trying to teach. This means that if teachers are to succeed, they must manage effectively. To the extent they can manage without coercion and persuade the students they manage that it is to their benefit to learn what is being taught, teachers will be successful. Again, making friends is essential to this process.

What Is to Be Learned from This Explanation

When we work with people (or even associate with people as friends), most of us have an agenda that we want them to accept. There is nothing wrong with having an agenda: What is wrong is that not nearly enough of us realize that if we are to achieve our agenda, we need to learn much more than most of us know now about how to manage people. Good managers, whom I call lead-managers, are always friendly; they never coerce and continually stress that what they want is the highest-quality performance that those they manage are capable of achieving. To get this quality, they continually ask the workers to evaluate their work and help them in every way they can to improve what they, the workers, believe they can do better.

To lead-managers, the welfare of the people they manage is more important than anything else. Lead-managers understand that consistent, quality performance cannot be forced. It is only achieved by workers who are treated in the way all human beings want to be treated, which is to be able to satisfy their basic needs as they work. Lead-managers understand what these needs are and that they must be continually kept in mind as they manage.

Therefore, to be more successful in all we do, we must realize that managing people effectively is by far the most difficult of all human endeavors, and managing resistant students so that they do quality work is the most difficult of all management assignments. If we can succeed in the schools, we will not only have done our society a great service, but we will have shown a way to solve the management problems that plague our country.

CHAPTER TWENTY-SEVEN

Taking Criticism and Rejection: The Teacher's Burden
BULLETIN #10, 2-20-91

When teachers accept the job of managing students (or principals the job of managing teachers and students), they must also learn to accept the resentment, criticism, ridicule, and blame that comes with the job. Teachers constantly have to deal with dissatisfied students whose behavior ranges from refusal to work to personal attacks as their way of expressing their dislike of what they are asked to do and/or how they are asked to do it.

Most teachers and principals handle disruptive students in the way they have seen them handled from the time that they themselves were students. They almost always wait until students disrupt before they deal with them. If doing this were effective, there would be few problems, but disruptions continue and may even be on the increase. Year after year, teachers and administrators do the same things that do not work because no one has succeeded in convincing them that there will never be a good way to solve these problems once they have occurred. The only way to solve them is to deal with them in a way that will prevent them from happening again.

To do this, however, we have to change the system. Joseph Juran, a colleague of W. Edwards Deming says, "When there is a problem, 85 percent of the time the problem will be with the system, not the workers."[1] In the case of rebellious students, I would say that this is an understatement—this problem is almost completely caused by the system. What is wrong is that it encourages teachers to deal with the behavior of rebellious students as if the behavior were a personal attack. As long as it is dealt with in this way, we will not prevent this problem. Teachers need to show students that they are not going to deal with attacks as if the students are attacking them personally. We are going to deal with them as if these attacks are problems that we can solve together. But teachers will have to learn to reject the present system in order to do this.

Teachers also should be aware that until they change the system and gain the skill to prevent disruption and abuse, they may vent their anger at the whole class and decrease their effectiveness with all their students. Too many teachers cling to the attitude, "You can't treat me like this," almost as if being hurt and angry will help them to deal with the problem. In doing so, however, they stick with a system that does not work, and they cut themselves off from any possibility of solving the problem through negotiation and compromise, the only ways it can be solved. The longer they maintain this righteous attitude, the more problems they will have with disruptive students. By staying with the system, teachers become obstacles to their own progress.

Right now the system tells teachers to deal with disruptive students punitively and show them who's boss. Punishment, however, is not a part of a Quality School Program. If you are a teacher in a Quality School and you are confronted by a disruptive student, you would 1) not immediately defend yourself as if you were being attacked personally and 2) not angrily counterattack as if you could squelch their behavior. As abusive as students may be, they are not really attacking you personally. Their rebellion is against a system of education that does not sufficiently take their needs into account. To them, you represent this system. Therefore, if the system is to be changed, you must change what you do.

I recognize that when students are disruptive or abusive, it is very difficult not to take what they do personally. I am aware that what goes through the minds of teachers being treated badly by students is, "I'm not going to take this from you or anyone else." At these tense moments, most teachers believe that they must put down the rebellion or risk losing the respect of the class. From the standpoint of teachers, I can appreciate that it appears that I am advocating that they take much more than they think they should.

This concern would be valid if all I were advocating was that they put up with what the student does. But I am suggesting much more than this. I am suggesting that teachers learn a new skill that earns the respect of all students and quickly reduces both disruption and abuse. As soon as they see that this skill is effective, they will gain confidence. They will know that they can handle recalcitrant students and, knowing this, should easily be able to absorb a little temporary abuse without being threatened.

What I am asking you to do is to try the principles of lead-management: When confronted by a disruptive student, do not threaten, get angry, or sulk. Teachers who are lead-managers deal with disruptive students calmly, recognizing that the students are rebelling against a frustrating system. It is the teacher's job to make the system less frustrating. No matter how abusive a student may be, teachers should respond by saying something like, "Look, you wouldn't be talking like this to me or doing what you are doing unless you were upset. But if you're upset, we have a problem that I think we can solve. We're not going to solve it by calling each other names or threatening each other. You come to school because you want to learn something useful—let's go to work on that."

Lead-managers do not focus on what the student did no matter how out of order it was. They never make statements like, "You can't do that," or "You can't say that." The student has already said or done it. There is no attempt to be righteous, to moralize, or to quote rules. Lead-managers know that they must try to get on friendly terms with these students, and that if they take the student's behavior personally, this cannot be accomplished.

They know that if they can get the students involved in doing some quality work, the problem will be solved: The student will soon forget what was said and become friendly. Everything the lead-manager does is to avoid the anger and tension that prevent this needed friendship. It is almost impossible for students to carry a grudge against anyone who treats them as I suggest.

At the time of the incident, the teacher acts as though no permanent harm has been done, which it hasn't, and that the only lasting harm that might possibly occur would be if the teacher failed to help the student work this problem out by getting him or her involved in useful schoolwork.[2] In working this way, lead-managers do not take the bait and reduce themselves to the student's level of ineffective behavior. The students are looking for someone to blame for their own unwillingness to put effort into their education. If the teacher rises to the bait with anger, the students have accomplished their purpose. In their mind is, "Why work for a teacher who doesn't like me? It's his or her fault that I am doing so poorly."

As much as students try to put blame on someone else, you must try to avoid the idea of fault completely. You accept that there is a problem. Whose fault it may be, if anyone's, has nothing to do with solving it. For example, explain to a student who says, "It's your fault I didn't do my homework; you didn't explain it enough" that all you care about is that he/she does it now. If the student needs a little extra help to get it explained and you don't have the time, find a student tutor who will help him/her get started. All that counts is getting it done now.

Tell the student that fault-finding is like finding your car with a flat tire and then spending an hour looking for the piece of glass or nail that punctured it. Wouldn't it be smarter to put on the spare and get going? As long as you try to deal with the student's anger, resentment, criticism, ridicule, and blame, you are in a poor position to solve any problem.

Teachers or principals who are lead-managers try to portray the attitude that they are competent to solve problems. They do not take criticism personally, and they have no interest in threatening or punishing. They are willing to listen to another side of the story and do not pretend to know all the answers. But they know that there are answers and that they and the student can work out most problems to the satisfaction of all parties. Nothing less is acceptable.

CHAPTER TWENTY-EIGHT

Counseling in the Classroom or In Other Group Situations
BULLETIN #14, 6-15-91

Learning to counsel noncoercively using reality therapy is an important part of the Quality School Training Program. Teachers think that they need to stop teaching and spend time counseling an out-of-order or upset student. They ask, "How can I do that?" The answer is, they can't. But this does not mean that teachers cannot counsel while they are teaching. They can do a great deal of counseling without stopping, or hardly stopping, what they are doing. How this is done is the subject of this bulletin.

It is unfortunate that in the minds of most people, including counselors, counseling is almost always pictured as a counselor and a counselee sitting by themselves in a quiet room talking to each other for at least a half an hour. Contrast this with what goes on in a classroom, and it is easy to see why most teachers do not think that learning to counsel is of much use to them. But this is not true. Once a teacher understands what counseling really is and also the control theory that underlies it, it will become apparent that reality therapy can be practiced by a teacher while he or she teaches without taking more than a few seconds away from regular activities.

As we teach it, reality therapy is divided into two major parts: 1) creating the counseling environment and 2) learning to use the procedures that lead to behavioral change. While both parts are important, the second part is not effective until the first (the proper counseling environment) has been created. Teachers need not fear that I am burdening them with extra work—the proper counseling environment and the most effective teaching environment are exactly the same.

For the students, this is a warm, comfortable, noncoercive environment. It is a talkative environment. There is always a great deal of dialogue between the teacher and all members of the class. All day long, you should work to create an environment in which students sense that they are free to talk to you without fear of criticism or punishment. At the same time, it is an environment in which you do not pay much attention to students' complaints and gripes. When students complain, you should say things like, "Okay, I hear you, but what can we do about it? Let's you and I talk it over as soon as we have a chance and work out a way to solve the problem." Or, "This is something that we all ought to talk about because it affects a lot of us and it can't be solved just by you and I talking." Keep emphasizing that problems are solvable and that griping is a waste of everybody's valuable time.

As you learn control theory, which underlies reality therapy, you will discover that what you are doing when you work to create the counseling environment is actually working to persuade your students to put you into their quality worlds. Once you are in their quality worlds, you have created this environment, and all you have to do is maintain it, which means to keep doing what you have been doing. It is from the position of being in their quality world that you can counsel to correct most classroom behavioral problems, even if you only have a second or two to devote to them.

When you envy the time that professional counselors seem to have, keep in mind that they need that time because when they sit down in a room to counsel someone they don't know; they have not had the chance that you have had to create and maintain the kind of environment that has persuaded your students to put you into their quality worlds. A professional counselor is starting from scratch and trying to do in twenty minutes what you have had weeks, even months, to accomplish. So don't think that their position is better than yours: It only seems that way. Unless they can succeed in persuading the students they are counseling to put them into their quality world (which many counselors do have the skill to do), they will not be effective.

Once you are in a student's quality world, that student will listen to you even if you only have a few seconds, because he/she believes that you are concerned with improving the quality of his/her life. You are a friend, never an adversary, and the more solidly you are in his/her quality world, the more easily you will be able to counsel. It is this accomplishment, getting into all your students' quality worlds, that prevents problems and leads me to claim that there are no discipline problems, only discipline incidents, in a Quality School. Discipline incidents cannot be prevented, but they are not important, because you can easily solve them through the counseling that you have now made possible by getting into the students' quality worlds.

Once there, you can put into practice the second part of reality therapy whenever there is a need, such as when a student is out of order. The second part of reality therapy is getting the student to evaluate what he/she is doing and, on the basis of this evaluation, decide to change to a more effective way to behave. Almost all students know when they are choosing to behave in a destructive or self-destructive way. The reason they continue to behave this way is because they have chosen not to evaluate what they are doing. The purpose of counseling is to confront them gently, but firmly, with what they are choosing to do. Once confronted by a teacher who is in their quality worlds, they have to evaluate what they are choosing to do. This is how control theory works. They cannot ignore a teacher who has done what is suggested here and who is now in their quality world. It is impossible.

In practice, all an effective teacher has to do to counsel most students in her class (for both minor and major incidents) is learn to make the proper confrontation. This means to use one or more of the following reality therapy comments or questions:

1. What's your plan?
2. What are you doing?
3. Is this the nice thing to do?
4. Could we talk a little later when we both have some time?
5. John, when you do what you are doing now, I just don't know what to do.
6. How is what you are doing helping me to teach this class?
7. Nancy, do you know you astound me?
8. Tod, could you stop what you are doing and help John?
9. Would you like me to ask Mary to help you?

I could write more of these, but it would be better to brainstorm when you discuss this bulletin and think of more on your own. These are enough for you to see that although all of these questions are confrontive and call the student's attention to his behavior, none of them are threatening, critical, or coercive in any way. All of them call the student's attention to what he/she is doing and some even offer help. Which one you use is something you will learn from experience. No harm can be done if you choose one that is not effective, because none of them will jeopardize your hard-won place in any child's quality world.

Once you have done your small part, the students will do the rest. They will evaluate what they are doing; they will see that it is not the thing to do; and if they know how (which most do), they will change. Even when you counsel in an office over a long period of time, this is what causes the change. What you may then do, which takes time, is work out a plan to change, but this is rarely necessary in a classroom. As stated, the students almost always know what to do, and if they get some help from you or another student, they are almost always capable of doing it. If a student has a serious problem that needs time and intensive counseling to work out, you can refer him or her to a counselor or set up a time to counsel the student yourself after school or during a break. This would not be a frequent thing in most schools. I suspect that even a teacher with many students would not find this necessary more than once a month. The advantage that you have over the school counselor is that you are already in the child's quality world; the counselor is not.

To facilitate the creation of the proper counseling-teaching environment and, through it, get into the quality worlds of the students in your class, I suggest that early in the school year you explain the way you intend to teach. Emphasize in this explanation that you will use no threats, punishments, or coercion, but that you will confront all students who behave discourteously. As an outgrowth of this explanation, have a discussion, answer their questions, and, finally, ask them to help you make the following large sign to display prominently in your class. Work out your own words if you wish, but try to include the ideas that are in the following:

In our class, if anyone, including the teacher, is upset or has any problem at all, we will talk it over and try to solve the problem. In solving the problem, we will never hurt, punish, criticize, or put any one down. We will always be willing to participate in a whole-class discussion, and anyone can ask for a class discussion at any time.

If you have a sign like this posted in your class and you act according to what has been suggested in this bulletin, you will have few problems with your students. This is not hard to do, and it could be the difference between enjoying and hating what you do. Although I used teaching as the example, this information is equally valid for anyone who works with groups of children or adults.

CHAPTER TWENTY-NINE

Dealing with Very Difficult Students
BULLETIN #17, 12-18-91

Recently I received a letter from a teacher in New Hampshire who is involved in the Quality School Training Program. She said that even though much was going well, she was having a lot of trouble with some eighth graders who were horrible both to each other and to the staff, especially as staff tried to work with the student's unacceptable behavior. Assuming her experience is shared by many others, I would like to explain how to deal with serious problem students, of any age, in a Quality School.

First, it is necessary to understand that the behavior of these students is their way to deal with a coercive system that has punished them for years for not being willing to expend effort to learn, often by rote, what seems to them to be a great deal of nonsense (see Chapters Twenty-One and Twenty-Two). In addition, they are punished for disobeying rules that have been forced upon them. They do not agree with many of these rules, but the system gives them neither a chance to express this disagreement nor an opportunity to participate in making the rules they are asked to follow. The vast majority of students do not rebel as these do, but over half express their dissatisfaction through apathy and low-grade work.

What we need to accept but do not want to is that we cannot coerce some students into accepting the nonsense that other students do. What they are doing is fighting back, which is their way to defend themselves against our coercion. This fighting back, however, does not work: The coercion is almost always increased, and what results is the destructive stalemate that prompted the letter from my New Hampshire correspondent. Unable to win their fight against nonsense, these students are increasingly frustrated and, in desperation, attack each other much as gang members do in many cities on a much larger scale.[1]

By the time they are serious problems, they have placed in their Quality Worlds as highly satisfying a destructive (and ultimately also self-destructive) picture of being at war with anyone who gets in their way, either other students or staff. And what we complain about is their continual attempt to satisfy this picture. The only way we can deal with these students successfully is to break the endless cycle: They act out and we punish; they increase their resistance and we increase the punishment.

The only way to break this cycle is for us, the staff, to take the initiative and stop the punishment. It needs to be done while they are still in school before they have committed serious crimes. Once they get arrested, our options are drastically reduced, and we may not be able to do much to save them from choosing to destroy their own lives and/or the lives of others.[2] Only through treating them with much less coercion than they expect, at best none, will these hardcore discipline problems be persuaded to take the "war pictures" out of their quality world.

This is easy to say, but very hard to do. It can only be accomplished by a staff who understands control theory and is willing to practice reality therapy counseling. Most school personnel, following their instincts, which are based on an erroneous theory (stimulus-response), will fall into the trap of dealing with this deviant behavior coercively, thereby increasing the problem. They will try to punish the wrongdoers and push them into doing what they want, and with almost all severe problem students, they will fail completely.

For the New Hampshire teacher or any other teacher, to stop punishing is difficult, because as soon as they try to stop coercing, they will be admonished from all sides: Staff, parents, and other students will say, "Get tough with them; that's all they understand." And in a sense the admonishers are right: Coercion and punishment is, indeed, all they understand—that is a lesson we have taught only too well. And if we continue to get tough with them, it is all they will ever understand. To do differently, we have to fight the immediate, simplistic stimulus-response urge to punish, far from dormant in all of us, that tempts us to move quickly and decisively in exactly the wrong direction.

WHEN WE ARE WORKING WITH BEHAVIORAL PROBLEMS SUCH AS THESE, THE ONLY EFFECTIVE TIME TO FIX THEM IS WHEN THEY ARE NOT BROKEN

We should try to stay calm in the face of any disorder the disruptive students create and look past the immediate situation. As urgent as any given situation may be, even the worst students are not at war with each other or us most of the time. When the bad behavior breaks out, as it may with little warning, it seems as if it will last forever, but it does not. When these students behave well, which is actually much of the time, we do wait with trepidation for the bad that will soon occur. We hope it will not but, of course, it does. If we are honest, we will see that there is nothing effective anyone can do at that given moment.

Therefore, with almost all problems of human disorder, there are no good solutions once a problem is actually occurring. Whatever solutions there may be are never immediate. The only chance of being effective is for us to act differently than we usually do when they are in good order. Only by doing this can we prevent instances of future acting out, and as we

do, we begin to solve the problem. Therefore, prevention
through teaching them better behaviors when they are in good
order, not intervention when they are at war, is the only
effective program.

A QUALITY SCHOOL IS A NEED-SATISFYING SCHOOL, AND
BECAUSE IT IS, IT IS NEVER COERCIVE

To set the stage for getting the longer periods of peace that
are needed to get the preventive program going, it is necessary
that it be made absolutely clear to the problem students that
no matter what they do, the staff will not become punitive or
coercive in any way. As stated in Chapter Fifteen, signs to this
effect should be posted all over the school and should stay
posted even if students like these make fun of them and taunt
the staff with inflammatory statements like, "This place sucks;
no one around here does anything no matter what we do."
This is an attempt on the part of these students both to justify
their actions and also to goad the staff into the reprisals that
feed war pictures into their Quality Worlds. As long as we do
not punish, it will be harder for them to become angry, and
we will be able to get started with what we have to do.

Therefore, no matter what they do, the message from the
staff has to be as follows: We run a caring school; teach useful
skills and knowledge; give all a chance to improve what they
do and, therefore, to succeed; talk to all students in a warm
and friendly way; teach them and encourage them to work
together; demonstrate that we know what we are doing and
that we believe it is good both for them and for us; and try as
hard as we can to persuade them to begin to do quality work.
In this school, the staff does not fail anyone: Any student who
is willing to work will ultimately succeed. We are aware of fun
and plan to help them to have as much fun as possible in what
they do everyday and also in planning enjoyable school activities. We also will always work with them to make what rules

we all agree we need and to change any rule that is not working.

Unless all these aspects of a Quality School are moving into place or are in place, there is nothing we can do to solve the problem of students seriously out of order either with us or each other. But as well as these conditions work for the out-of-order students, they work even better for all students. When these conditions are in place, there will be no discipline problems, and what the teacher from New Hampshire is complaining about will become a thing of the past. Behavior problems with students who are so out of order that we do not know what to do with them do not occur in Quality Schools.

Our experience at Apollo with many hostile students like these has been that in our useful, no-nonsense classes, with caring teachers encouraging them to do quality work and with no compulsory schoolwork or homework, there is little trouble. If at your school, these students are subjected to compulsory homework and useless desk work (like filling out dittos) and are taught with little attempt to talk with them and to get them involved in discussions of what it is you are trying to teach that is useful in their lives, there is little hope of solving the problem. But if we put into practice what is suggested in Chapter Fifteen, they will be unable to resist the temptation to begin to learn. Keep in mind that if they are in school, they have some sort of picture in their Quality World of wanting to learn. The desire may not be strong, but it exists and, if we follow Chapter Fifteen, we will succeed in tapping it.

It is in the ostensibly academic discussions of history that we can, if we are wise, relate their warlike behavior with each other to wars past and present. If we can succeed in teaching them that they are doing what frustrated people have always done since civilization began, which almost always has led to misery, then we can swing the talk over to what they are choosing to do with each other. From that we can move into reality therapy and ask them if what they are choosing to do will help them to get what they want. Then with education, they can move from fear to respect. And then well before trouble breaks out or when we see that it is about to start, we can step in and ask if we can work out a plan to avoid what is going to happen.

We can also make sure that when they pass from class to class or congregate on the school grounds during lunch or before or after school, we are out there with them. There is no better preventive for student unrest than a teacher or administrator circulating among the students and, with some subtlety, drifting into the groups of students who are most likely to attack each other. The attacks almost always begin verbally and, if we are there when this occurs, we can blunt the attack with our presence.

Where we choose to stand, whether we joke or make light banter, whether we distract them with an interesting bit of conversation, ask them for advice or a favor, inquire about a girlfriend—all these gestures are important. There is nothing that will substitute for it if we want to work with these students successfully. What this will accomplish is to allow them is to get to know us as caring, noncoercive people. It will also allow them to save enough face, as they restrain themselves because of our presence, so that for a while they can abandon their warlike stance. It is only the presence of a supportive faculty person acting as I suggest above that will allow them to do this. They know this, and they will welcome your presence if you adhere to the noncoercive approach that makes you acceptable to them. They may still make remarks as to your ineffectiveness because you no longer are punitive, but you should remind them that this is what you believe in and you have no intention of doing what you do not think is right.

Be somewhat aggressive in countering their disbelief in your nonpunitive approach by asking them as individuals, "When has punishment or force ever helped you?" As much as they profess their belief in this stimulus-response approach, you will be surprised that in almost the same breath they will say, "It never works with me or any of my friends." Don't show surprise in this complete contradiction of what they profess to believe, just say, "That's why we don't use it around here; we agree with you completely. It does not work."

It may, however, come to a point with some students that they will not behave even if you do the above. Send them to the office and let them cool down. Do not attempt to talk with them when they are fighting or screaming at each other. If they are chronic offenders, tell them that you do not know what to do. Ask them if they have any dissatisfaction with the school and, if it even approaches a Quality School, they will say that school is okay, it's the kids who are lousy here. Tell the chronic offenders that the school will not change. It is nonpunitive and we are continually trying to make it a better place to learn useful material. Tell them, "This school is becoming a good place and will even get better if students like you will give it a chance."

A QUALITY SCHOOL IS NOT A PERMISSIVE
SCHOOL—STUDENTS WHO ARE NOT IN GOOD ORDER
CANNOT BE IN SCHOOL UNTIL THEY ARE ORDERLY

Any student who will not make a workable plan to get along without attacking students, staff, or property cannot be in school; destructive behavior will not be tolerated in any school that is even close to becoming a Quality School. First they can be offered the option of the time-out room, where they can be offered counseling and also do their work if they wish. But if they won't behave in this room, they should be sent home. If they want to do their schoolwork at home, all their teachers will do is give them some work so they can try to keep up. In a Quality School, if they want to accept this help, a student tutor will also be assigned to help them at home. After at least three days, if they want to try to come back to school, they can come back if they are willing to present some kind of a written plan for how they are going to avoid trouble. In this plan they should agree to evaluate their own progress.

If they make it, fine; if not, send them home to try again after three days and do this as long as they want to try. There is no limit to these trials. They will be kept on the school roll for the rest of the year. If they do not choose to follow the rules this year, they can try again next year if they have a plan in hand when they come to register.

A Quality School does not depend on peer pressure to keep order; it depends on peer modeling. As the vast majority of students in a Quality School will model good order, the out-of-order students will have no grounds to accuse the school of being lax and to claim that their trouble is the school's fault. What they will learn is that the school will not punish them for being out of order. But at the same time, they will learn that the school will not tolerate disorder. Any disorder no matter how slight must be dealt with first by the teachers and then by the administrators or counselors.

They will learn that they must be orderly or they cannot be in the school. Since they will see students who used to be out-of-order now doing well, they will want to be in the school too. Because a Quality School is a desirable school, being out of school will not be seen by the disorderly student as getting away with anything or hurting the school. They will almost always see it as a foolish choice.

When they come back to school, as they will if the approach suggested in this bulletin is followed faithfully, you should not remind them that they have lost the war and you have won. No one should ever say things like, "Aren't you glad that you are now in order?" Avoid like the plague saying "I told you so" in any shape or form. Accept them back as if they had done little or nothing, but involve them in the class discussions that, in a Quality School, are held to try to figure out a way to solve any significant problem as soon as it arises. As stated, let nothing go by and deal with everything in the way suggested here.

Keep your problem students in mind for anything that might go on in the school that would interest them. Don't settle for good behavior, but try to get them involved in quality schoolwork or quality extracurricular activities. These warlike students have a lot of energy and, if you can tap it productively, you will find that they are very capable and can be as strong a force for good as they were for bad. Never give any student the least impression that he or she is too tough for you to handle or that you are in any doubt about what you do. Send the message loud and clear, "We are on the right track; we know what we are doing, and the quicker you join us, the better off we will all be.

CHAPTER THIRTY

A Proposal for Creating Quality Secondary Schools

BULLETIN #16, 08-10-91

If they are dedicated to the ideas and on good terms with their staffs, it should not be too hard for principals of elementary schools, alternative secondary schools (like the Apollo School) and for very small secondary schools (less than 300 students) to persuade at least half the teachers to sign the Quality School Contract. It will be much more difficult for a principal of a large high school, junior high, or middle school to get half the faculty to agree. On the staff of most large secondary schools, there are too many skeptics and too much inertia to get a new idea started in the whole school. The only way to overcome this resistance is to create a model, and the model I suggest is the Q-School.

The Q-School is a small, academic school that will operate as a Quality School in the same building as the regular school. To create it will take an especially strong commitment from the principal, because he or she has to be able to run two academically separate schools under one roof for several years. But if it works, it will provide a solid model that can be gradually enlarged as more teachers and students see the advantages of a Quality School. If you are a secondary school administrator who is intrigued by the idea of moving your school to a Quality School, you should start laying the groundwork as soon as you make up your mind to move in this direction.

Before I describe the Q-School, I must acknowledge that I am aware of the difficulty of trying to run two separate schools under one roof. Competitiveness and jealousy between both the staffs and students of the two schools is inevitable to the point where, in petty ways, each may try to sabotage the other. To try to do it without firm support from both the superintendent and the school board will be very difficult. But if we want quality secondary schools, I do not believe we have any viable option other than to try to create an on-site model.

The Q-School

The Q-School is a small alternative school that will operate as a separate academic school within the secondary school. It could start with as few as 100 students and five to ten teachers. The number of teachers would vary, depending on whether they teach full- or part-time in the Q-School. The Q-School should be restricted to academics—all involvement in vocational courses or in extracurricular activities, such as sports and music, should be in the regular school. It should function with regular hours so that a special bus schedule is not needed. If it is in a high school that starts in the ninth grade, all ninth- and tenth-grade students should be eligible to apply for admission and all teachers for a place on the teaching staff. If the high school starts in the tenth grade, I would start the Q-School with tenth grade students only. If it is in a middle school, all grades could be represented. If the school is successful, it will expand with students who enter in subsequent years, assuming enough additional faculty can be recruited to take care of this expansion.

I suggest that the Q-School have an initial charter of one academic year. A self-evaluation procedure for the whole project developed by a committee of students, teachers, parents, an administrator, and a board member should be put in place to evaluate the school. At the end of the school year, based on that evaluation, a decision should be made to continue or abandon the project.

What follows are some suggestions: If you want to expand upon them, feel free to do so. We will learn from what we do, and we will share what we learn in our conferences and in these bulletins. I am available for telephone consultations for all schools that have signed the contract and have joined the Quality School Consortium.

Description of the Start-up Procedures

During the present academic year, the principal (or people assisting the principal) should begin talking to all the teachers, parents, and students to explain the project. From these people, a start-up committee led by the principal and made up of interested students, teachers, and parents and, if possible, joined on occasion by a supportive superintendent and school board members, should begin to talk to the community about the project. By the end of the school year, the teachers and students who will form the Q-School should be selected from those who apply.

Each school should work out its own selection procedures, but the Q-School should be open to all who apply—both teachers and students. The number of students who can be accommodated will be determined by the number of teachers who apply. All teachers must sign the Quality School Contract. All students and their parents should sign a statement that says that they have attended meetings and are aware that the Q-School will be as close as they can make it to the Quality School described in Chapter Fifteen. This bulletin should be made available to all who are interested in being a part of the Q-School.

It should be made clear from the very beginning to all who

are interested that the educational philosophy of the Q-School will be the definition of education stated in Chapter Twelve: EDUCATION IS THE PROCESS IN WHICH WE DISCOVER THAT LEARNING ADDS QUALITY TO OUR LIVES

It will be up to the principal to help make the Q-School happen. He or she will be in charge of the project, and this bulletin is my first attempt to help with what needs to be done. As I hear from principals who are trying to get started, I will do all I can to give additional help. I strongly suggest that as part of the principals' commitment to this project, they agree to teach at least an hour a week in the Q-School so that they are seen clearly as teachers as well as administrators. What is taught is up to them, but they should try to teach something that is not a part of the regular curriculum. Everyone should teach in a Quality School.

In selecting applicants for the staff, the principal will try to find as many teachers as possible to teach full-time in the Q-School. Usually he or she will have to select some teachers who will teach only part-time because they have skills, like an ability to teach calculus, that cannot be totally removed from the regular school. All teachers who are selected for the Q-School will be asked to commit themselves in writing to the Quality School Consortium by signing the Quality School Contract on behalf of the Q-School.

When the Q-School reaches the upper grades, it is possible that there may not be enough Q-School students to fill some of the electives, like chemistry or physics. Being involved in two schools will create some adjustment problems for both teachers and students, but nothing that cannot be solved. Having some students and teachers in both schools will provide the assessment committee with a good source of information as they go about trying to assess the effectiveness of the Q-School.

The Q-School will be a much different school from the

regular school. How it differs is described in detail in Part One of this book, and in *Schools Without Failure.* All the information in these books is applicable to the Q-School. Detailed information is also supplied in these reference bulletins and the specifics of the Q-School are well summarized in Chapter Fifteen.

There would be an emphasis on community service, but this service would never be pure physical labor. It would always have an intellectual component—something the students learned in school that they could put to work in the community. An example would be studying the local environment and a plan to correct some deficiency that was brought out by the study so that both the students and the community could profit from what the students had learned. The ramifications are endless. Given this opportunity, students would be creative and parents and teachers would pitch in with advice and help.

The Curriculum

In the beginning, I suspect that the curriculum of a Quality School would be similar to that which is taught in the regular school—the difference would be how it was taught. By the second semester, or even earlier, I would hope that the teachers would begin to veer from what they had taught for years to teach more of what they thought was important. The students would tend to be more involved, as teachers who were more interested would tend to pique their interest.

To prepare students for a successful life, proficiency in three skills is almost mandatory. These are writing, math, and speaking, and they would be emphasized. Of these, speaking is perhaps the most important, yet it is an almost totally neglected part of the curriculum in almost all schools. Even from our best schools, the vast majority of students who graduate have almost no ability to speak competently on an intellectual subject. Since success in almost every field, as well as in our personal lives, depends on the ability to speak clearly and sensibly, every teacher in the Q-School would focus on teaching students this skill and giving them a lot of opportunity to practice it. All students who graduated from a Q-School would be able to speak well.

The same is true for writing. National assessment tests show that students cannot express themselves well on paper. For example, fewer than 3 percent of graduating seniors can write a good letter. Since essay tests would be the standard for assessment in a Q-School, learning to write well would be a natural outcome. By the end of the tenth grade, all students would have been taught to write on a computer, using a standard word-processing program, as this is the tool that almost all people who write now use. Students would have had enough practice in good writing to assure that this skill would be firmly in place by the time they graduate.

I suggest that all students in the Q-School be required to study math for at least two years. This would not be done as it is now in separate courses that tend to confuse and fragment what is the most logical and continuous subject taught. Instead, based on what we have learned at Apollo (see Chapter Twenty-Three), almost all students would accept this requirement willingly, and many would want to continue beyond the two years. All students who enter the Q-School would be given a math book that starts with basic arithmetic and asked to show the teacher (or a teaching assistant) the level at which they are competent. If all they could do was add and subtract, they would start at that point. If they were skilled in algebra or beyond, they would start there. They would move ahead as they continued to show competence and go as far as they could in the next two years.

There would be no pressure. They would learn at their own

rate, ask and receive help as needed from each other and from the teacher or a student teaching assistant. When they thought they knew what to do, they would call the teacher over and work one or two sample problems for the teacher, explaining what they are doing as they do it. When both they and the teacher were satisfied that they had mastered that level, they would move on. While this method of instruction is not effective for most subjects, it is wonderfully effective for math, which is always logical and continuous. We learned at Apollo that students love to learn math this way. Many would opt for more years, and in four years, quite a few would begin calculus. Taught this way, students would enjoy math and all would learn far beyond the minimal competencies that are achieved by so few now.

Teachers in a Q-School would be treated as professionals. They would be trusted to teach what they believed were the most important aspects of their subjects. There would be no restriction on what they could teach except in cases where they could not convince the students that the material would ever add quality to their lives. Given this opportunity, most competent teachers would have no trouble persuading students to go along. Teachers in a Q-School would know that the skill of teaching is not to try to force knowledge or skills on students, but to convince them that what is taught is useful and has the potential to add quality to their lives. This would be the most obvious skill of the teachers in a Quality School: The chance to teach this way would be the main attraction of teaching in a Q-School.

Basically, the job of the teacher would be to teach what is useful and sensible to the students. Useful, however, would not be restricted to the pragmatic. It could be aesthetically useful, entertaining, or fun. Teachers would be responsible for assessing what the students had learned, but not responsible for comparing students with each other or discovering which students learned the most or the least. Students could be assessed in any way the teacher wanted, with one exception: They could not be assessed with what is called an objective test, which calls for them to know a fact or make a guess such as on a multiple-choice test—probably the worst of all assessment instruments. They could be given essay tests or be assessed orally, singly or in groups. They could also demonstrate that they could use what they have learned through written work like notebooks or portfolios. It would be up to the student and the teacher to work out ways that students could be assessed fairly and accurately.

Teachers and students would plan large projects that could involve up to the whole school for several weeks. Students would study recognized local, national, and world problems like low voter turnout, AIDS, economic recessions, uninsured drivers, environmental pollution, school failure, and crime and punishment. In these studies, the students would cover the social, moral, and economic effect of these problems on their community, the state, the country, and the world. Students would be urged to come up with recommendations for solving these problems and maybe figure out ways to get government officials to listen to what they had to say.

Responsibility

Students would be taught that they are responsible for all that goes on within their school. In math class, they would study the finances of the school in depth and be urged to make recommendations as to how to reduce spending and use the budget better. For example, the students would be taught how the school is maintained and asked to figure out ways in which they could aid not only in its maintenance but in the improvement of the physical plant. They would not be asked just to provide labor but to study what is the best approach to improving the school, as if they were contractors who were given contracts for improving the school plant. Everything they did would be part of an educational program that they could then apply to their lives later on.

They would be asked to take responsibility for each other, to investigate the various problems students have in school, and to come up with ways to prevent these problems as well as to help each other to solve them. Regular town meetings would be held in which any and all concerns about the school could be aired for discussion. Committees could be set up to make recommendations to deal with those that the group decided needed to be addressed.

The responsibility for what goes on both in and out of class would be shifted from the staff and administration to the students, with the staff and administration acting as facilitators and consultants. If we are to have responsible students, they must be given the responsibility to do all they can to make their school the best possible place it can be. They would learn good citizenship through studying and assuming their responsibilities as citizens of their school.

Summary

With no coercion and in an atmosphere of warmth and concern for all, the Q-School would be an educational experience unlike any that students had ever had and much different from any that their parents and teachers ever had. The theme would be quality work and self-responsibility, and the goal of all students would be to discover that education is the most powerful tool available to improve the quality of their lives. All would be involved in taking responsibility for everything that went on in the school.

The staff would be there to help students get the education that all students want, not to make them learn and punish the ones who did not learn enough. There would be no elitism. All would be eligible for whatever the school had to offer. It would be up to each of them to discover what was needed to get a quality education for themselves and to help each other get the most from the school.

The Quality School Training Program

The Quality School Consortium and the Quality School Training Program have been conceived by William Glasser, M.D. Under the direction of Dr. Glasser, the program will be offered through the Institute for Reality Therapy, 7301 Medical Center Drive, Suite 104, Canoga Park, CA 91307. Phone: (818) 888-0688; fax: (818) 888-3023.

Part One: General Information for Interested School Principals

Many people have called or written to express an interest in finding out how their school can begin the process of moving toward becoming a Quality School as outlined here. Rather than answer each inquiry individually, I would like to outline the procedure for any school to use to enroll in the Quality School Training Program and begin the first phase of what is anticipated to be a four-phase process. If after reading the book and this program description you are interested in moving forward with Phase One, please request the following from the Institute: 1) contract, 2) discussion guide, and 3) list of materials.

Enrolling in the training program also means becoming a member-in-training of the Quality School Consortium. Beyond the cost of purchasing a copy of *The Quality School* for each staff member and paying a $50.00 enrollment fee, Phase One of the training program costs nothing. It will, however, require that the school sign a contract as explained in Part Two of this description of the program.

The Quality School Consortium is not meant to be an exclusive group. Schools already enrolled in other programs are more than welcome to join, as the concepts of the Quality School will help any program to succeed. The purpose of the training program is to move enrolled schools to the point where they become certified as Quality Schools. A goal of the consortium will be to develop a cadre of indigenous consultants who will travel to other schools, both in and out of the consortium, to help teach the Quality School concepts.

The consortium will also hold conferences so that members can get together to exchange ideas that they have found to be useful as they move toward becoming Quality Schools. It is anticipated that most of the conference sessions will be led by our own "homegrown" experts. I would hope that member schools will volunteer to host these conferences so that they can show others what they have accomplished. Ultimately, the consortium members working together will develop standards for what the members agree should be called a Quality School. Schools designated as such will receive certification and become both models and resources for other schools who want to get started in the process.

It is my belief that Phase One is the crucial part of the training program. Any school that takes the time and makes the effort to learn all that is in this book will have little trouble moving ahead through the next three phases of the program. I suspect that most schools will be able to complete this first phase in a year, but there is no hurry. Schools should take the time needed for all committed staff to learn, in depth, what a Quality School actually is and to begin to put into practice the three main elements of such a school. These are:

1. Persuading all students to think about what is quality schoolwork and what is quality in their lives. With this awareness, they will develop a sense of how important it is to make quality a part of all they do.
2. Persuading all students to evaluate the quality of all they do in school.
3. Managing both students and teachers without the use of any coercion; in Quality School terms, converting completely from boss-managing to lead-managing.

I believe that unless the school is led by its principal and can make a substantial start toward accomplishing all three of the above elements on its own in Phase One, there is little chance that it will become a Quality School.

Part Two: Specific Information About the Quality School Training Program

The following steps explain the training program as it is presently conceptualized. While everyone who has anything to do with the school should be given the opportunity to read these steps, I address them to the school principal, because the principal must lead the move to quality education. The teaching staff, however, should be specifically encouraged not only to read these steps but also to read all of the initial material sent to the school. It is important that you understand these steps. If you have any questions about any of them: call, fax, or write the Quality School Training Program of the Institute for Reality Therapy, and, to the extent we can, we will provide advice and support.

PHASE ONE—LAYING THE FOUNDATION

1. Read the book yourself. No matter how you found out about the quality school, the first step for you, the principal of the interested school, is to read this book. Before you go any further, you might want to meet with a group of administrators from other schools with whom you are friendly and go through the book with them. This will help you to get comfortable with the ideas even before you present them to your own staff. If several principals in your group decide to go ahead with Phase One, you might want to continue these meetings to support each other and to exchange ideas. The Institute will provide a discussion guide for Part One of the book upon request.

2. Provide copies of the book to administrative staff and significant others. If after reading this book very carefully you are interested in enrolling your school in Phase One of the training program, then provide copies of the book both to your administrative staff and to your immediate superior in the central office. If you are the principal of a small school with no administrative staff, ask at least three of your most dedicated teachers to volunteer to participate in the administrative task of first reading and then discussing the book. Tell the whole staff what you are doing and make sure that the staff approves of the teachers who have volunteered. If you are in a secondary school, you may want to ask at least three willing students (who are representative of and also acceptable to most of the student body) if they would volunteer to be a part of this preliminary, administrative study group. They will provide needed student support to the program as it develops and, if it continues

into Phase One, continue to be an important part of the study group.

3. Discuss with administrative staff the first three chapters (refer to the discussion guide). Arrange to meet with your small administrative group as it reads the book in order to discuss the ideas—especially those ideas in the first three chapters. Begin these meetings by explaining that you want to begin to lead the school toward becoming a Quality School but you want to enlist their support before you approach your teachers. You and/or someone you designate whom this group will accept should lead these initial discussions, but you must attend all these meetings to show that you are committed to the process. From a careful reading of the book, you should be prepared to answer any questions that arise from the text.

4. Distribute copies of the book to each teacher as well as other members of your staff.

5. Arrange meetings with your staff to discuss the first three chapters and the contract. After they have the book, arrange a regular meeting time in which you will lead enough meetings so that the first three chapters of the book can be discussed in depth. At the first meeting, tell them that you want to enroll the school in the Quality School Training Program and explain the program to them. Tell them that you will ask them to make up their minds about joining the program after you have discussed the first three chapters. Also tell them that only this meeting is compulsory. Take your time; make sure that these discussions are not hurried and that all of the staff understands what they are committing themselves to do if they agree to sign the contract.

6. The contract. To become affiliated with the Quality

School Consortium, it is necessary that the principal, almost all administration and at least 50 percent of the teachers sign a contract committing themselves to the process of working together with the goal of making their school a Quality School. The contract is in two parts: Part A, to be signed by the principal and almost all administrators; Part B, to be signed by at least half the teachers. This contract is available upon request from the Institute.

7. Signing the contract. If half or more of the teaching staff agree to commit themselves to Phase One of the training program, they should—after reading the contract carefully—sign Part B of the Phase One Contract enclosed in the material sent to you. Some teachers will be wary of signing. They have never done anything like this and do not trust the process. If they want to join without signing and you feel they are committed, you can sign on their behalf. However, our experience is that teachers who do sign demonstrate more commitment to the process. To enroll your school in Phase One, however, we must have a commitment from at least half the teaching staff. Send the signed contract with the $50.00 school enrollment fee to the address on the contract and we will enroll your school in Phase One of the program.

8. Use of the discussion guide. Enclosed with the start-up information is a discussion guide that lists questions and topics for each chapter of *The Quality School*. This guide should be used in all meetings with staff, starting with the initial administrative meeting. While this discussion guide should be followed faithfully, it is also wise to add to it and enrich it as you or your staff see fit. If you have a large staff, you might want to break the large group down into smaller groups for these discussions. If you do this, you or someone who is skilled at

leading discussions should always be present, no matter how small the group. You should rotate so that you are present at as many meetings (large and small) as you can fit into your schedule, but you should always be present and presiding at all meetings of the whole staff. In all the training that takes place in a Quality School, the staff must experience continuous administrative support. Just telling them that they have your support is not enough.

9. Information on control theory which underlies the Quality School Program. For further information about the control theory explained in *The Quality School,* it is suggested that you and all of the administrative staff read *Control Theory* and *Control Theory in the Classroom,* but these are not required reading. If, before (or after) starting Phase One with your staff, you want a local representative of the Institute for Reality Therapy to explain control theory and reality therapy, which underlie the Quality School concepts, this can be arranged by calling or writing Linda Harshman at the Institute for Reality Therapy. Instructors will be available at a reasonable fee; but it should be understood that their expertise is in control theory and reality therapy, not in the concepts and procedures of the Quality School. If, however, you would like a consultant who has direct knowledge of how to get started in implementing the Quality School concepts, we can also arrange this for you.

PHASE TWO—INTENSIVE WEEK TRAINING

1. From early experience, it is strongly suggested that schools do not start Phase Two of the training program before they have finished Phase One. This means that

the school principal has led (directly or indirectly) all those who have signed the Phase One contract through the whole book and that there has been a substantial reduction of coercion in the whole school. Specifically, there are now fewer threats or punishments both in and out of the classrooms. What has been accomplished should be documented by listing what used to be done that was coercive and what the school is doing now in these same situations that is much less coercive or non-coercive. This documentation should be sent to Dr. Glasser. He will review it and decide if the school is ready for Phase Two. If the school is not ready, he or one of his representatives will be in touch with the school to work out what further needs to be done to get ready for this second phase. If Phase Two is started prematurely, it will not be effective; money and effort will be wasted.

2. Phase Two must involve all of the administration plus as many teachers who signed the contract in two weeks of intensive training (four and a half days for each week) and a supervised practicum. This training is called intensive because it is limited to twelve participants in each group. The participants are trained in both reality therapy and control theory. The goal is to teach as many of the staff as possible how to manage, teach, and counsel students noncoercively. In Phase One, they began this on their own, and now they will get specific instruction on how to do it more effectively. To those who may think that I am putting the cart before the horse, I can only say that I have done it for years the "correct" way and it does not work. Until the staff has struggled and, to some extent, succeeded on their own, they will not be committed enough to get full benefit from the training.

The two intensive weeks need to be taken approximately one year apart and involve a practicum in between.

3. The training will be offered by instructors from the Institute who have had some special training in the Quality School ideas. We will offer what we call "closed" training for your group so that the instructor can focus on the problems inherent in moving toward becoming a Quality School. The cost of the training will be approximately $400.00 per person per week. A minimum requirement is that each school needs to have at least one group go through two intensive weeks of training. It is suggested that all who sign the contract have this training; if this is beyond the financial resources of the school, we will work out a way to move ahead with just this minimum amount. If you have trouble raising the money, we will put you in touch with principals who have figured out how to do this. Some of them are quite ingenious—what worked for them may work for you.

PHASE THREE—STUDENT TRAINING PHASE

Phase Three, the Student Training Phase, will be designed to teach all students in the school enough control theory so that they can use it in their lives and in their education. This training will be done by teachers at your school who volunteer and who have been specially trained by your Institute instructor to do this. This program will mostly utilize the Choice Drug Abuse Prevention Program that is already in place and the best way, we believe, to teach students, especially grades 4 through 9, control theory. The program is eligible for financial aid through the federal drug abuse prevention funds that are presently available, and it should not be an added expense to the school. Moreover, we will be able to assist you in working out a package that is affordable for your school. This phase could start as early as the second year and will usually overlap with Phase Two. It is important to note that the Choice program is in no way designed to address drug problems per se, but to teach students control theory so that they will be able to make more effective choices in their life, including deciding not to use drugs.

PHASE FOUR—THE INTEGRATION PHASE

Phase Four has yet to be developed. It is anticipated that this is the part of the program which will be developed jointly by people in the consortium itself and the staff of the Institute for Reality Therapy. It will stress the development of lead-teaching and also focus on how we must change the curriculum so that what we ask students to learn will, in itself, persuade them to expend the effort to do quality work. All students doing a significant amount of quality work will be the ultimate criteria for whether a school has become a quality school. It is anticipated that most of the consultants for this phase will be drawn from the training programs run by the consortium and should be available at very low fees to schools enrolled in the program.

RESOURCES AND MATERIALS

1. We have a list of books and materials that should be very helpful for a school staff to use in all phases of the program. The use of these materials is neither necessary nor mandatory, but we would be remiss if we did not indicate that they were available. To save money, it is also possible that the members of the consortium who are near each other will decide to buy this material as a group and share it as needed.
2. Since it is impossible to estimate what it will cost to

administer the consortium, answer questions and give support, set up the indigenous training programs and conferences, evaluate the progress of member schools, and perform other services that will be needed, it is difficult at this point to know what membership dues will be. It is likely that the fairest way would be to assess each school in the consortium for yearly membership dues based on the number of teachers who sign the Phase One contract. It is my idea that, starting in 1991, all schools who become members will send a representative to a yearly business meeting where, based on experience, these representatives will decide what these dues should be. If we mostly use our own indigenous "experts," the cost should be low.

3. The one-time $50.00 enrollment fee will cover as much support as we can give to your school. Please write to us if you have any questions, and I will answer by audiocassette. I will make these audiocassettes available at our cost to other schools who inquire if any material like this is available. Within reason, I will answer your phone calls and even (if possible) visit your school. I hope to spend a lot of time in the next five years visiting Quality Schools and talking to students and staff.

Thank you for your interest in the Quality School ideas. I look forward to working with you for many years to come.

William Glasser, M.D.

Notes

PREFACE

1. Shayle does not know the source of this material. If any reader knows, we will be happy to attribute it properly in a future printing.

CHAPTER ONE. Quality Education Is the Only Answer to Our School Problems

1. Further information about Deming is published in Dr. Myron Tribus, *Selected Papers on Quality and Productivity Improvement.* This book can be obtained by sending $15 to the National Society of Professional Engineers, P.O. Box 96163, Washington, D.C. 20090-6163.

2. See the article by James Risen, *Los Angeles Times,* May 20, 1989, pp. 1, 18.

3. *Los Angeles Times,* February 1, 1989, p. 4.

4. W. Edwards Deming, *Out of the Crisis* (Cambridge: Massachusetts Institute of Technology, Center for Advanced Engineering Study, 1982).

5. National Commission on Excellence in Education, *A Nation at Risk: The Imperative for Educational Reform* (Washington D.C.: U.S. Government Printing Office, 1983).

6. Linda M. McNeil, *Contradictions of Control: School Structure and School Knowledge* (New York: Routledge, 1986).

7. *Los Angeles Times,* April 27, 1989, Metro Section, p. 1.

8. William Glasser, *Control Theory in the Classroom* (New York: Harper & Row, 1986).

CHAPTER TWO. Effective Teaching May Be The Hardest Job There Is
1. See Chapter One, Footnote 6.
2. Linda M. McNeil, *Phi Delta Kappan,* March 1988, p. 485.
3. Linda M. McNeil, *Phi Delta Kappan,* January 1988, p. 337.

CHAPTER THREE. We Need Noncoercive Lead-management from the State Superintendent to the Teacher
1. A good review of the research on what is essentially lead management (he calls it "system 4") is included in Rensis Likert, *Past and Future Perspectives on System 4,* 1977. This paper can be obtained from Rensis Likert Association Inc., 630 City Center Building, Ann Arbor, MI, 48104.
2. Ellen Flax, "New Dropout Data Highlights Problems in the Middle Years," *Education Week,* Vol. VIII, No. 30, April 19, 1989.
3. See Chapter One, Footnote 4.

CHAPTER FOUR. Control Theory and Motivation
1. Stanley M. Elam, "The Second Gallup/Phi Delta Kappa Poll," *Phi Delta Kappan,* June 1989, p. 787.
2. Ron Harris, *Los Angeles Times,* May 29, 1989, p. 1.

CHAPTER FIVE. The Quality World
1. See the dedication for more information about this school.

CHAPTER SIX. How We Behave: Quality Work Feels Good
1. See the major book on control theory: William Glasser, *Control Theory* (New York: Harper & Row, 1984).

CHAPTER SEVEN. Quality Schoolwork
1. See McNeil, *Contradiction of Control,* for documentation of this claim.
2. Robert Pirsig, *Zen and the Art of Motorcycle Maintenance* (New York: Morrow, 1974).

CHAPTER EIGHT. Grades and Other Basics of a Quality School

1. Jay Matthews, *Escalante: The Best Teacher in America* (New York: Henry Holt, 1988), p. 271.

2. This is a test given by the Educational Testing Service (ETS) in Princeton, New Jersey. A score of 3 or better (5 is the top score) qualifies a student to take a higher level course in that subject in college.

3. See Chapter Four, Footnote 1.

CHAPTER NINE. Building a Friendly Workplace

1. One of the best volunteer programs was initiated by Bill Borgers, now superintendent of the Dickinson, Texas, School District, when he was principal of Harlingen High School. Contact Borgers in Dickinson if you want some hints on how to get a volunteer program started.

CHAPTER TEN. Dealing with Discipline Problems

1. See the footnote on school volunteers in Chapter Nine.

CHAPTER ELEVEN. Creating the Quality School

1. Mary Walton, *The Deming Management Method* (New York: Perigee Books, 1986) p. 35.

2. Training in reality therapy and control theory is available through The Institute For Reality Therapy, 7301 Medical Center Drive, Canoga Park, CA 91307.

3. Gerald Coles, *The Learning Mystique* (New York: Pantheon, 1988).

CHAPTER TWELVE. Defining the Educational Terms We Talk About

1. This is the control theory definition of quality. In this case, it means that what you are learning increases your ability to satisfy one or more of your basic needs.

CHAPTER TWENTY-THREE. Evaluating Students in a Quality School

1. At Apollo, teachers and students are called by their first name. Since there is no coercion, there is no power struggle, so being on a first-name basis tends to increase respect. We are all very comfortable with this practice.

2. See Chapter Twelve for the definitions of education, teaching, and managing.

CHAPTER TWENTY-SEVEN. Taking Criticism and Rejection: The Teacher's Burden

1. For a good explanation of Deming's and Juran's work in Japan read: Dobbyns, Lloyd & Crawford-Mason, Clare (1991): *Quality or Else,* Houghton Mifflin, New York.

2. See Chapters Twenty-One and Twenty-Two.

CHAPTER TWENTY-NINE. Dealing With Very Difficult Students

1. For a chilling description of this process see Leon Bing, *Do or Die* (HarperCollins, 1991).

2. For confirmation of this claim, see *Do or Die.*

WILLIAM GLASSER is a board-certified psychiatrist who is best known for his book, *Reality Therapy,* a method of psychotherapy which is now taught all over the world. Early in his career Dr. Glasser became interested in mental health, and to further that interest began working in public schools. His thesis was that school failure was very destructive to the mental health of the failing child and, as documented in his book *Schools Without Failure,* he does not believe that any child should be failed in school.

Dr. Glasser later became involved with a new theory of how human beings function, "control theory." While not the originator of this concept, he has published two books, *Stations of the Mind* and *Control Theory,* on this important new theory. His most recent interest is in the application of control theory to education. His first book on this process was *Control Theory in the Classroom.* Dr. Glasser believes that understanding control theory is necessary if we are to make progress not only in schools but in all the other areas where we need to improve. He continues to write and lecture on these ideas.